PAUL PHILIP **LEVE**

LOVE
AND THE
MESSIANIC
AGE

MESSIANIC
LUMINARIES
SERIES

STUDY GUIDE
AND COMMENTARY

First Fruits of Zion is a 501(c)(3) registered nonprofit educational organization.

Vine of David is a publishing arm of the ministry of First Fruits of Zion dedicated to resurrecting the voices of Messianic pioneers and scholars of the past. If you would like to assist in the publication of more works like *Love and the Messianic Age*, please visit **www.vineofdavid.org** to learn about sponsorship, volunteer, and partnership opportunities.

Fourth Edition 2012
Printed in the United States of America

ISBN: 978-1-892124-34-0

Contributors: Toby Janicki, D. Thomas Lancaster, Brian Reed
Editors: Toby Janicki, D. Thomas Lancaster

Cover Design: Avner Wolff

Special thanks to the volunteer review team

Vine of David

PO Box 649, Marshfield, Missouri 65706–0649 USA
Phone (417) 468–2741, www.ffoz.org

Comments and questions: www.ffoz.org/contact

Also available from Vine of David: *Love and the Messianic Age*

First Fruits of Zion: www.ffoz.org
Vine of David: www.vineofdavid.org

PAUL PHILIP **LEVERTOFF**

LOVE
AND THE
MESSIANIC
AGE

MESSIANIC
LUMINARIES
SERIES

STUDY GUIDE
AND COMMENTARY

VINE OF DAVID

TABLE OF CONTENTS

FOREWORD

If I speak in the tongues of men and of angels, but have not love, I am a noisy gong or a clanging cymbal. (1 Corinthians 13:1)

When Paul Philip Levertoff wrote *Love and the Messianic Age,* modern Messianic Judaism did not yet exist. Levertoff confessed faith in Yeshua as the Messiah of Israel shortly after graduating from yeshiva. He was a teenager. It was the end of the nineteenth century. Levertoff announced his newfound faith in Yeshua the Messiah to his family in Orsha, Belarus. His father thought he had lost his mind and locked him in his room, hoping he would come to his senses. That night Levertoff slipped out through his bedroom window and never returned to Orsha. But the Jewish world of Orsha never left him.

Prior to becoming a believer, Levertoff swam in the sea of *Talmud* as a star pupil at the Volozhin Yeshiva. He was fluently conversant with the obscure and cryptic, esoteric works of Jewish mysticism. That background gave him a completely different perspective on the Gospels and the writings of the apostles. He recognized themes, ideas, and concepts in the Gospels that were prominent in Jewish mysticism and Chasidus. He wondered how any could hope to really grasp the message of the New Testament if they were unfamiliar with the Jewish background.

THE HEBREW-CHRISTIAN CHURCH

Levertoff's family in Orsha did not take the news of his conversion well. They locked him in his room. Levertoff left through his bedroom window, found himself cut off from his community, disowned by his family, penniless and alone. No Messianic synagogue existed for him to join. He had only the mainstream church. Levertoff eventually became an ordained member of the Anglican confession.

Nevertheless, Levertoff's greatest dream was to see the establishment of what he called the "Hebrew-Christian Church," a denomination within Christianity consisting of churches practicing a version of Judaism believing in Yeshua as Messiah, employing synagogue liturgy, and meeting on the biblical days of worship—not a sectarian movement, but rather a "group within the [universal]

Church composed of racially, intellectually and spiritually conscious Jews who, having accepted Christ and become conscious Christians, refuse to renounce their Jewish identity—since they believe this to be enriched and completed in Christ—but instead demonstrate to the Jewish and to the Christian worlds the fact that Christ may be worshiped and His Life lived in Jewish ... terms."[1] Towards that end, Levertoff and his family spent more than thirty years pioneering a congregation of that type in London. Levertoff felt that he was laying the groundwork for the Hebrew-Christian Church.

When he first published *Love and the Messianic Age*, he was just beginning that work at Holy Trinity in Shoreditch, London, where he had established the first real Messianic congregation in the modern era. *Love and the Messianic Age* is part of the groundwork he laid. Levertoff believed that the mystical philosophies of Chasidic Judaism could serve as a model for Jewish believers in the Hebrew Christian Church.

NOT A BOOK FOR EVERYBODY

Love and the Messianic Age is not a book that will appeal to everyone. It is not easy reading. It deals with large abstract theological concepts in a summary form. Levertoff's language is terse, densely packed, and often as cryptic as the sources he is citing.

Love and the Messianic Age is not like Christian devotional material. It reads more like poetry than prose. It aims for an academic readership, but its simple, sincere faith-perspective disqualifies it from serious academic consideration. It inherits Neo-Platonic philosophical ideas about the soul and creation which it inherits from its Chasidic sources. It liberally quotes mystical Jewish sources, which many Messianic readers regard as off-limits.

Kabbalistic literature is, generally speaking, comparable to a large, sprawling city with many treacherous back alleys, dangerous neighborhoods, and sudden, unexpected dead ends. Even with a good map and a good sense for direction, the visitor is likely to find himself lost and confused, and may easily stray into a bad part of town. Rather than trying to find your way through this maze-like metropolis on your own, we recommend you follow a reliable guide. Paul Philip Levertoff is just such a guide.

Still, if mysticism makes you uneasy, this is probably not a book for you.

LOVE AND THE MESSIANIC COMMENTARY

When we decided to reprint Levertoff's *Love and the Messianic Age*, I asked our staff to write a brief commentary which would help the modern reader navigate that otherwise obscure and sometimes difficult-to-understand book. *Love and the Messianic Age* makes only passing references to large mystical concepts which will likely pass over the heads of the uninitiated. To assist readers in unlocking the contents of *Love and the Messianic Age*, Vine of David has created this accompanying study guide that expands on Levertoff's concepts, explains them, and connects them to the words of Yeshua and the apostles.

---

[1] Paul Levertoff quoted by Olga Levertoff, "Diary of an Optimist," *Church and the Jews* 106 (January 1936): 15.

When he came to faith in the Messiah, Levertoff recognized that the Gospels and the other Apostolic Writings had much in common with Chasidic thought, philosophy, and theology. Toby Janicki, Brian Reed, and D. Thomas Lancaster, co-authors of the *Love and the Messianic Age Commentary and Study Guide*, have had a similar experience, although from the opposite direction. All three of them were raised as Protestant Christians, but when they began to study Jewish sources, they were astounded to realize that the great, mystical writings of the Chasidic teachers had a lot in common with apostolic thought, philosophy, and theology.

In this book, our writers explain Levertoff's concepts and to bring additional insights from the world of Jewish literature. More than that, they draw out intriguing parallels from the Gospels and Epistles. The final result is more than a simple commentary on another book; it is a plunge into the deepest waters of New Testament mysticism and apostolic theosophy. The short, bite-sized commentaries will also serve well as a type of daily devotional. I hope you will find the commentary on *Love and the Messianic Age* as inspiring and revolutionary as I have.

REMEMBERED FOR GOOD

Love and the Messianic Age is an important book both for Messianic Judaism and for Christianity as such. It opens a field of inquiry and reflection which encourages us to internalize the spiritual truths of theology and of our faith in Messiah. It causes us to consider our relationship with God, our motivations for serving him, and how our interactions with God and Torah can be expressed in hearts of joy, acts of love, fervent prayer, and sincere repentance. Most importantly, Levertoff's work demonstrates just how mysterious and wonderful the gospel message actually is.

It is my prayer that the name of Paul Philip Levertoff will be remembered for good.

Boaz Michael
20 IYYAR 5769

PREFACE

PAUL LEVERTOFF, CHASIDUS, AND THE ZOHAR
PREFACE TO *LOVE AND THE MESSIANIC AGE*

This little book forms the basis of lectures on "Chasidic Teaching in the Light of the New Testament."

In the preface to *Love and the Messianic Age*, Paul Philip Levertoff outlines his purposes for writing the book. Levertoff intends "to prove that traditional orthodox Judaism has no lack of spiritual fervor."[1] "Paul Levertoff was brought up in a Chasidic atmosphere. This means that Judaism was a spiritual thing, not just a legalistic religion."[2] However those on the outside may perceive it, Judaism is not a religion of rituals, void of feeling and spiritual ecstasy. Instead, the spiritual, theological, and philosophical ideals of Chasidic Judaism are sometimes similar to and even overlap those of the Messianic faith.

Levertoff's goal is to create a "short study" that displays the similarities of the two paths of faith—a work of comparative religion, so to speak. *Love and the Messianic Age* focuses on the teachings of Chasidic Judaism, comparing them with those of the apostles, and primarily focusing on the Gospel of John. Levertoff sees the mystical and transcendent Chasidic movement as possessing "an almost Johannine coloring."

The focus of the book is on the concept of love and the way it is expressed in Chasidic writings and the Apostolic Writings. Levertoff says that the difference between Chasidic and Christian love "is not a difference of degree, but of quality, a difference between expectation and realization." By saying this, Levertoff means to depict the New Testament faith as a solid, physical realization of

---

[1]   This and all following quotations without a footnote reference are from *Love and the Messianic Age.*

[2]   Beatrice Levertoff, "Thirty Years Work," *Church and the Jews* 180 (July 1954): 3.

the ideals espoused in Chasidism: "Everything here [in Chasidic teaching] is shadowy, afar, and undefined … unlike the New Testament, where everything is real, present, 'bodily.'"[3]

To understand *Love and the Messianic Age* and to understand Paul Philip Levertoff, it is first necessary to understand Chasidism. Levertoff was from a family with Chasidic leanings and Chasidic heritage. His mother was a grand niece of Rabbi Schneur Zalman, the first Rebbe of the Lubavitch Chasidim.[4] Zalman was a disciple of the Maggid of Mezeritch who was, in turn, a disciple of the Baal Shem Tov, the founder of the Chasidic movement. Levertoff's *Love and the Messianic Age* is a distillation of Chasidic teaching, particularly that of his illustrious ancestor Schneur Zalman.

INTRODUCTION TO CHASIDUS

The Chasidim are a mystical, orthodox sect of Judaism known for their piety, ecstatic worship, esoteric scholarship, and devotion to God. The Chasidic movement began with the teachings of their charismatic leader, the Baal Shem Tov, in the mid-eighteenth century. The Baal Shem Tov taught that the important thing in religion is not formula, dogma, and ritual, but faith, passion, soulful connection, and the experience of God.[5] The Chasidic movement sparked a revolution in Poland and Eastern Europe that in scope could be compared to the Protestant Reformation in Christianity.

Eighteenth-century Judaism in Eastern Europe had become stagnate in sterile religious formalism, more academic than spiritual. Where Jewish mysticism was incorporated, it was systematized and utilized as a type of gloomy asceticism, more appropriate for monks in a Christian monastery than for the average Jew. Chasidism (or Chasidus), the teaching of the Baal Shem Tov, reached deep into earlier spiritual streams of Judaism, drawing inspiration from the wonder-working rabbis of the apostolic and Talmudic eras and from the pulsing spiritualisms preserved in the mystical schools. The aim of Chasidism was not to change Judaism; it was to change the individual Jew. The Baal Shem Tov did not seek to alter Jewish belief; he sought to quicken the soul of the believer. In this regard, the Chasidic movement is paralleled by a much earlier Jewish reform movement, that of the apostles and first followers of Yeshua of Nazareth. Chasidus brought a flourishing revival—a stream of religious enthusiasm—into moribund, rabbinical Judaism.

---

[3] Paul Levertoff, *Die religiöse Denkweise der Chassidim* (Leipzig: J. C. Hinrichs, 1918). Passage translated by Johann Stoll.

[4] Levertoff's father, Shaul Levertov, was said to be a descendant of Zalman as well, but the original records have been lost. See Moshe Levertov, *The Man Who Mocked the KGB* (Brooklyn, NY: self published, 2002), 9.

[5] Some scholars speculate that the Baal Shem Tov was heavily influenced by a dissenting sect of the Greek Orthodox Church. See Yaffa Eliach, "The Russian Dissenting Sects and Their Influence on Israel Baal Shem Tov, Founder of Hassidism," *Proceedings of the American Academy for Jewish Research* 36 (1968): 55–83. Shimon Dubnov even points out how the stories of both Baal Shem Tov and Yeshua circulated orally for about two generations after they passed away before being written down. See Shimon Dubnov, *Toldot HaChassidut* (Tel Aviv, Israel: Dvir Co., 1959), 41.

THE BAAL SHEM TOV

The Chasidic movement began with a simple peasant named Israel ben Eliezer.[6] He earned an early reputation as a healer and miracle-worker. People soon began to refer to him as "The Master of the Good Name," i.e., the Baal Shem Tov. He acquired wide popularity within peasant-class Jewry in Poland and Russia. His teaching emphasized sincere love for God, simple faith in the power of prayer, and passionate devotion to HaShem. He placed compassion and spirituality above Talmudic scholarship and taught that a simple man's earnest prayers are more precious to God than the most erudite cogitations of halachic hair-splitting and ceremonial observances.

In the mid-eighteenth century, the Baal Shem Tov formed a school of disciples in the Podolian town of Medzhybizh. Those disciples disseminated his teachings and founded Chasidic Judaism. They became the heads of the various sects of the Chasidic movement.

Sects of Chasidim are characterized by radical discipleship to a rebbe—a great rabbi and spiritual leader over a community. The disciple of such a rebbe is called a *Chasid* (חסיד), a biblical Hebrew word that means "devoted one." In Chasidic Judaism, the disciples of a rebbe regard their teacher as a *tzaddik* ("righteous one," צדיק). To the Chasidim, the *tzaddik-rebbe* was a prophet, miracle-worker,[7] saint, and intermediary between them and God—a living link to God. A Chasidic rebbe is to his Chasidim a small version of what Moses was to Israel.

SCHNEUR ZALMAN AND CHABAD

Paul Philip Levertoff's grand uncle, Rabbi Schneur Zalman of Liadi (1745–1813) learned Chasidus from Rabbi Dov Ber, the Maggid of Mezeritch, one of the prominent disciples of the Baal Shem Tov. Schneur Zalman was born in Lionza, a Polish town in the province of Mohilev, only fifty miles from Orsha, Belarus, where Paul Levertoff was born. Schneur Zalman, a descendant of the Maharal of Prague, was an early prodigy with an enormous intellect. He authored numerous works of Jewish literature, including a revised siddur, Chasidic discourses, and a revision of the *Shulchan Aruch*. Despite his scholarship, Schneur Zalman was characterized chiefly by his piety, his ecstatic devotion in prayer, and his ardent attachment to HaShem:

> This was actually heard from my master and teacher, Rabbi Schneur Zalman, when he was in a state of d'veikut [spiritual ecstasy] and would exclaim: "I want nothing at all! I don't want Your Gan Eden [Paradise], I don't want Your Olam Haba [World to Come] … I want nothing but You alone!" (Menachem Mendel of Lubavitch, the Tzemach Tzedek)[8]

---

6   See Appendix Two: Sketches of the Chasidic World, "The Life of the Baal Shem" for Levertoff's own overview of the life of the Baal Shem Tov.

7   See Appendix Two: Sketches of the Chasidic World, "Kabbalistic-Chasidic Miracle Stories" for Levertoff's account of a miracle story of Rabbi Isaac Luria and his disciple.

8   Rabbi Schneur Zalman, *Journey of the Soul: A Chasidic Discourse by Rabbi Schneur Zalman of Liadi* (trans. Ari Sollish; Brooklyn: Kehot Publication Society, 2004), 13.

Schneur Zalman quickly became a leading figure in the Chasidic movement. His three brothers, Yehudah Leib, Mordechai, and Moshe, joined the growing ranks of his disciples. (Levertoff's mother was a granddaughter of one of them.)

In his teachings, Schneur Zalman labored to unite the spiritual ecstasy and mystery of Chasidus with the academic rigor of traditional Judaism. He rejected the blind-faith approach adopted by many Chasidic proponents and advanced a more rational and scholarly discipline which traced Chasidic mysticism to its sources in the Bible, the *Talmud,* and kabbalistic literature. His method of study came to be called ChaBaD (חב״ד), an acronym for the three Hebrew words *Chokmah* ("Wisdom," חכמה), *Binah* ("Understanding," בינה), and *Da'at* ("Knowledge," דעת). He published his teachings in an anthology titled *Likkutei Amarim* (*Collected Discourses*). The book is better known as the *Tanya* (*It was taught*), named after the first word of the book. The *Tanya* is a systematic exposition of the teachings and philosophy of Chasidus, and it remains a veritable bible of Chasidic thought for the Chabad Lubavitch movement today.

Schneur Zalman and the Chasidic heritage loomed large in Levertoff's mind. "To his father, his grandfather, and to his mother's uncle, the famous Rabbi Schneur Zalman, he felt he owed his own preparation for, and understanding of the teaching of Jesus."[9] Levertoff draws much of the material in *Love and the Messianic Age* from the *Tanya* and other writings of Schneur Zalman. Shortly before his death, Levertoff told his wife that he had seen his deceased parents and Schneur Zalman. She said, "In his last hours he talked with them, and assured me that they were now 'of the Kingdom' and awaiting his coming."[10] Levertoff rose from his sick bed and danced a Chasidic dance of joy before he died.

THE CHASIDIC GOSPELS

Orsha, Belarus, where Levertoff grew up, was home to a large Jewish population served by two primary synagogues. One of these was a *Mitnagdim* synagogue. They called themselves *Mitnagdim* ("opponents") because they opposed the Chasidic movement. The *Mitnagdim* represented a more traditional, sober approach to Judaism. They rejected the excesses, emotional ecstasies, and mystical esotericism of the Chasidim. The other synagogue in Orsha was a Chasidic synagogue called Reb Boruch's Schul.[11] They were known for their loud, Pentecostal-styled prayer services, joyous singing, and dancing. The Levertoff family with their Chasidic lineage and connections most likely attended the latter: Reb Boruch's Schul.

When Paul Philip Levertoff first read the Gospels, he felt that they had far more affinity with the Chasidic world than they did with Christianity and the Gentiles who revered them. He found the Gospels to be thoroughly Jewish, and conceptually similar to Chasidic Judaism. All of the concepts

---

9   Beatrice Levertoff, "Thirty Years Work," 4.

10   Ibid.

11   Ironically, though he retained his Chasidic leanings throughout his life, Levertoff later studied at the prestigious Volozhin yeshiva under Rabbi Naftali Zvi Yehudah Berlin (the Netziv), who was a staunch *mitnaged*, an opponent of the Chasidic movement. For more on the Netziv and the Volozhin yeshiva, see Baruch HaLevi Epstein, *My Uncle the Netziv* (Brooklyn, NY: Mesorah, 1988). One of the Netziv's more famous works has been translated into English as *The Path of Torah* (trans. E. Greenman; Jerusalem, Israel: Urim, 2009).

were present: rebirth of the soul, spiritual endowment, personal relationship with God, emphasis on joy and love, the priority of repentance, Messianic hope, and, most of all, attachment to a rebbe-tzaddik through discipleship. In this case, however, the rebbe was Yeshua of Nazareth. Levertoff wondered how Gentile Christians could hope to comprehend Yeshua and His words without the benefit of a classical Jewish education or of experience with the theological philosophies of the Chasidim.

Levertoff's *Love and the Messianic Age* is a short, English version of his much longer dissertation, *Die religiöse Denkweise der Chassidim* (*The Religious Ideas of the Chasidim*) where he first laid out his ideas about Chasidus and the New Testament. In the introduction to *Die religiöse*, Levertoff makes some sweeping comparisons between Chasidic philosophy and that of the apostles:

> Even though it has many of its roots in rabbinic legality, Chasidism delivered to Ghetto-Jewery a world of new religious anticipations, new value judgements, new strengths, and a vivid desire for personal redemption. Chasidism, like Christianity, aims at the completion of the personality in the alliance of life and love with God. The Chasid would agree with the Apostle Paul [in 1 Corinthians 2:14], that "the man without the Spirit does not accept the things that come from the Spirit of God, for they are foolishness to him, and he cannot understand them, because they are spiritually discerned." [12]

Along similar lines, Paul Levertoff's daughter Olga described Chasidism in her book, *The Wailing Wall:*

> The Chasidic, i.e., mystical movement of the eighteenth century, released all the incipient mysticism in Judaism. Jewry has always repressed this tendency, preferring to be known to the world as a legalistic rather than as a contemplative people. Yet genuine Jewish spirituality is found in Chasidism and in the [esoteric] movements which preceded it ... Chasidim often do dance to the glory of God; but they do more than that. They have produced a type of mysticism, piety and meditation which approaches uncannily near to the Christian method and spiritual language. Jewish mysticism at its best does really equal, or almost equal, the mysticism of, say, St. John of the Cross. [13]

TZADDIKISM

One critical aspect of Chasidic theology that Levertoff does not deal with in *Love and the Messianic Age* is *tzaddikism*—the concept of connection to God by means of attachment to a righteous person. It seems like a strange omission from a book comparing New Testament and Chasidic philosophy. There is no other point of congruence between the two so startling as the Chasidic

---

[12] Paul Levertoff, *Die religiöse*. Introduction passage translated by Johann Stoll.

[13] Olga Levertoff, *The Wailing Wall* (London: A. R. Mowbray & Co. Ltd., 1937), 35–36. St. John of the Cross (1542–1591) was a Spanish priest and mystic who was an important contributor to the Catholic Reformation.

belief in a righteous intermediary who bridges the gap between God and man, calls disciples to follow him, atones for his followers through his personal suffering, lifts the prayers of his disciples to God, and imbues the sinful among his people with his own personal righteousness so they might find justification before HaShem. Though Levertoff does not include a study of *tzaddikism* in *Love and the Messianic Age,* he was no stranger to the notion. To provide readers of this exposition with an overview of the concept, we have included an article, "The Exalted Rebbe," by Toby Janicki of First Fruits of Zion in Appendix One at the back of this book.

PAUL LEVERTOFF AND THE ZOHAR

The writers plunge the reader into a welter of ideas, strung together in sentences three pages long, out of which he at last emerges excited and breathless.

Mysticism is the study of the mystical, that is, the unseen ways in which God runs the universe and reveals Himself to the world. For example, the prelude to the Gospel of John is a classic example of early apostolic mysticism.

In *Love and the Messianic Age,* Levertoff liberally quotes the *Zohar* (and other mystical literature derived from it) for purposes of comparing and contrasting those teachings with Christian spirituality. Levertoff's employment of the *Zohar* and mystical literature poses a problem for some within Messianic Judaism, where that same literature is sometimes regarded as dangerous and even occult material.

As Levertoff says, the *Zohar* is the "'Bible of the mystics'—which, in common with most bibles, is more talked about than known."[14] Jewish mysticism is often wrongly identified with hocus-pocus and occultism. Although those elements are present in medieval books of mysticism, they are present in Christian mystical writings from the same era as well.

At First Fruits of Zion, we routinely consult all branches of Jewish literature for insight into the Apostolic Scriptures, including arcane texts like the *Zohar.* Our use of such material or quotation of select passages should never be regarded as an endorsement of the whole. The literature of mystical Judaism sometimes does contain problematic passages, magical-type prescriptions, Gnostic-styled concepts, and flights into fantastic contemplation.[15] The same could also be said of other ancient sources such as the *Talmud* and midrash, sources which are recognized as valuable in theological discussion but are not always to be taken literally. In those cases, the benefits of these literary works outweigh their deficits, inasmuch as they provide invaluable context to the Gospels and the writings of the apostles, and they contain undeniable, stunning parallels to the teachings of Yeshua. When studying Jewish sources, it is not necessary to endorse the whole gamut of the literature to profit immensely from the content.

---

[14] Paul Levertoff, "Some Aspects of Jewish Mysticism," 23.

[15] For a refutation of the idea that much of the content Jewish mysticism comes from Gnosticism, see Moshe Idel, *Kabbalah: New Perspectives* (New Haven, CT: Yale University Press, 1988). Idel argues, contrary to the popular theories of scholars such as Gershom Scholem, that instead these mystical concepts developed within the "wellsprings of Judaism" itself and that instead Gnosticism was influenced by Judaism.

AUTHORSHIP OF THE ZOHAR

In a 1934 article, Levertoff provided an overview of the *Zohar* as follows:

> In its present form, the *Zohar* first appeared in Spain in the thirteenth century, and while purporting to be but a commentary on the Pentateuch, it is in reality a thesaurus of mystic contemplations on the Divine Transcendence and Immanence, on Creation and Redemption, on God and Israel, on Israel and the world, on this world and the world to come, on holiness and the "other side"—i.e., sin, on life and death, on Paradise and Hell. It is written in Aramaic, and is ascribed to the second century Galilean Rabbi, Simeon ben Yochai.[16]

The academic community regards the *Zohar* as "pseudepigrapha," a word which refers to texts whose claimed authorship is unfounded. A pseudepigraphic work is simply one whose real author attributed it to a figure of the past. Though it purports to be the work of Shimon ben Yochai (an apostolic-era sage), scholarly consensus regards the *Zohar* as a medieval creation.[17] In this regard, it can be compared to the book of Enoch, a first-century apocalypse that claims to be written by Enoch, the ancestor of Noah.

For that reason alone, the *Zohar* should not be regarded as literally true or historically accurate. Instead, it is more like a window into the world of Jewish esoteric thought. In that world, the reader quickly becomes lost in its wild maze of obscure conjectures and bizarre expositions. Despite all that, Messianic Judaism should not regard the *Zohar* as a banned book. Instead, the *Zohar* is a wealth of amazing parallels to the thought and theology of the apostolic writers. When Levertoff first encountered the Gospels, those parallels inspired him to look deeper into the New Testament, a process which eventually led him to faith.

CONTENT OF THE ZOHAR

In her book, *The Wailing Wall*, Levertoff's daughter Olga provides an entertaining introduction to the *Zohar*:

> The "*Zohar*," or "Brightness," … is the most important mystical work produced by Jewry in the Middle Ages. The *Zohar* influenced profoundly the mystical thought of future generations; it was also known to Christian scholars of the period, and was a mine of theosophical and Gnostic-styled lore, as well as weird and pseudo-scientific ideas about astronomy, astrology, physiognomy, and other ingenuities. Purporting to be the work of Shimon ben Yochai, a second century rabbi, it was supposed to have been discovered by Moses de Leon (1230–1305) who later asserted that he had written it himself. In reality, it is quite obviously the work of many authors. Much of the material goes back, in all probability, to a very early date, perhaps indeed to

---

[16] Paul Levertoff, "Some Aspects of Jewish Mysticism," 20.

[17] For arguments for an earlier dating of the *Zohar*, see Rabbi Menachem Mendel Kasher, "HaZohar (The Zohar)," *Sinai* 50 (1958).

the second or even the first century, but its sources and its authors lie buried in the past and its whole history is wrapped in obscurity. It is a literary curiosity, a historical enigma. Its style is cryptic to the point of being perfectly incomprehensible at times. It purports to be a commentary on the Pentateuch. So it is, but not in the least a commentary on the Pentateuch as we read it. Every word and syllable, every phrase and every incident has an inner-supernal meaning, and these meanings build up into a sort of code of imagination, an airy structure on a quite different plane of reality. And everything is twisted out of its mundane context in order that it may yield a "supernal" implication. The book is therefore not the slightest use as commentary on the Pentateuch. But as a guide to the intricacies of Jewish mystical thought, as a signpost to a strange dream-country which has its own solidity and its own verities, which in time one comes to recognize with a sort of familiarity—as such a pointer, the *Zohar* is extraordinarily illuminating. It is written mostly in Aramaic, and in a kind of cryptic abbreviated and allusory style which resembles nothing so much as some sort of "supernal" shorthand.[18]

Paul Levertoff maintained that, although the *Zohar* was written in the thirteenth century, it contained material inherited from earlier sources and schools of Jewish tradition—a conglomeration of early Jewish sources and spiritual constructs anthologized into the *Zohar*. Levertoff's view is supported by several critics today, including the respected scholar of Jewish mysticism, Moshe Idel, of Hebrew University.[19]

THE SONCINO ZOHAR

When the Soncino Press undertook to translate the *Zohar* to English, their translators became bogged down in the cryptic Aramaic, unable to complete the more difficult volumes of the translation. Incredibly, Soncino asked Paul Philip Levertoff for assistance. Levertoff agreed to help with the translation and singlehandedly translated the two remaining untranslated volumes: the whole, tangled commentary on Exodus. However, Soncino wanted to leave his name off of the publication because, in Jewish circles, Levertoff was infamous as an apostate and a believer in Jesus. The editors at Soncino felt that having his name on the publication would damage their credibility and feared that subscribers would cancel their subscriptions to the publication. Levertoff insisted that if they were to use his work, they place his name on the translation. Soncino eventually conceded, but they insisted on placing the other translators' names alongside his, even on the volumes he had produced independently.[20] The Soncino version of the *Zohar* is still the most popular English edition.

The *Zohar* has often been misunderstood and misused. In 1933 the propaganda ministry of Nazi Germany circulated a pamphlet misquoting a passage from the *Zohar* in a manner calculated to lend credence to the old European blood-libel. In an attempt to refute the Nazi smear, a German

---

18   Olga Levertoff, *The Wailing Wall*, 36–37.
19   Idel, *Kabbalah: New Perspectives*.
20   Beatrice Levertoff, "Ten Years at Holy Trinity, Shoreditch," *Church and the Jews* 94 (January 1933): 18.

Zionist Jew traveled to England to find a Jewish scholar who could correctly translate the passage. He tried several experts in rabbinical texts, but the scholars all referred him to Levertoff. Levertoff was able to quickly translate the passage and provide the man with the refutation he sought.[21]

In Christianity and Messianic Judaism today, the *Zohar* is feared because of its strange, secretive content. Anti-Semites depict the *Zohar* as a Satanic menace. To Levertoff, though, the numinous world of thought in the *Zohar* made a ready bridge between the charismatic, Chasidic Judaism he grew up with and faith in Yeshua, the Messiah of Israel.

CHRISTIANITY AND THE ZOHAR

In terms of providing perspective on the Gospels, the *Zohar* has so much to offer that the first translation out of Aramaic was commissioned by the Church. By the time of the Protestant Reformation, both Protestant and Catholic scholars had begun to dig into Jewish mysticism. Christian Hebraists delighted to find within it many amazing affinities with the gospel and the doctrine of the Incarnation. Spurred on by such exciting discoveries, the Church ordered a version of the *Zohar* translated into Latin.

Jewish scholar Yehudah Liebes notes that the affinity between Christianity and the mysticism of the *Zohar* exceeds the natural expectation of comparative religious studies. In an article titled "Christian Influences in the Zohar,"[22] he suggests that some of the concepts in the *Zohar* might have entered Judaism under the influence of early Christianity. He cites examples of high Christology, messianic sonship, messianic interpretations of Genesis 1:1, and other items, which all seem to betray a Christian sway. Alternatively, the *Zohar* can be simply understood as expanding on the same Neo-Platonist reflexes present within classical Judaism that influenced and informed the spiritual worldview from which our Gospels emerged.

In one long, breathless passage from his journal, *The Church and the Jews,* Levertoff describes the central thrust of the *Zohar* as follows:

> The final aim and all-pervading theme of the whole *Zohar,* and the reason at the back of the whole order of its philosophy [is] the desire to effect and complete the unity of all things in one volume of glory and perfection—union of the different aspects of the Divine Personality; union of the two ultimate aspects of the universe, Justice and Mercy; union of the celestial and terrestrial spheres; union of God and Man. But whereas in too many modern minds too great a stress is laid upon this last unifying intent in its subjective aspect, in the minds of the unknown spiritual artists whose testament and apologia the *Zohar* is, even the mystical ideal of fusion with the Divine is subject to, and but a part, of the yet higher aim of glorifying ever more perfectly the Divine Itself. Thus Man becomes at once more humble and more noble—an instrument only, but actually an instrument with power to exalt and aid the splendor of the majesty of the Most High! No theory of worship can approach this in its dignity, its objectivity, its stupendous simplicity. There is no room here

---

[21] Paul Levertoff, "The Religious Tragedy of Judaism," *Church and the Jews* 100 (July 1934): 11.

[22] Yehudah Liebes, "Christian Influences in the Zohar," *Immanuel* 17 (Winter 1983/84): 43–67.

for mere emotional satisfaction, self-glorification or cold righteousness: everything glows and burns with the bright steady flame of self-forgetful ecstasy, of will concentrated fiercely on one point and to one end, of heart subdued by the discipline of the spirit until the point is reached where the suppliant becomes the giver, the co-operator, the partaker of delight, one with the celestial life of praise, his heaven begun while yet on earth, this world being but a prefiguring of what is above, man but a lesser copy of angels, his world a lesser heaven, or, if he will it so, a lesser Gehenna, if he choose to be ruled by those principalities of evil, the rulers of "the other side" who are yet themselves within the Creator's scheme, being the "Lords of Judgment" by whose accusations the self-destroyed soul may be duly punished, though even for such there is some final hope. In this all-embracing scheme of life, whose universe, being at once limitless and God-created, must of necessity include all things in the gigantic sweep of Divine intention, the incomprehensible is not caged nor is poetry tied down into bundles of formalism, but, perhaps because of the long silent watches of mystical contemplation which at last receive their reward in this wise—for "at present there is indeed an appearance as of separation between the Creator and His Creation ... because of the scum of wickedness which as yet still clings to the hem of the garment of righteousness, and therefore although even in this time we proclaim the Unity we do so silently ... But in the time that is to be, when the Messiah will reign and sin be banished, then shall that unity be proclaimed openly ..." —the Divine somehow comes down at some unremarked moment into the simple ways of men and is found in their midst become familiar and comprehensible at last: and what wealth of Christ-ward implication could one find in an interpretation of the *Zohar* in the light of Messianic fulfillment![23]

In an article from another issue of the same journal, Levertoff reflects upon the *Zohar* with a similar rhapsody, comparing it to a deep-set jewel:

> In spite of its peculiar (and often bizarre) idiom and method the *Zohar* is as a jewel set very deep. It is bright, and gleams, but such radiance has to be sought. The masters of its mysteries did not desire knowledge of such mysteries to be widespread; rather, they veiled the glories of which they were cognizant, and guarded the hidden beauty with jealous secrecy. Its language is curt, pre-supposing intimate knowledge of all the sources mentioned in its obscure references: its phraseology is soaked in allusions, not only Biblical but apparently—contemporaneous; allusions which fascinate by their very elusiveness ... But when the beauty is revealed, and the incomprehensible made plain, what splendor remains! How the jewel glows and lightens in its dusty setting! What glories flash and beam within its strange radiant depths! [24]

---

[23] Paul Levertoff, "Worship," *Church and the Jews* 94 (January 1933): 6–13.

[24] Paul Levertoff, "Some Aspects of Jewish Mysticism," 20.

For Paul Philip Levertoff, the value of the *Zohar* did not lie in its veracity or historical reliability, but in the broad strokes of its spiritual vision. In one stunning passage from *The Church and the Jews,* Levertoff laments the absence of such passionate spiritual vision among his fellow churchmen, and he even suggests that the cryptic world of the *Zohar* could be regarded as a common ground between Christians and Jews:

> If Christians could but attain to a vision of the essence and core of their own faith of one thousandth the intensity wherewith those Zoharitic Rabbis plumbed the depths and scaled the heights of infinitude, they might become more worthy of their title, and even show to others a worthier, more thrilling, less man-exalting path to more distant but O more glittering and lightful stars. How petty, how earthbound, how much a clod the *Zohar* makes one feel! Undoubtedly, the vision and the ardor which crams its tantalizing pages hardly needs re-focusing, with Christ as its centre, to make it a [veritable] bible not only of Jewish but of Christian and above all of Hebrew-Christian mystics—and what mystics ought not they to be![25]

In *Love and the Messianic Age,* Levertoff does not assume that the *Zohar* or any of the Chasidic and rabbinic sources he quotes are authoritative or should be received unquestioned by believers. Instead, he uses them to paint the broad landscape of Jewish mysticism for his readers. He does this in order to show us that the Gospels are part of that same landscape of literature.

The reader who feels wary of a book such as *Love and the Messianic Age* that so liberally cites mystical Jewish literature will do well to remember that the apostolic faith as expressed in the Gospels, the Epistles, and Revelation is also a mystical expression of Judaism. One should keep in mind that the various ideas and concepts presented in *Love and the Messianic Age* need not be accepted at face value. Instead, they are simply presented for purposes of comparison and contrast with the teachings of Yeshua and the apostles. In any case, Paul Levertoff is a safe and reliable guide in the strange and sometimes unsettling paths of esoteric Jewish thought and theology.

---

[25] Paul Levertoff, "Worship," 6–13.

1

KNOWLEDGE AND LOVE

TWO APPROACHES TO FAITH

Mysticism in theology differs from perspectives which are more scientifically logical. (31)

There are two different approaches to faith: a mystical approach and a rational approach. In popular religious terms, one might contrast the "charismatic" against the "academic."

The rational approach to theology attempts to provide a consistent and comprehensive system for belief—something akin to a math equation. Anything inconsistent with that systematic theology is rejected as irrational.

A mystical approach distrusts a theology which rejects ideas and experiences simply because they do not fit into the rational box. For the mystic, the value of the irrational can be proven simply by the existence of life around us. Life itself is irrational and unpredictable.

Our experience of life gives life meaning to us. Similarly, our experience of faith is what makes faith meaningful. Our experience with God cannot be reduced to an objective equation any more than the love between a man and woman can be reduced to a biological necessity.

FACTS AND FEELINGS

The paramount difference between the two begins at the outset, when each defines its sources of knowledge concerning the relations between God and man. (31)

The rational approach to theology is different from the mystical approach. The two approaches differ the most when explaining God's interaction with man.

For the rationalist, religious experiences—interactions with the Divine—must be analyzed and tested against objective data. If the experience proves to be consistent with the expectations of the rational system, then the experience can be considered valid. A subjective experience with God must be discounted, because it cannot be objectively tested.

The mystic, however, thinks differently. To the mystic, objective "religious data" has no important value "except as it is caught up into the realm of subjective experience." He is less concerned with the facts, and more concerned with experience. The mystic not only wants to know what is true; he wants to experience what is true. The facts are important when they are "caught up into the realm of subjective experience and found to have affinity therewith. The actual feeling, the excitement, has essential value to the mystic."

The rationalist desires to explain God. The mystic desires to feel Him.

THE TWO KINDS OF KNOWLEDGE

🌿 *There are two kinds of knowledge. (32)*

Chasidic theology teaches that there are two types of knowledge.

The first type is that which is attainable through the study of creation and the divine "character imprinted thereon." That is to say that by carefully observing the universe, a man can deduce a great deal about the Creator. Paul refers to natural revelation like this in the first chapter of Romans:

> That which is known about God is evident within them; for God made it evident to them. For since the creation of the world His invisible attributes, His eternal power and divine nature, have been clearly seen, being understood through what has been made, so that they are without excuse. (Romans 1:19–20)

The second type of knowledge is that of the "inner being of God." According to Levertoff, this latter type is a progressive knowledge. Study of the knowledge of the inner being of God leads to love of Him, and, as a result of this love, a person is brought to "the actual vision of Him." That is to say, through knowing the "inner being of God," a person comes to intimately know God. The inner being of God is revealed through our Master who said, "If you knew Me, you would know My Father also."[1]

THE VISION OF GOD IN THE MESSIANIC AGE

🌿 *To attain this vision—the actual sight of God—is the highest aim; it is a consummation which will not be reached until the Messianic Age. (32)*

Seeing God (allegorically speaking) is the highest aim of the Jewish mystic and Chasid. In this present age, HaShem is concealed from His creation, but in the coming age, He will be fully revealed:

> The presence of G-d is not truly revealed at present. At best we can attain knowledge of His existence, and not comprehension of His nature. Only in the future will the prophecy be fulfilled "Your teacher will no more be hidden (Isaiah 30:20)," for His

---

[1] John 8:19.

true nature will be revealed then. But now, this nature is not revealed, so the soul is in a constant state of thirst.[2]

Our, souls are enclothed in a bodily form, which prevents us from perceiving G-dliness directly. It is only in the Messianic Future to Come that the body, too, will become so spiritually pure as to accommodate such perception ... as it is written, "And the glory of G-d shall be revealed, and all flesh shall perceive together" (Isaiah 40:5).[3]

This vision of God will be revealed in the Messianic Age and the hunger and thirst of the soul will be satisfied.[4] This future vision is spoken of through Moses and the prophets.

Though "it has not appeared,"[5] the vision of God that Moses and the prophets promised will ultimately be realized in the Messianic Era and the World to Come. The book of Revelation offers us a brief glimpse into this promised vision. In Revelation 22:4 it is stated that "they will see His face, and His name will be on their foreheads."

The mystic and Chasid lives his daily life in this present world eagerly anticipating that future realization. Levertoff points out that in mystical literature, the words "See now that I, I am He" (Deuteronomy 32:39) are prophetic of the day when "all flesh will see it together" (Isaiah 40:5) in the Messianic Era:

> Similarly it is written, "See now that I, I am he" (Deuteronomy 32:39), to show that there is no division between the upper and the lower. See now, in this way, when there are righteous men in the world, blessings are sent to all worlds." (*Zohar* I, 87b [Soncino]).[6]

Thus, the mystic is seeking the knowledge of HaShem that will be revealed in the Messianic Era when "we will see Him just as He is."[7] Yet, he is seeking to understand this knowledge in the here and now.

---

[2] Rabbi Shalom DovBer, *Kuntest Umaayan: Overcoming Folly, A Chasidic Treatise by Rabbi Shalom DovBer of Lubavitch* (trans. Zalman Posner; Brooklyn: Kehot Publication Society, 2006), 105–106.

[3] *Torah Or*, Genesis16 (Wagshul).

[4] Matthew 5:6, Revelation 7:16.

[5] 1 John 3:2.

[6] Cf. *Tanya* 36. See Psalm 17:15. Note also the words of the Master in Matthew 5:8, "Blessed are the pure in heart, for they shall see God." Compare this with Psalm 24:3–5; Psalm 51:10.

[7] 1 John 3:2.

THE SINGER AND THE PAINTER

🖋 *The picture is not the artist, nor is the voice of a singer the personality of the man. (33)*

Levertoff offers us an explanation of the two types of knowledge by means of two illustrations: those of a singer and a painter. Creation is like a picture painted by HaShem. It displays His power, His magnificence, and His attributes. However, there is a limit to how much we can learn about a painter from staring at his painting. Just as the picture is not the artist, HaShem transcends creation. In the same way, we may know the voice of a gifted singer without personally knowing the singer, because the voice is not the singer. The mystic wants more than knowledge about God; he wants to know God. He wants to know the artist who made the painting. He wants to know the singer who sang the song.

CHILDREN OF WISDOM

🖋 *We know God best when we know Him in His holiness and wisdom and love, apart from His creation. (33)*

Knowledge of HaShem Himself is the only true way to know Him. In the Hebraic sense, "knowing God" implies "intimate relationship" with God.

According to Levertoff, we know HaShem best through His holiness and wisdom. His holiness and His wisdom are found in the Torah.[8] The apostles also speak of wisdom being closely connected to HaShem's essential being:[9]

> We speak God's wisdom in a mystery, the hidden wisdom which God predestined before the ages to our glory … which things we also speak, not in words taught by human wisdom, but in those taught by the Spirit, combining spiritual thoughts with spiritual words. (1 Corinthians 2:7–13)

A child is born from the union of both a father and a mother. The Holy One and His wisdom may be allegorically referred to as Father and Mother.[10] The child of God is one who is born of the Father and Mother both—that is to say that faith in God must be paired with obedience to His wisdom. "Wisdom is vindicated by all her children."[11]

---

[8]   1 Peter 1:15–16 quoting Leviticus 11:44ff., 19:2, 20:7.

[9]   E.g. Ephesians 3:10; Colossians 1:9. Cf. James 1:5, 3:17.

[10]   This is most evident in Proverbs where Solomon states that the goal is "to know wisdom and instruction" (Proverbs 1:2). Throughout the book of Proverbs, Solomon instructs his readers to hear "your father's instruction" (Proverbs 1:8); wisdom is personified with the feminine. Since all wisdom comes from HaShem, it may be said that He is the Father whose instruction Solomon calls his reader's attention to hear. Wisdom (which is a feminine word in Hebrew) is personified as a caring mother. For example, see Proverbs 6:20 which states "My son, observe the commandment of your father and do not forsake the teaching of your mother."

[11]   Luke 7:35.

The Messiah is the personification of HaShem's wisdom. Paul states that in the Messiah "are hidden all the treasures of wisdom and knowledge."[12] In Messiah is the "manifold wisdom of God."[13] This is further stated in 1 Corinthians: "But by His doing you are in Messiah Yeshua, who became to us wisdom from God."[14] Therefore, we may know HaShem best through His Son, who says, "Believe in God; believe also in me" (John 14:1).

SHOW US THE FATHER

🖋 *Only Moses had, to some extent, this vision; yet it is the business of all to try and reach this stage. (33)*

The Torah says that, out of all the prophets, only Moses attained a clear vision of HaShem. "He beholds the form of the LORD."[15] The *Zohar* discourses on the difference between Moses' vision of HaShem and that of the other prophets:

> Moses was separated by many degrees from all the other prophets, who bore the same relation to him as an ape to a human being. Other prophets beheld visions in a glass that did not illumine, and even so they did not venture to lift up their eyes and gaze above … nor was their message given to them in clear terms. Not so was Moses, the faithful prophet: he saw his vision in a luminous glass and still stood upright, and he dared to raise his head and gaze upwards, like one to whom his neighbour says: Lift up your head and look me in the face in order that you may know what I say. So Moses raised his head without fear and gazed at the brightness of the supernal glory without losing his senses like the other prophets, who when they prophesied were bereft of their faculties and became transformed and knew nothing at all of this world. Not so Moses, for even while he was in that exalted grade he did not lose his faculties, and straightway after gazing on the brightness of the heavenly glory he returned to the camp to speak to them concerning all their requirements, and his mind was as clear as before, and more so. (*Zohar* V, 268b–269a [Soncino])

Nevertheless, attaining a pure revelation of HaShem is a goal worthwhile for everyone to seek. In the Gospel of John, the disciple Philip said, "Lord, show us the Father, and it is enough for us."[16]

Moses states that "you will seek the LORD your God, and you will find Him if you search for Him with all your heart and all your soul."[17] Jeremiah says, "You will seek Me and find Me when

---

12 Colossians 2:3.

13 Ephesians 3:10.

14 1 Corinthians 1:30.

15 Numbers 12:8.

16 John 14:8.

17 Deuteronomy 4:29.

you search for Me with all your heart."[18] However, before one can see this vision of HaShem (so to speak) one must know how to search for Him. Our Master tells us to "search the Scriptures"[19] because they testify of Him.

The vision of HaShem is best acquired through imitation of our Master; as Paul stated, "Be imitators of me, just as I also am of Messiah."[20] When we behold the Son and live in imitation of Him, we are able to see HaShem (so to speak). It is not that we are literally seeing HaShem, for it states, "You cannot see My face, for no man can see Me and live!"[21] Rather, we are seeing wisdom and holiness personified. This is found in our Master's reply to Philip's request: "Have I been so long with you, and yet you have not come to know Me, Philip? He who has seen Me has seen the Father; how can you say, 'Show us the Father'?"[22]

THE PURE IN HEART

🖎 *However, it is characteristic of him who longs to see the King and to be received by Him, that he keeps himself undefiled and walks in His way. (33)*

To behold HaShem one must keep himself pure. Our Master said, "Blessed are the pure in heart, for they shall see God."[23] He warns us that the things which come out of a man's heart and out of his mouth are the things that defile him.[24] The impurity of our own hearts obscures our vision of the King.

His sacrifice was intended "to purify for Himself a people for His own possession."[25] Purification comes through obedience; as it is stated, "Since you have in obedience to the truth purified your souls."[26] Purification also comes through confidence in the Messiah's return and our resurrection from the dead, as it says, "And everyone who has this hope fixed on Him purifies himself, just as He is pure."[27]

---

[18] Jeremiah 29:13.

[19] John 5:39.

[20] 1 Corinthians 11:1. Cf. 1 John 2:6.

[21] Exodus 33:20.

[22] John 14:9.

[23] Matthew 5:8.

[24] Matthew 15:11.

[25] Titus 2:14.

[26] 1 Peter 1:22. Cf. Levertoff's reference to 1 John 3:2–4. See also Psalm 24.

[27] 1 John 3:3.

PROPERTY OF THE MESSIANIC AGE TO COME

🌿 *The knowledge of God which the Chasid thus seeks to cultivate belongs, strictly speaking, to the Messianic world to come. (33)*

The mystic strives after the knowledge of HaShem which is to be revealed in the Messianic Era. Levertoff states, "In the Messianic Age the knowledge of God will no longer be merely intellectual apprehension but actual realization in experience."

When Messiah comes, the veil will be lifted and all humanity will come into an intimate knowledge of God and experience with God.[28] We will be like men born blind, suddenly receiving the gift of sight. The intimacy and experience of God that will be ours when Messiah returns is the joy for which we long.

However, the mystic does not wait for the Messianic Era to experience God; he seeks the vision of HaShem in the here and now. Our Master's words allude to this when He calls us to "repent, for the kingdom of heaven is at hand."[29]

Although the kingdom of heaven is not yet realized and fully revealed, it actually is, in a sense, attainable now. The minute one takes upon himself the yoke of heaven, he immediately is granted a foretaste of the Messianic Era to come. Our Master speaks of this paradox when He says, "An hour is coming, and now is …" The words "an hour is coming" refer to the Messianic Age. The words "and now is" refer to our experience of the Messianic Age in this present era.

> An hour is coming, and now is, when the true worshippers will worship the Father in spirit and truth. (John 4:23)
>
> An hour is coming and now is, when the dead will hear the voice of the Son of God, and those who hear will live. (John 5:25)
>
> Do not marvel at this; for an hour is coming, in which all who are in the tombs will hear His voice. (John 5:28)
>
> An hour is coming when I will no longer speak to you in figurative language, but will tell you plainly of the Father. (John 16:25)

"An hour is coming" when the Son of Man will return and the Messianic Age will commence. But the hour has already come and "now is" in the sense that He has come once already. In a spiritual and intangible sense, the era of Messiah is already under way. Though the hour is still coming, it already is now. The more we seek after our Master, obey Him and the instruction of the Torah, the greater and purer our vision and the greater our foretaste of the Messianic Age.

---

[28] Jeremiah 31:34.

[29] Matthew 4:17.

A TIME OF PREGNANCY

🌿 *The present age is a time of pregnancy. (34)*

The era in which we currently live is likened to a time of pregnancy. This is similar to the words of our Master in the Gospels of Matthew and Mark. Our Master tells us that the events before His return "are merely the beginning of birth pangs."[30] In Jewish eschatology, the years that precede the coming of Messiah are known as the "birth pangs of the Messiah."[31]

Levertoff's sources depict the people of God in this era as embryonic. We are spiritually undeveloped. In our current, embryonic state, "it has not appeared as yet what we will be. We know that when He appears, we will be like Him."[32] In that hour we will be born, so to speak.

The period of birth pangs ending in the Messianic Era is alluded to in the words of our Master:

> Truly, truly, I say to you, that you will weep and lament, but the world will rejoice; you will grieve, but your grief will be turned into joy. Whenever a woman is in labor she has pain, because her hour has come; but when she gives birth to the child, she no longer remembers the anguish because of the joy that a child has been born into the world. Therefore you too have grief now; but I will see you again, and your heart will rejoice, and no one will take your joy away from you. (John 16:20–22)[33]

RACHEL WEEPING FOR HER CHILDREN

🌿 *The mother of Israel weeps because the Shechinah has departed. (34)*

The prophet Jeremiah poetically depicts the Babylonian exile as the matriarch Rachel weeping, watching her children being led away into captivity. "Rachel is weeping for her children," He says. "She refuses to be comforted for her children, because they are no more" (Jeremiah 31:15).[34]

Levertoff depicts Rachel as weeping not only for the captives of Israel but also for the Shechinah, as HaShem's Dwelling Presence accompanies the Israelites into exile. Judaism teaches that the Shechinah departed the Temple and went into exile with Israel.[35] The departure and exile of the Shechinah is a biblical concept. It is described in Ezekiel: "Then the glory of the LORD departed from the threshold of the temple and stood over the cherubim."[36]

---

[30] Matthew 24:8. Cf. Mark 13:8.

[31] For a collection of sources on the eschatological use of the birth-pangs imagery, see Raphael Patai, *The Messiah Texts* (Detroit: Wayne State University Press, 1988), 95–103.

[32] 1 John 3:2.

[33] Cf. *Igeret HaKodesh* 25 and *Tanya* 17.

[34] Cf. Matthew 2:18. In Jewish mysticism Rachel becomes "the personification of Zion as a maternal figure" (cf. Galatians 4:26). See Gershom Scholem, *On the Mystical Shape of the Godhead* (New York: Schoken Books, 1991), 145.

[35] Cf. b.*Megillah* 29a. See also Levertoff's, "The Shechinah Motif in the New Testament Literature," (Lecture, Society of the Study of Religions, 1951), republished in *Messiah Journal* 100 (Spring 2009), 43–49.

[36] Ezekiel 10:18.

In Levertoff's sources, Rachel symbolizes the Shechinah going into exile and weeping over the children of Israel:

> The Shekinah replied with tears: "… Look away from me, I will weep bitterly" (Isaiah 22:4), as much as to say, "Seeing that my children have gone into exile and the Sanctuary is burnt, what is there left for me that I should linger here?" And the answer of the Holy One, blessed be He … was "Refrain thy voice from weeping [and your eyes from tears; for your work will be rewarded … and they will return from the land of the enemy] (Jeremiah 31:16). (*Zohar* I, 203a [Soncino])

> Hence it is written, "A voice is heard in Ramah, Rachel weeping for her children because they are not"; or, as we should rather translate, "He is not" (*enennu*), referring to the Holy King who had gone aloft and was not in her midst. R. Hiya asked: "From what place did She begin to go into exile?" He replied: "From the Sanctuary, where Her abode was." (*Zohar* III, 20b [Soncino])

That the Shechinah sojourns with Israel in exile can be demonstrated from the Torah; as it says, "I will go down with you to Egypt, and I will also surely bring you up again."[37] This may also be learned from the apostles: "Do you not know that you are a temple of God and that the Spirit of God dwells in you?"[38]

Through repentance we hasten the day of the coming of our righteous Messiah[39] and thereby draw His Presence out of exile.

THE LION AND THE LAMB

The Messianic days are days in which all creation, even the very animal world, will know God as in days before the fall. (34)

At the culmination of the period of the birth pangs, the Messianic Era will begin. In that day, all creation, even the animal world, will return to the Edenic state. Isaiah offers us a glimpse into this era: "And the wolf will dwell with the lamb, and the leopard will lie down with the young goat, and the calf and the young lion and the fatling together; and a little boy will lead them."[40]

---

[37] Genesis 46:4.

[38] 1 Corinthians 3:16. Cf. Ephesians 2:21–22.

[39] 2 Peter 3:9–12.

[40] Isaiah 11:6. Cf. Isaiah 65:25.

MORE PERFECT THAN SINAI

> *The Messianic revelation will be more perfect than the revelation at Sinai. (34)*

The revelation of the Messianic Era will surpass even that of the giving of the Torah at Mount Sinai. At Sinai, only Israel witnessed the revelation of HaShem's glory. In the Messianic Era, the whole world will witness the majesty of the Holy One. At Sinai, HaShem was cloaked in darkness and the people remained distant, as it says, "So the people stood at a distance, while Moses approached the thick cloud where God was."[41] In the Messianic Era, "your Teacher will no longer hide Himself, but your eyes will behold your Teacher,"[42] and "all flesh will see [Him] together."[43] The revelation in the Messianic Era will never cease. "The nations will walk by its light, and the kings of the earth will bring their glory into it."[44]

That the Messianic revelation surpasses the revelation at Sinai is also made explicit in the Epistle to the Hebrews: "For [Messiah] has been counted worthy of more glory than Moses."[45]

> For you have not come to a mountain that can be touched and to a blazing fire, and to darkness and gloom and whirlwind, and to the blast of a trumpet and the sound of words … but you have come to Mount Zion and to the city of the living God, the heavenly Jerusalem, and to myriads of angels, to the general assembly and church of the firstborn who are enrolled in heaven, and to God, the Judge of all, and to the spirits of the righteous made perfect, and to Yeshua, the mediator of a new covenant, and to the sprinkled blood. (Hebrews 12:18–24)

THE DIM MIRROR

> *All we see now is the mirrored reflection; then it will be the reality that we see. (34)*

In this present age, our vision of the Messianic Era is a "mirrored reflection." That is to say that even our clearest perception of HaShem in this world is, at best, an obscured one. The apostle Paul used the same symbolism when contrasting our vision in this present world and the vision of HaShem that will be ours in the Messianic Era: "For now we see in a mirror dimly, but then face to face; now I know in part, but then I will know fully just as I also have been fully known."[46] The sages made a similar statement while contrasting the prophetic stature of Moses with that of the other prophets:

---

41 Exodus 20:21.

42 Isaiah 30:20.

43 Isaiah 40:5.

44 Revelation 21:24. Cf. Isaiah 60:3.

45 Hebrews 3:3. Cf. Hebrews 2:2–3.

46 1 Corinthians 13:12. Cf. "speculum … אספקלריא (*Ispaqlarya*) deriving from Greek, *speklon*, 'mirror, window pane,' and Latin, *speculum*, 'mirror'" (Daniel C. Matt, *The Zohar Pritzker Edition: Volume Three* [Stanford, CA: Stanford University Press, 2006], 31).

What is the difference between Moses and all other prophets? ... The other prophets beheld their prophetic visions through nine mirrors ... but Moses beheld his [prophetic visions] through one mirror, as it is said [in Numbers 12:8], "With him I speak mouth to mouth, even openly, and not in dark sayings." The Rabbis said, "All the other prophets beheld their visions through a blurred mirror ... but Moses beheld his visions through a clear mirror, as it is said [in Numbers 12:8], "He beholds the form of the LORD." (*Leviticus Rabbah* 1:14)

Also the *Zohar*:

Our teachers have laid down that Moses derived his prophetic vision from a bright mirror, whereas the other prophets derived their vision from a dull mirror. So it is written concerning Ezekiel: "I saw visions of God" [Ezekiel 1:1], whereas in connection with the difference between Moses and all other prophets it says: "If there is a prophet among you, I the Lord will make Myself known to him in a vision.... My servant Moses is not so, who is faithful in all my house: and with him I will speak mouth to mouth" [Numbers 12:7–8]. (*Zohar* II, 82b [Soncino])[47]

Moses was considered the greatest of the prophets because of his pure vision of HaShem. In Exodus 33:23, HaShem says, "I will take My hand away and you shall see My back, but My face shall not be seen." The other prophets saw even less of HaShem—a reflection, so to speak, through multiple mirrors or lenses.

Our Master is greater than Moses and the other prophets. He is the only one to have seen the Father. John spoke concerning our Master: "No man hath seen God at any time; the only begotten Son, which is in the bosom of the Father, he hath declared him."[48] Note also John 6:46: "Not that anyone has seen the Father, except the One who is from God; He has seen the Father."

TABERNACLE AMONG MEN

God has shown Himself a king who desires to make His abode with us here below. (35)

Levertoff's Chasidic sources offer two illustrations of God's love for man. On the one hand, God is compared to a king who has compassion on a poor man and brings him to live in the king's palace. On the other hand, God is compared to a king who so loved his people that he forsook his palace and went to dwell among the common people. So great is the love of HaShem for us that He desired "to make His abode with us here below."

The sages teach that it was HaShem's original intention to allow His Shechinah to dwell within man. Exodus 25:8 states, "Let them construct a sanctuary for Me, that I may dwell among them." However, the Hebrew text may also be read, "Let them construct a sanctuary for Me, that I may

---

47   See also *Zohar* I, 170b, II, 23b, V, 268b–269a.

48   John 1:18 (KJV).

dwell *within* them" [emphasis mine]. HaShem's original desire to dwell with His people will be achieved in the Messianic Era: "Behold, the tabernacle of God is among men, and He will dwell among them, and they shall be His people, and God Himself will be among them."[49] But that original desire is already being fulfilled through the bestowal of the Holy Spirit upon the disciples of Messiah. "You are a temple of God, and the Spirit of God dwells in you."[50]

NEW JERUSALEM

> *[His] one desire is to draw his subjects to himself; a king who also, out of love for his own, forsakes his palace and dwells among his people in order to unite himself with them, that they may see more of his glory and learn more of his character. (35)*

HaShem originally desired for His Presence (Shechinah) to dwell inside of each individual Israelite. Due to the sin of the golden calf, HaShem confined His Presence to the Tabernacle instead. Nonetheless, the Tabernacle alludes to the Messianic Era when the people will become a living Temple of God.[51]

After the final judgment of all mankind, HaShem will reveal a new heaven and a new earth. During this time, a New Jerusalem will come down out of heaven. The difference between New Jerusalem and the Jerusalem which housed the Temple of God in this world is that there will be "no temple in it, for the Lord God the Almighty and the Lamb are its temple."[52] There will no longer be a need for HaShem to conceal His presence, for the world will be restored to its former Edenic state. This can be compared to a king who loved his people so much that he left his palace to dwell among them.

It is this vision for which the mystic strives—to experience as much of New Jerusalem as possible even before its actual arrival. The mystic strives to "draw near to God"[53] in this present era so that God will draw near to him.

TZIMTZUM

> *In creation God has by an act of self-limitation created. (35)*

The mystic asks how God can be completely infinite and a "consuming fire,"[54] a God which no man can see and live,[55] and yet interact with His creation and finite human beings. The answer

---

49 Revelation 21:3.

50 1 Corinthians 3:16. Cf. Ephesians 2:21–22.

51 Cf. 1 Corinthians 3:16–17.

52 Revelation 21:22.

53 James 4:8.

54 Deuteronomy 4:24 and Hebrews 12:29.

55 Exodus 33:20.

is that HaShem must conceal Himself to some extent in order to interact with mankind and the rest of finite creation.

Jewish mysticism explains that creation can exist and God can interact with creation only because He has deliberately limited Himself through contraction of His infinite being. This "self-limitation" of the infinite God is one of the fundamental principles of mystical thought. In Levertoff's sources, God's act of self-limitation is known as *tzimtzum* (צמצום) which means "contraction" or "concealment."

If HaShem did not first reduce Himself and limit Himself, we would be completely incapable of comprehending or withstanding the full revelation of God. Even Moses was hidden in the cleft of the rock and granted only a glimpse of God's back, as it were, as He passed by. If God did not first limit and humble Himself (so to speak), we could not begin to conceive of Him.

> Rabbi Yochanon said, "Wherever you find the greatness of the Holy One, blessed be He, you will also find his humility." (b.*Megillah* 31a)

Rabbi Yochanon means to tell us that if we have tasted of the glory of God, in any measure, we should know that it is only because God first humbled Himself enough for us to perceive Him. "Will God indeed dwell on the earth? Behold, heaven and the highest heaven cannot contain You."[56]

EIN SOF

🌿 *The proof of God's love lies less in the fact that He raises creatures to Himself, than in that He stoops to have His tabernacle among men and thus reveal Himself to them. (35)*

Levertoff states that it was only "by an act of self-limitation" that HaShem created humans who are capable of "realizing their self-hood, and then, of realizing Him, their Creator, and of receiving Him into their innermost life as their Father and King." Had God not limited Himself, it would have been impossible to create other "selves," because His infinite character would have filled and consumed all.

God conceals His presence as it descends from the loftiest heavens to the level of man upon earth. "The higher a being, the lower he is able to condescend," Levertoff writes.

The opposite is also true: The higher man ascends spiritually, the greater his vision of God, so to speak. Paul alludes to something like such an ascent when he speaks of being "caught up to the third heaven."[57] However, in light of Paul's words about ascending, man can only ascend so high; there is a level of God that man cannot comprehend, nor can he see. The Kabbalists refer to this ultimate, completely concealed level of God as the *Ein Sof* (אין סוף), which means the infinite

---

56 1 Kings 8:27. Cf. Philippians 2:5–8.
57 2 Corinthians 12:2.

unknowable God. This is the level at which "no man can see Me and live."[58] This is the level at which our Master rests; as it says, "No one has seen God at any time. The only begotten Son, who is in the bosom of the Father, He has declared Him."[59]

Even though HaShem is concealed from mankind, He nevertheless makes Himself known so that man, in turn, may know Him.[60] If not for the concealment of *Ein Sof,* the God who is a consuming fire could not "tabernacle among men and thus reveal Himself to them."

A HUMBLE DISH

✍ *The prophets always compare the ideal wonders of the Messianic Age with the wonders of divine providence in the deliverance of Israel from Egypt. (36)*

When we read the prophets' descriptions of the Messianic Era to come, we would expect them to compare the wonders and miracles of that age to those of the creation of the universe. Instead, they compare the Messianic Era to the Exodus from Egypt. For example, consider the following passage from Jeremiah:

> "Therefore behold, days are coming," declares the LORD, "When it will no longer be said, 'As the LORD lives, who brought up the sons of Israel out of the land of Egypt,' but, 'As the LORD lives, who brought up the sons of Israel from the land of the north and from all the countries where He had banished them.'" (Jeremiah 16:14–15)[61]

Levertoff says, "The great significance of the redemption from Egypt is not the revelation of God's power, but of His condescending love for Israel." He uses a parable to explain the difference. HaShem's act of creating the universe is compared to a king who invited a great host of men to a banquet at which they ate from the finest of dishes. HaShem's act of personally intervening and redeeming Israel from Egypt is compared to the king selecting one simple dish from the table and

---

[58] Exodus 33:20. A similar concept is found expressed by Christian writers such as Basil of Caesarea: "If the energies descend to us, the essence [of God] remains absolutely inaccessible" (*To Amphilochius* 32 [Lossky]), and John of Damascus, citing John 1:8, "The Deity, therefore, is ineffable and incomprehensible" (*An Exact Exposition of the Orthodox Faith* 1:1 [Salmond]). Cf. Romans 1:19. God therefore was only knowable through his "energies" and not in his "essence." Gregory of Palamas writes, "There exists, then, an eternal light, other than the divine essence; it is not in itself an essence—far from it—but an energy of the Superessential" (*Triads* 3:2:14 [Gendle]). He felt that through the energies we "become partakers of the divine nature" (2 Peter 1:4). See Vladimir Lossky, *In the Image and Likeness of God* [Crestwood, NY: St. Vladimir's Press, 2001], 56. In Chasidus the *Ein Sof* reveals himself to the world through ten *sefirot* ("emanations," ספירות). This is also similar to how Saint Nikitas Stithatos quantifies God's energies down into a decad (*The Philokalia* 99). See G. E. Palmer, Kallistos T. Ware, and Philip Sherrard, *The Philokalia* (4 vols.; England: Faber & Faber, 1986), 4:173 n1. The fourth-century church writer Saint Jerome specifically mentions ten divine names for God used in the Bible in his third letter to Marcella (*Letter #25*). Rabbi Abraham Zacuto (15th century) writes in his *Sefer HaYuhasin* that Jerome was referring to the *sefirot.*

[59] John 1:18 (NKJV).

[60] Cf. Romans 1:20.

[61] Cf. Jeremiah 23:7–8.

personally carrying it to his friend for the two of them to privately enjoy together. The redemption from Egypt reveals HaShem's humility and His love for Israel.

THE CHARIOTS OF GOD

> ✐ *The "Fathers"—Abraham, Isaac, and Jacob—are called "the chariots of God." (36)*

A chariot is a vehicle steered only by the will of its driver. If the driver directs the chariot to the left, it goes to the left; if to the right, it goes to the right. The chariot has no will of its own; it only responds to the will of the driver. Levertoff cites the *Midrash Rabbah* as stating that the patriarchs are "the [*merkavah*, מרכבה] chariots of God."

> Rabbi Shimon bar Lakish said, "The forefathers [Abraham, Isaac and Jacob] are [God's] chariot, for it says [in Genesis 35:13], "Then God went up from [Jacob]." … and it says [in Genesis 17:22], "God went up from Abraham," and [in Genesis 28:13] it says, "Behold, the LORD stood [upon him]." (*Genesis Rabbah* 82:6)

The *Tanya* comments on this passage:

> "The patriarchs are truly the chariot," for all their organs were completely holy and detached from mundane matters, serving as a vehicle solely for the Supreme Will alone throughout their lives. (*Tanya* 23)[62]

A similar thought is expressed by Ignatius who writes that we are all "God-bearers."[63] Every person should endeavor to become a "chariot" steered only by the will of HaShem.

THE DIVINE SOUL AND THE ANIMAL SOUL

> ✐ *Every Israelite is supposed to possess two souls: a "divine" soul, which comes directly from God Himself, and a "natural" or "animal" soul, which comes from the "other side" of God. (36)*

Jewish mysticism speaks of two distinct souls which comprise a human being. Man contains a "divine" soul and an "animal" soul. The divine soul (*neshamah*, נשמה) is that preexistent aspect of the soul, the "breath" of God which He breathes into human beings. It is a portion of His own

---

[62] See also *Tanya* 18, 37, and 39. In Chassidic thought the tefillin symbolize that Israel is to serve as a carrier of the Shechinah. The Hebrew letter *shin* (ש) on the head tefillin represents God's name *Shaddai*. Chassidic thought teaches that the *shin* also stands for the word Shechinah which begins with *shin*. See Rabbi Bachya on this in Rabbi Isaiah Horowitz, *Shney Luchot Habrit* (trans. Rabbi Eliyahu Munk; 3 vols.; Jerusalem: Lambda Publishers, 1999), 2:571. He bases his comments on Ezekiel 10:19 where it says that "the glory of the God of Israel was over them."

[63] Ignatius, *Epistle to Ephesians* 9.

essence and is that aspect of man that survives death. The animal soul (*nefesh*, נפש) is our mortal vitality, our sense of self and sentience. It is thought, speech, and action.[64] When the body dies, the animal soul perishes with it, but the divine soul returns to its source.[65]

Both the *nefesh* and the *neshamah* are mentioned in Genesis 2:7:

> Then the LORD God formed man of dust from the ground, and breathed into his nostrils the breath of life [*neshamah*, נשמה]; and man became a living being [*nefesh*, נפש]. (Genesis 2:7)

The animal soul is not evil, for it also comes from God. The mystics say the animal soul is derived from the "other side of God," His "back" so to speak. Though the animal soul is not intrinsically evil, its inclination and appetites are carnal and material. Therefore, its influence over man leads us toward selfishness, lust, greed, and sin. However, the animal soul can be harnessed and brought under the influence of the divine soul and into the service of HaShem.

The divine soul is the source of our innate thirst for God. In the biblical text, it is referred to most often as the "spirit" (not be confused with the Spirit of God, or the Holy Spirit). According to apostolic theology, this spirit within man is dead until it is quickened by salvation and brought to life and communion with the Holy Spirit.

According to some schools of Jewish mysticism, a Jew receives a godly or "divine soul" by virtue of being a son of Abraham. This divine soul is in addition to the "animal soul" which every human being and living creature possesses. The people of the nations, however, possess only the animal soul and not a divine soul.[66] This concept is at odds, however, with the teaching of the apostles, which states, "But as many as received Him, to them He gave the right to become children of God,

---

[64] In Chabad Chasidus, the animal soul (*nefesh haBahamit*, נפש הבהמית) is contrasted against the divine soul (*nefesh Elokit*, נפש אלקית), but both are called *nefesh*, the general term for soul. However, *neshamah* is a more specific term for the divine soul and can be used in contrast to the animal soul.

[65] "Then the dust will return to the earth as it was, and the spirit will return to God who gave it" (Ecclesiastes 12:7). Levertoff also cites Aphraates, *Homilies* 6:14 (Hendrickson): "For when men die, the animal spirit is buried with the body, and sense is taken away from it, but the heavenly spirit that they receive goes according to its nature to Christ."

The terminology of *nefesh* and *neshamah* is inherently ambiguous and *nefesh* has a broad semantic range of application which at times may encompass the more specific term *neshamah*. In this respect, it shares the same ambiguity as the English word "soul." Further confusing matters, in the biblical text, the term spirit (*ruach*, רוח) can stand for God's intangible essence, any being of the unseen world, supernatural endowment, the immortal element of man's being, a particular inclination, or even just the wind. Judaism has traditionally understood "spirit" in Ecclesiastes 12:7 to refer to the immortal soul of man (*neshamah*).

[66] The *Testament of the Twelve Patriarchs*, as Levertoff notes, mentions man possessing various spirits. This is on a different level than the mystical concept of certain people possessing two souls; yet there is nonetheless some connection. In the *Twelve Patriarchs* the spirits are viewed more as temperaments.

even to those who believe in His name, who were born, not of blood nor of the will of the flesh nor of the will of man, but of God."[67]

Paul also states that "if you belong to Messiah, then you are Abraham's descendants, heirs according to promise,"[68] and as a result Abraham is "the father of us all."[69]

Regarding the concepts of the "animal soul" and the "divine soul," compare Paul's words contrasting the deeds of the flesh with the fruits of the Spirit.[70]

REVEALING THE IMMORTAL SOUL PLANTED WITHIN

As the grain must enter into the earth in order to bring forth fruit, so must [the Divine] soul enter into man's innermost nature and be quite absorbed by it, if it is to bring forth spiritual fruit. (37)

The mystics compare the divine soul placed within the body to a seed planted in the earth. God has planted within the human being a soul (*neshamah*) with godly and immortal potential. The Messianic Age is the time of harvest when the fruit of every soul will be revealed.

The soul planted within us brings forth godly fruit only after diligent work. "That which you sow does not come to life unless it dies."[71] Just as the soil must be worked before the seed will sprout, man's flesh[72] must be "ploughed and prepared." That is to say, a man's flesh must be made to conform to the desires of the Spirit and divine soul. Man must "lay aside the deeds of darkness"[73] and "not participate in the unfruitful deeds of darkness."[74] The apostles considered "repentance from

---

[67] John 1:12–13. Apostolic passages like Romans 6:6–7, 2 Corinthians 5:17, and 1 Peter 1:23 can be seen as indicating that all men receive rebirth of the soul in Messiah and are not the same as they formerly were without him, but the apostles never indicate that Jewish people inherently possess a more exalted spiritual essence than that of Gentiles.

Concerning the doctrine that every Jew possesses two souls see *Tanya* 1–2. Also see Paul Levertoff, "Some Aspects of Jewish Mysticism," *Journal of the Transactions of the Victoria Institute* 65 (1933): 71–87. In the lecture presented therein, Levertoff offers insights comparable to, and at times identical with, the present work, *Love and the Messianic Age*. The lecture in the journal consists primarily of thoughts on Jewish mysticism as found within the *Zohar*. On page 87, Levertoff contrasts the concept that only a Jew possesses a divine soul by virtue of being a son of Abraham: "I need only refer to John 1:2–13, to show the contrast between this Gnostic conception and Christian truth, but nevertheless, the very thought-forms and the sometimes almost Johannine colouring of some portions of the *Zohar*, which deal with the 'unio mystica' of the soul with God, have not infrequently led a 'Zoharic' Jew onward toward the mystery of Christ."

[68] Galatians 3:29. Cf. Romans 7:14–25.

[69] Romans 4:16.

[70] Galatians 5:19–23. Also Gregory of Palamas taught that men should "unite in themselves the created and the uncreated, to become, so to speak, persons of two natures." See Lossky, *In the Image and Likeness of God*, 65.

[71] 1 Corinthians 15:36.

[72] The flesh may be compared with the soil of the ground. Cf. Genesis 2:7.

[73] Romans 13:12.

[74] Ephesians 5:11. Cf. Ephesians 4:22 and Colossians 3:8–9.

dead works,"[75] i.e., from the deeds of wickedness, to be one of the foundational and elementary teachings about Messiah.[76]

The imagery of a seed waiting to sprout to fruition is alluded to by James when he states, "Therefore, putting aside all filthiness and all that remains of wickedness, in humility receive the word implanted, which is able to save your souls."[77]

THE BLOSSOMING SOUL

🌿 *It all depends upon the receptiveness of the human personality and whether it has proved a fertile soil in which the heavenly seed can develop. (37)*

The divine soul has the potential to take root and grow or to wither and fail. Failure to become a "vessel of God's love" results in "absolute isolation" and "self-righteousness." Self-righteousness is a quality which our Master often rebuked in the hypocritical members of the Pharisees. However, allowing God's love to work in a person allows one to "come to such close fellowship with God, as to be completely united with Him." Levertoff says that a "man whose love for God is perfect" becomes "a living expression of God." This is comparable to Paul's remarks regarding the Corinthian congregation: "You are our letter, written in our hearts, known and read by all men."[78] Our Master was a perfect vessel for God's love, a living expression of God.

HEPHTZI-BAH AND BEULAH

🌿 *In the Messianic times the Holy Land will be called "the land of God's pleasure." But even now this is, in a measure, true of those men who have become temples of the divine love; they are the land of God's pleasure. (38)*

In the Messianic era, God will call the people of Israel by the name *Hephtzi-bah* (חפצי בה), which means, "My delight is in her," and the land of Israel by the name *Beulah* (בעולה), which means, "Married."

> It will no longer be said to you, "Forsaken," nor to your land will it any longer be said, "Desolate"; but you will be called, "My delight is in her," and your land, "Married"; for the LORD delights in you, and to Him your land will be married. For as a young man marries a virgin, so your sons will marry you; And as the bridegroom rejoices over the bride, so your God will rejoice over you. (Isaiah 62:4–5)

---

[75] Hebrews 6:1.

[76] Ibid.

[77] James 1:21. Compare also the Master's parable of the sower in Matthew 13:18–23, 36–43.

[78] 2 Corinthians 3:2.

The Land of Israel, transformed into paradise, and the people of Israel, redeemed and no longer forsaken, are the objects of God's affection, delight, and pleasure in the Messianic era. This mystical "union will be fully revealed" when the Messiah takes His bride. "Let us rejoice and be glad and give the glory to Him, for the marriage of the Lamb has come, and His bride has made herself ready."[79]

However, Levertoff's sources explain that there are some who experience a foretaste of this marriage by becoming "temples of the Divine Love" in this present era. The person who becomes a vessel for God's love has already entered into a "spiritual marriage" with God.

These are people who desire to make their bodies into dwelling places of the Shechinah, vessels fit for the service of HaShem in order that through them, God may dwell among men. The Messiah is the ultimate and perfect example of such a dwelling: "And the Word became flesh and tabernacled among us."[80] This verse may also be understood as "tabernacled *in* us" (author's emphasis).

The Messiah's body became a dwelling for the Shechinah, for "all the fullness to dwell in Him,"[81] a fullness of the Deity dwelling in bodily form.[82] As Levertoff states in his commentary on Matthew 28:20:

> Christ is the Shekinah, i.e., the visible Presence of God. His Presence is the Presence of God. In these last verses we find perhaps the grandest conclusion that any book could have—recalling us to the knowledge of Jesus the glorified and timeless, leading and guarding His people in all ages into union with the Father.[83]

TEMPLE OF THE HOLY SPIRIT

They experience the "divine soul" which is in them to work out His purpose. (38)

With the Messiah as our example of godly living and by virtue of His Spirit dwelling within us, we become "tongues as of fire"[84] which collectively make up the dwelling of the Shechinah in exile, the Temple of the living God. Those who hear His voice become God's household: a "holy temple in the Lord" and "dwelling of God":

> God's household, having been built on the foundation of the apostles and prophets, Messiah Yeshua Himself being the corner stone, in whom the whole building,

---

79 Revelation 19:7.

80 John 1:14 (author's translation).

81 Colossians 1:19.

82 Cf. Colossians 2:9.

83 Paul P. Levertoff, *St. Matthew* (London: Thomas Murby & Co., 1940), 101. Cf. also *Igeret HaKodesh* 25. Cf. the saying, "If two sit together and interchange words of Torah, the Divine Presence abides between them" (m.*Avot* 3:3 [Hertz]), with Matthew 18:20, "For where two or three have gathered in My name, I am there in their midst."

84 Acts 2:3.

being fitted together, is growing into a holy temple in the Lord, in whom you also are being built together into a dwelling of God in the Spirit. (Ephesians 2:19–22)

By virtue of the Messiah being a dwelling for the Shechinah, we, as the body of Messiah, are the abode of God upon the earth. If we allow the Messiah to dwell in our hearts through faith[85] and if we "know the love of Messiah which surpasses all knowledge,"[86] then we will cause the "growth of the body for the building up of itself in love."[87]

THE DISEASE OF SELF-SATISFACTION

God will remove the disease of self-satisfaction and self-righteousness from humanity. (38)

In the Messianic Era, HaShem will remove the heart of stone from humanity and give them a heart of flesh.[88] The "heart of stone" is the self-satisfied person who does not seek God. Instead, he is content with his own being and seeks only after his own inclinations. His self-righteousness consists in perceiving himself to be his own master:

> There is a way which seems right to a man, but its end is the way of death. (Proverbs 16:25)

Such a person cannot know God because he knows only himself. He is blind to spiritual reality. In the Messianic Age, though, every man will know God.[89] The prophet Zephaniah says, "For then I will remove from your midst your proud, exulting ones, and you will never again be haughty on My holy mountain."[90] As we submit to the rule and reign of HaShem by taking upon ourselves the yoke of His kingdom, we may taste of that future era today.

ADAM KADMON

Man, as he now is, is an incomplete being; the more he opens his heart to the divine influences, "the more he grows into the image of the ideal man laid up in heaven." (38)

In his discussion of humanity, Levertoff mentions the concept of "the ideal man laid up in heaven." He says that the more man opens his heart to HaShem, the closer he is conformed to the image of that "ideal man."

---

[85] Cf. Ephesians 3:17.

[86] Ephesians 3:19.

[87] Ephesians 4:16.

[88] Cf. Ezekiel 36:26.

[89] Jeremiah 31:34.

[90] Zephaniah 3:11.

In Jewish mysticism, the "ideal man laid up in heaven" is called *Adam Kadmon* ("primordial man," אדם קדמון). In Levertoff's mystical sources, the concept of *Adam Kadmon* is connected with the concealment of God (*tzimtzum*). The *Adam Kadmon*—the divine human being—is the result of HaShem's initial concealment after *tzimtzum* occurred. In the later mystic book *Etz Chayim*, he is referred to as "the great light … the precursor of everything."[91]

Musings about a heavenly Adam were born out of a conflict between the idea that God is incorporeal—that is, without image and form—and the idea that man is created in the image of God: "Then God said, 'Let us make man in Our image, according to Our likeness" (Genesis 1:26). Therefore it was interpreted that the physical Adam was created in the image of a heavenly Adam.[92] *Adam Kadmon* is God's "blueprint form for man."[93]

As Levertoff states in his note, "Both St. Paul and Philo must have known an old tradition [about *Adam Kadmon*]."[94] Philo mentions the primordial man in his *Allegorical Interpretation*:

> The races of men are twofold; for one is the heavenly man, and the other the earthly man. Now the heavenly man, as being born in the image of God, has no participation in any corruptible or earthlike essence. But the earthly man is made of loose material, which he calls a lump of clay. (*Allegorical Interpretation* 1:12)

Further in Philo's *On the Confusion of Tongues* he writes:

> I have also heard of one of the companions of Moses having uttered such a speech as this: "Behold, a man whose name is the East!" [Zechariah 6:12]. A very novel appellation indeed, if you consider it as spoken of a man who is compounded of body and soul; but if you look upon it as applied to that incorporeal being who in no respect differs from the divine image, you will then agree that the name of the east has been given to him with great felicity. For the Father of the universe has caused him to spring up as the eldest son, whom, in another passage, he calls the firstborn;

---

91 Donald Wilder Menzi and Zwe Padeh, *The Tree of Life* (New York: Arizal Press Publications, 2008), 6. Possibly this is a mystical reflection on Genesis 1:3.

92 Ibid. Cf. *Zohar* I, 13b. Cf. also the interpretation of Genesis 9:6 in Aryeh Kaplan, *The Bahir* (Lanham: Rowman & Littlefield Publishers, 2004), 4.

93 Kaplan, *The Bahir*, 95. See also Ezekiel 1:26.

94 Although the doctrine of *Adam Kadmon* was not fully developed until the Middle Ages and later, these concepts existed in some form at the time of Paul's writing. In an article about *Adam Kadmon*, Moshe Idel argues that the later mystical literature "preserved earlier theoretical conceptions and committed them (in some cases for the first time) to writing." See Moshe Idel, "Enoch is Metatron," *Immanuel* 24/25 (1990): 238. We can find traces of this in early rabbinic literature. Ginzberg feels there is a veiled reference to *Adam Kadmon* in m.*Avot* 3:14 where Rabbi Akiva cites Genesis 9:6 instead of the typical Genesis 1:27 while discusses man being created "in the image." He writes that "in the image" is not a substitution for "in the image of God" but rather refers to in the image of Adam (Louis Ginzberg, "Adam Kadmon," *Jewish Encyclopedia* 1:181–183.). See also b.*Ketubah* 7b–8a. Additionally, we see a possible illusion to this in Rabbi Meir's use of "Likeness on High" (*Avot deRabbi Natan* 39). For a discussion of the early development of this in the concept of *Metatron* and its relationship to the New Testament see Shlomo Pines, "Form(s) of God: some Notes on Metatron and Christ," *Harvard Theological Review* 76:3 (1983), 269–288. There is even a variant text of b.*Sanhedrin* 38b that comments on Exodus 24:1 stating, "This is Metatron, who is the lesser HaShem [*HaShem katan*, ייי הקטן]." See Gershon Scholem, *Kabbalah* (New York, NY: Meridian, 1978), 377–378.

and he who is thus born, imitating the ways of his father, has formed such and such species, looking to his archetypal patterns. (*On the Confusion of Tongues* 14)[95]

Paul also alludes to *Adam Kadmon* imagery when he states: "Just as we have borne the image of the earthy [i.e., Adam], we will also bear the image of the heavenly [i.e., Yeshua]."[96] He notes that "the first man is from the earth, earthy; the second man is from heaven."[97]

If a man fails to open "his heart to the divine influences," he remains earthly and will never ascend beyond the level of Adam, the first man. However, if one opens his heart and soul to receive the divine light and is therefore receptive to the HaShem's Spirit, then he will continuously grow into the image of the heavenly Adam—the image of God in which man was created. Paul says Messiah "will transform our lowly body to be like His glorious body."[98]

MORE ON THE HEAVENLY MAN

🌿 *The ideal man laid up in heaven. (38)*

In Romans 5:14, Paul says that Adam was "an impression of Him who was to come."[99] That is to say that Adam was made in the image of Messiah. This teaching is very similar to the esoteric idea of *Adam Kadmon* described above. Another connection in Jewish literature between *Adam Kadmon* and Messiah can be found by comparing two different versions of the same midrash on Genesis 1:2. *Genesis Rabbah* 2:4 (Soncino) states: "'And the spirit of God hovered': this alludes to the spirit of Messiah"; whereas the same midrash in *Midrash Tehillim* 139:5 has (Braude) "the spirit of Adam."[100]

This connection is made more explicitly in the early sectarian, Jewish-influenced *Clementine* literature, where Yeshua is identified with *Adam Kadmon*:

> Although indeed He was the Son of God, and the beginning of all things, He became man; Him first God anointed with oil which was taken from the wood of the tree

---

[95] See also *On Creation* 46 and *On the Confusion of Tongues* 28.

[96] 1 Corinthians 15:49.

[97] 1 Corinthians 15:47. For a discussion of *Adam Kadmon* imagery in the New Testament see Joachim Jeremias, "Αδαμ" in *Theological Dictionary of the New Testament* (ed. Gerhard Kittel; 10 vols.; Grand Rapids: Eerdmans, 2006) 1:141–143. Additionally Samuel Tobias Lachs suggests that the reason Luke's genealogy goes back to Adam may "be indicative that Luke had the *Adam Qadmon* concept in mind, i.e., that Jesus is the reappearance of primordial man, *Adam Qadmon*." See Lachs, *A Rabbinic Commentary on the New Testament: The Gospels of Matthew, Mark, and Luke* (Hoboken, New Jersey: KTAV Publishing House, 1987), 48. It is also possible for an *Adam Kadmon* background to be seen for Colossians 1:15–19. Verse 19 states, "for all the fullness to dwell in Him," which Moshe Idel sees as implying that "he apparently comprises both the image of the Creator and the Creation" [in later Jewish mysticism the *sefirot*], which is similar to legends about *Adam Kadmon*. See Idel, *Kabbalah: New Perspectives*, 112–122. Cf. Ephesians 4:12–16; Romans 12:4–5; 1 Corinthians 12:24–26; Philippians 2:6–11 and Colossians 1:15–20.

[98] Philippians 3:21. Cf. Gershom Scholem, *On the Mystical Shape of the Godhead* (New York: Schocken, 1997), 278 n.19.

[99] The Greek *tupos* (τυπος) in Romans 5:14 is a word meaning "impression" or "stamp made by a die."

[100] Also *Genesis Rabbah* 8:1. See Ginzberg, "Adam Kadmon," 1:181–183.

of life: from that anointing therefore He is called Christ. (*Recognitions of Clement* 1:45 [Coxe])[101]

The pregnant language of the "tree of life" recalls the Garden of Eden and doubtlessly alludes to the concepts of *Adam Kadmon*.

ADAM, DAVID, AND MESSIAH

The ideal man laid up in heaven. (38)

Levertoff states in a footnote "Adam [אדם] stands for Adam [א], David [ד], Mashiach [מ], the ideal man and his historical prototypes."[102] Rabbi Menachem Nochum Twerski of Chernobyl (18th century) elaborates on this idea:

> This unification [of speech and thought] is a construction of the stature of the Messiah as [explicated] in the dictum of the Besht, let his soul be in heavenly treasure: Each and every one of Israel has to repair and prepare the part of the stature of the Messiah which belongs to his soul, as known. Because 'aDaM is the acronym of Adam, David, Messiah. The stature of Adam has been from the beginning of the world to its end, as the souls of all the Israelites were comprised in him. Afterwards, his stature has been diminished by the sin. So also will the stature of the Messiah be complete, [formed] out of all the souls of Israel, which are six hundred thousand, as before the sin of Adam. This is the reason why each and every one of Israel has to prepare that part which is the aspect of Messiah that belongs to his soul until the entire stature is restored and rebuilt and a complete and everlasting unification is complete, may it be fast in our time.[103]

The themes in Rabbi Twerski's words are quite similar in content to Paul's in Romans chapter 5:

> Therefore, just as sin came into the world through one man, and death through sin, and so death spread to all men ... Yet death reigned from Adam to Moses, even over those whose sinning was not like the transgression of Adam, who was a type of the one who was to come ... Therefore, as one trespass led to condemnation for all men, so one act of righteousness leads to justification and life for all men. For as

---

[101] See also 1:28 and *Clementine Homilies* 3:20. See Ginsburg, "Adam Kadmon," 182. According the fourth-century Roman philosopher Marius Victorinus, some of the Jewish believers taught that Yeshua "is Adam himself, and is the universal soul" (Stephen Andrew Cooper, *Marius Victorinus' Commentary on Galatians* [New York: Oxford University Press, 2005], 265–266). The Church Father Epiphanius wrote about this belief amongst the Jewish believers as well: "For some of them even say that Adam is Christ—the man who was formed and infused with God's breath" (Frank Williams, *The Panarion of Epiphanius of Salamis: Book I* [New York, Brill, 1997], 121).

[102] For a fuller discussion of this acronym see Moshe Idel, *Messianic Mystics* (New Haven, CT: Yale University, 1998), 189ff. and Scholem, *Kabbalah*, 334–335.

[103] Translation from Idel, *Messianic Mystics*, 221.

by the one man's disobedience the many were made sinners, so by the one man's obedience the many will be made righteous. (Romans 5:12–19)

Rabbi Schneerson expands on this idea:

> The Meor Einayim writes, in the name of the Baal Shem Tov, that "every Jew must rectify and prepare that part of Moshiach's 'body' that is relevant to his [personal] soul." That is, each Jew has within his soul part of Moshiach's soul. He continues: "As it is known, the letters of the word adam (man) are the beginning letters of Adam, David, Moshiach." Every person called "adam" (and all Jews are called adam) has in himself the levels of Adam, David and Moshiach. Adam—because all men are his offspring. David—because he is "King of Israel," and the king is the life and existence of the country and its citizens. Likewise, every Jew has part of Moshiach's soul within him.
>
> Since the purpose of everything is the concrete result that must eventuate, the Meor Einayim continues to say, "every Jew must prepare that part of the level of Moshiach applicable to his soul, until all the 'body' will be rectified and prepared, and there will be a general unity speedily in our days." In other words, the service of every Jew is to awaken and reveal the level of "Moshiach" in his soul, and to ensure that this "Moshiach" will redeem him and everything related to him. This is his personal redemption, similar to the general redemption through Moshiach.[104]

1 Peter 1:11 also talks about the "spirit of Messiah" in the prophets and Galatians 4:6 states that, "God has sent the Spirit of His Son into our hearts."[105] The practical implication of this is that we can begin the final work of Messiah now by refining ourselves in preparation for His coming.

THE EXALTED MESSIAH

☙ *The Messiah will reach a far higher state of perfection than man can ever reach. (38)*

The prophet Isaiah describes the Messiah, saying, "Behold, My servant will prosper, He will be high and lifted up and greatly exalted."[106] In the Apostolic Writings, this prophecy is connected to Messiah, but in mystical sources, it is also related to the *Adam Kadmon* mentioned previously.

---

[104] Menachem M. Schneerson, *Sichos in English Volume 17* (Brooklyn, NY: Sichos in English). See also Rabbi Abraham Stone, *Highlights of Moshiach* (Brooklyn, NY: Sichos in English, 1992), 17–18.

[105] "Spirit" in Hebrew is ruach (רוח) and can refer to "soul" as well.

[106] Isaiah 52:13.

The Messiah is the only man to have seen God,[107] and He "was in the beginning with God"[108] and shared glory with the Father "before the world was."[109] In Jewish mysticism, the Messiah is said to reside at the level of *Adam Kadmon*. Because of this lofty dwelling at which no other resides, He is called "very high."

Paul refers to Messiah as the *Adam* who is "from heaven"[110] and "the image of the invisible God."[111] Messiah is "the radiance of [God's] glory and the exact representation of His nature"[112] and has therefore "inherited a more excellent name"[113]—the Son of God—as it is written, "You are My Son, today I have begotten You."[114]

Levertoff says that during the Messianic Era "everything in Nature—even evil itself—will be absorbed in God." This will be the time when "all things are subjected to Him,"[115] and "the last enemy that will be abolished is death."[116]

THE SABBATH REST OF THE SOUL

The partial rest which the pious experience now is often contrasted with that "Sabbath of the soul" in the Messianic times which God is preparing for those who love Him. (39)

Levertoff's sources speak of the Messianic Era as Sabbath rest. The weekly Sabbath is a foretaste of the coming "Sabbath of the soul." Each weekly Sabbath is a glimpse of "the perfect Sabbath of God." The writer of the book of Hebrews uses the same imagery: "So there remains a Sabbath rest for the people of God. For the one who has entered His rest has himself also rested from his works, as God did from His."[117] It is possible for man to experience a measure of the Messianic Sabbath by resting "according to the commandment"[118] today.

To properly enjoy the weekly Sabbath, a person has to prepare provisions for the Sabbath in advance. Similarly, man must "be diligent to enter that rest, so that no one will fall."[119] Man must prepare himself in this world so that he may enter the eternal Sabbath of the Messianic Era:

---

[107] Cf. John 1:18.

[108] John 1:2.

[109] John 17:5.

[110] 1 Corinthians 15:47.

[111] Colossians 1:15.

[112] Hebrews 1:3.

[113] Hebrews 1:4.

[114] Hebrews 1:5; Psalm 2:7.

[115] 1 Corinthians 15:28.

[116] 1 Corinthians 15:26.

[117] Hebrews 4:9–10.

[118] Luke 23:56.

[119] Hebrews 4:11.

> Do you not know that [the world to come] is like the Sabbath and that [this present world] is like the eve of the Sabbath? If a man does not prepare his meal on the eve of the Sabbath, what will he eat on the Sabbath?" (*Ruth Rabbah* 3:3)

If we prepare ourselves in this world for the world to come, then we will bask in the Divine Light[120] and enjoy the Sabbath of the soul. These are the ones who will "rest from their labors, for their deeds will follow them."[121]

A DAMAGED WORLD

🖝 *The world is made for man, but when he becomes a slave of this world and separates himself from God, he does harm not only to his own nature but to the whole creation.* (39)

If a man becomes "a slave of this world," he separates himself from God. This separation not only does harm to our "own nature but to the whole creation." The principle of our sin actually damaging God's creation is illustrated by the sin of Adam. One man's sin did great harm to the entire world; as the Apostle Paul says, "Through one man sin entered into the world, and death through sin, and so death spread to all men."[122]

All of creation suffers as a result of the fall of man in the Garden of Eden, as stated in the Book of Jubilees:

> And on that day was closed the mouth of all beasts, and of cattle, and of birds, and of whatever walks, and of whatever moves, so that they could no longer speak: for they had all spoken one with another with one lip and with one tongue. And He sent out of the Garden of Eden all flesh that was in the Garden of Eden, and all flesh was scattered according to its kinds, and according to its types unto the places which had been created for them. And to Adam alone did He give (the wherewithal) to cover his shame, of all the beasts and cattle. (Jubilees 3:28–30 [Charles])

In the Messianic Era, the creation will be returned to God's original intent. The Apostle Paul explains, "For the creation was subjected to futility, not willingly, but because of Him who subjected it, in hope that the creation itself also will be set free from its slavery to corruption into the freedom of the glory of the children of God."[123]

Just as Adam's sin damaged the whole of creation, so do our sins bring harm to the world. Conversely, repentance and godliness bring correction into the world. Once man recognizes the Creator and no longer thinks of himself but thinks rather only of submitting himself to the Divine Will—that is the Torah—he fulfills the role for which he was created. However, as long as man

---

[120] Cf. Revelation 22:5.

[121] Revelation 14:13.

[122] Romans 5:12.

[123] Romans 8:20–21.

"becomes a worshiper of himself," he will continue to subject the Creation to pain and suffering, himself included. Man must realize that he is not "separate from God, the Creator of all." He can be a partner with God, so to speak, in repairing His creation through obedience to HaShem. To the extent that he does, he is already reaching into the Messianic Era.

THE LOWER WATER WEEPS

> *Everything is longing for the Messianic redemption, through which God's immanence will be fully realized. "The lower water weeps: 'I want to be with the King.'" (40)*

In Levertoff's sources, the created world's longing for the Messianic redemption is depicted by the lower waters weeping and saying, "I want to be with the King." Levertoff explains that the "lower waters" are those that were separated on the second day of creation when God "separated the waters which were below the expanse from the waters which were above the expanse."[124] After each of the six days of creation, the Torah says, "And God saw that it was good," except at the completion of the second day, on which the upper and the lower waters were separated. Jewish mysticism sees the "lower waters" as symbolizing the material world, while the waters above symbolize the spiritual world. Levertoff explains:

> The idea underlying this symbolic interpretation is evidently suggested by the difference between the tangible heaviness of the ocean and the aerial lightness of the clouds, and perhaps also the fact of tides governing the seas, while clouds float hither and thither at the whim of the wind.

To say that "the lower water weeps: 'I want to be with the King,'" is to say that the material world mourns its separation from God. This is based upon a midrashic treatment of Psalm 93:3 which says, "The floods have lifted up, O LORD, the floods have lifted up their voice, the floods lift up their pounding waves."

By way of switching vowel points, the midrash interprets "the floods lift up their pounding waves (lit. "their roaring" *dokyam*, דכים)," as if the lower waters are saying "We are crushed (*dakkim*, דכים): receive us; we are broken; receive us."[125] Thus the lower waters that have been released from the "fountains of the deep"[126] are seen as crying out to the heavens to be reunited

---

[124] Genesis 1:7.
[125] *Genesis Rabbah* 5:3 (Soncino).
[126] Genesis 7:11.

with HaShem. They want to be reunited with the upper waters. This is therefore a metaphorical picture of all creation groaning to be reunited with the King in the Messianic redemption.[127]

Since "the whole creation groans and suffers the pains of childbirth together until now,"[128] it is man's task to become one with his Father in heaven and therefore fulfill his divine task, and in turn to elevate all of Creation to the King and ease its suffering.

Once man accepts the yoke of Heaven, he realizes that his soul groans along with "the imprisoned soul of nature," just as Paul states: "We ourselves, having the first fruits of the Spirit, even we ourselves groan within ourselves, waiting eagerly for our adoption as sons, the redemption of our body."[129] Sanday and Headlam write, "Not only does creation groan, but we Christians groan: our very privileges make us long for something more."[130] He must therefore become a partner with HaShem in finishing the world in order to prepare it for the Messianic Era. Man was thus entrusted with the task of repairing that which he ruined. Then "the wolf will dwell with the lamb."[131]

RELEASING SPARKS

When all our thoughts and actions are the outcome of divine inspiration, then we unite everything that is seemingly separated from and independent of God with Him. (40)

All things originated with God. Therefore a man of faith should strive to unite all things with God by revealing their godly potential and bringing them into His service. In so doing, a man can cooperate with God "in His redemptive activities and prepare the way for the Messiah." By collecting and elevating the so-called "divine sparks" that are hidden throughout creation, man has "the privilege and joy of becoming [HaShem's] fellow-worker in this world, in natural as well as in spiritual life."

In these last generations before the return of our righteous Messiah, the responsibility of elevating creation by bringing it into the service of HaShem is more important than ever, "for we are God's fellow workers; you are God's field, God's building."[132] In this service of elevating all things to

---

[127] By putting John 7:37–38 back into Aramaic, it may be possible to see this concept on the lips of Messiah (See Rendel Harris, "Rivers of Living Waters," *The Expositor* 8th series, 20 (1920): 197–202.) In most English translations we read: "Jesus stood and cried out, saying, "If anyone is thirsty, let him come to Me and drink. He who believes in Me, as the Scripture said, 'From his innermost being will flow rivers of living water.'" When this is put back into Aramaic we have the Scripture the Master is quoting as: "Out of his throne shall flow rivers of living water." In other words the upper waters will flow down and be reunited with the lower waters, thus creation will be restored and redeemed. This concept is reiterated in Revelation 22:1 "Then he showed me a river of the water of life, clear as crystal, coming from the throne of God and of the Lamb." Sanctus of Vienna describes being strengthened as he is martyred by the "heavenly fountain of the water of life, flowing from the bowels of Christ" (Eusebius, *Pamphilius* 5:22). The joining of the waters, which begins with a flow from Heaven, metaphorically represents a return to the perfect state of unity before Creation.

[128] Romans 8:22.

[129] Romans 8:23.

[130] W. Sanday and Arthur C. Headlam, *International Critical Commentary to the New Testament: A Critical and Exegetical Commentary on the Epistle to the Romans* (New York: Scribner, 1896), 209.

[131] Isaiah 11:6.

[132] 1 Corinthians 3:9.

God and a godly purpose, some laid a foundation and others are building on it.[133] In the Messianic Era, when this service is complete, "each man's work will become evident."[134]

THE DIVINE SPARKS

❧ *There are some men who love God for His own sake and search for the divine sparks which are scattered in this world, in man and Nature, and try to bring them back to their source. (41)*

Jewish mysticism teaches that when man sinned and fell in the early days of Creation, he shattered the world. This shattering, according to Chasidic philosophy, sent *nitzotzot* ("sparks [of godliness]," ניצוצות) into the world.[135] This is an esoteric way of speaking of the godly source and potential inherent in all things: the world, man, and nature—even in a fallen world.

In the view of Jewish mysticism, man's task in life is to find, reveal, and release the divine element in every aspect of life. This is more than simply recognizing that all things proceed from God. It is the attempt to harness all things for God and bring all things into His service. Such service includes returning man to HaShem's Torah as well as using all that God entrusted to us for the sake of good.

Levertoff contrasts three types of men. Some men are absorbed in materialism and have no love for God. Such a man has no awareness of the godly potential inherent in the material world. Others are eager to please God in order to merit rewards in the world to come, but they do not serve Him out of love. Such a man thinks only of his own spiritual future and has no interest in the potential inherent in the material world. A third type of man serves God out of love for Him alone and so endeavors to bring the material world into His service, thereby bringing the divine sparks in creation back to their source.

---

[133] Cf. 1 Corinthians 3:10.

[134] 1 Corinthians 3:13.

[135] The sparks were originally contained in vessels. When these vessels were broken, the shards fell throughout the universe and became *kelippot* ("shells," קליפות). The *kelippot* are the evil forces that prevent the "divine sparks" from rising heavenward again. Some scholars suggest that the image of the "shells" goes back to an earlier concept called *chochmat ha'egoz* ("the wisdom of the nut," חכמת האגוז). The *chochmat ha'egoz* concept may go back to the Talmudic period and possibly even earlier. See A. Altmann, "'Eleazar of Worms' *Hokhmath Ha-'Egoz*," *Journal of Jewish Studies* 11 (1960): 101–113 and Joseph Dan, "*Hokhmath Ha-'Egoz*, Its Origin and Development," *Journal of Jewish Studies* 17:1–2 (1966): 73–82. Some believe that the developed doctrine of *shevirat hakelim* ("breaking of the vessels," שבירת הכלים) originated with Issac Luria (1534–1573). See Gershom Sholem, *Major Trends in Jewish Mysticism* (New York: Schocken Books, 1961), 265ff.

GOD REVEALED IN A HUMAN BEING

🌿 *God, by virtue of His character, needs a being to whom He can reveal Himself,*
whom He can love, and through whom He can shed abroad His light and
life. (41)

In a certain sense, God does need man. However, a king is not a king unless he has subjects over whom he rules. Levertoff cites a midrash about the creation of man that illustrates the point:

> The Torah replied and said to [Hashem], "Sovereign of the worlds! If there be no host for the king and if there be no camp for the king, over whom does he rule? If there be no people to praise the king, where is the honor of the king? The Holy One, blessed be He, heard this and it pleased Him." (*Pirke de Rabbi Eliezer* 3 [Friedlander])

According to Levertoff, God needs man primarily for the purpose of revealing His love. God displays His love to man.[136] When man receives that love, he can recognize his Creator in it and learn to serve Him out of love. He may then display God's love to others. Thus God is revealed to human beings through human beings.

Levertoff's words may also be understood to refer to the Messiah, the "being" to whom God reveals Himself. The Messiah is the ultimate example of one who accepts God's rule "voluntarily." By learning obedience, the Messiah was made perfect.[137] Yeshua is the one to whom God reveals all things concerning the attributes and nature of the Divinity. God reveals Himself to the Messiah, and in turn the Messiah reveals the Father to us; as stated, "He who has seen Me has seen the Father."[138]

Messiah reveals this love of God to us, and we are, in turn, able to love God just as our Master did. Our love of the Messiah is the fullest expression of the descent and ascent of this love of God. "He who has My commandments and keeps them is the one who loves Me; and he who loves Me will be loved by My Father, and I will love him and will disclose Myself to him."[139]

THE RESERVOIRS OF GOD

🌿 *The ultimate issues of this truth are of the most vital and cosmic significance,*
for God Himself is affected by our life. (41)

Levertoff compares man to a suckling child and God to a nursing mother. The child's nursing directly affects the mother. The more the child nurses, the more milk the mother generates; the less the child nurses, the less milk produced.

---

[136] Cf. 1 John 4:7–14.

[137] Cf. Hebrews 5:8–9.

[138] John 14:9.

[139] John 14:21.

Human beings have a similar effect on God, so to speak. The Torah says, "The LORD saw that the wickedness of man was great on the earth, and that every intent of the thoughts of his heart was only evil continually. The LORD was sorry that He had made man on the earth, and He was grieved in His heart."[140] Paul also speaks of this when he says, "Do not grieve the Holy Spirit of God, by whom you were sealed for the day of redemption."[141] If it is possible for human beings to grieve God so that He withdraws from man, it must also be possible to find favor in His eyes and draw down His lavish grace. "For He gives the Spirit without measure."[142]

GIVING AND RECEIVING

> *In like manner, the reservoirs of God are increased the more we draw from*
> *them for holiness, grace, and love. (41)*

The more we draw nourishment from sources of godliness the more godliness is poured out upon us. This may be learned from the verse that says, "Give, and it will be given to you. They will pour into your lap a good measure—pressed down, shaken together, and running over. For by your standard of measure it will be measured to you in return."[143] Levertoff's sources say that, on the other hand, "'If Israel neglects the will of God, the higher Powers wax feeble.' There is a reciprocal giving and receiving."

However, it is said that in the Messianic Era "they will not teach again, each man his neighbor and each man his brother, saying, 'Know the LORD,' for they will all know Me, from the least of them to the greatest of them," declares the LORD, "for I will forgive their iniquity, and their sin I will remember no more."[144] Of that day God says, "My salvation will be forever, and My righteousness will not wane."[145]

VESSELS OF LOVE

> *We must try our best to become vessels for God's love, guard our hearts*
> *wherein dwells the divine spark and preserve it undimmed and entire, and*
> *flee from "Egypt" in order to experience God's revelation on "Sinai." (41–42)*

"Love is from God; and everyone who loves is born of God and knows God."[146] Before a man can receive the revelation of God's love (which is compared to Sinai) a man must leave behind the old

---

[140] Genesis 6:5–6.

[141] Ephesians 4:30.

[142] John 3:34.

[143] Greek text of Luke 6:38, 12:20, 48 and 16:9 where "they" is used as a circumlocution for God. See also m.*Avot* 4:4,5, and b.*Yoma* 39a.

[144] Jeremiah 31:34.

[145] Isaiah 51:6.

[146] 1 John 4:7.

life of sin (which is compared to Egypt). Levertoff likens us to vessels which must be emptied out before we can be refilled with God's love. He says, "We must first try to clear away the thorns and weeds—hatred, jealousy, and lust—from the vineyard of the soul, so that which is good in us may be separated from that which is evil." The Apostle Paul says, "If anyone cleanses himself from these things, he will be a vessel for honor, sanctified, useful to our Lord, prepared for every good work."[147] When we clear the body of the impurities that hinder our service to God, we become "His workmanship, created in Messiah Yeshua for good works, which God prepared beforehand so that we would walk in them."[148] Then God is able to fill us with His love and sanctify us unto Himself.

DESCENT OF THE SOUL

> *The divine love which is revealed in the mystery of the human personality, in "the descent of the soul, in order to inhabit a material tabernacle." (42)*

The mystics teach that the godly soul leaves its abode in the heavens to inhabit an earthly body. As noted above, this descent of the soul is derived from a mystical reading of Genesis 2:7, where HaShem breathes life into Adam[149]:

> Then the LORD God formed man of dust from the ground, and breathed into his nostrils the breath of life [*neshamah,* נשמה]; and man became a living being [*nefesh,* נפש]. (Genesis 2:7)

The common biblical Hebrew word for "soul" is *nefesh,* (נפש), but *nefesh* is seldom used to refer to the immortal, spiritual element of the divine soul. Instead, *nefesh* refers to a person's life-force, vitality, and psyche. The *nefesh* is essentially the "self" and the "personality." The mystics describe the *nefesh* as a man's thought, speech, and action. Even animals have a *nefesh.* In Chasidic philosophy, the *nefesh* is equivalent to the "animal soul."

The Hebrew word for "breath" is *neshamah* (נשמה). The same word is commonly used in Judaism to refer to the divine soul. By reading *neshamah* as soul, one may understand the "breath of life" God breathed into Adam as the divine, preexistent soul being imparted into human flesh and binding to the *nefesh.*[150] Philo of Alexandria comments on Genesis 2:7:

> For the essence of the soul of man is the breath of God, especially if we follow the account of Moses, who, in his history of the creation of the world, says that God breathed into the first man, the founder of our race, the breath of life; breathing it into the principal part of his body, namely the face, where the outward senses are

---

[147] 2 Timothy 2:21.

[148] Ephesians 2:10.

[149] See the Ramban and Bachya on Genesis 2:7.

[150] Compare the Jewish-Christian document *Recognitions of Clement* 4:9 (Coxe): "When God had made man after His own image and likeness, He grafted into His work a certain breathing and odour of His divinity, that so men, being made partakers of His Only-begotten, might through Him be also friends of God and sons of adoption."

established, the body-guards of the mind, as if it were the great king. And that which was thus breathed into his face was manifestly the breath of the air, or whatever else there may be which is even more excellent than the breath of the air, as being a ray emitted from the blessed and thrice-happy nature of God. (*The Special Laws* 4:123)[151]

The *nefesh* (personality) and *neshamah* (divine soul) are connected, but remain distinct. At death, the *nefesh* perishes with the body, but the *neshamah* returns to HaShem. Second-century church theologian Tatian shares a similar view but follows the conventions of the apostolic writers by referring to the heavenly soul as the spirit: "For the dwelling place of the spirit is above, but the origin of the soul is from beneath."[152]

THE KING'S SON

❧ *A king had an only son who was pure, wise, and good, having never known evil. (42)*

Levertoff relates a parable wherein the soul is compared to a prince sent by his father to travel abroad. God is compared to the king who sent his son out into the world. The soul is compared to the prince who withstood the temptations of the world before returning to his father the king. The world is compared to the soul's sojourn on earth wrapped in human flesh.

That the soul preexists is an idea central to Judaism.[153] This was based on verses like, "The spirit will return to God who gave it"[154] and can be seen most prominently in the *Talmud,* which says, "The Son of David will not come before all the souls in [the repository of souls] are used; since it is said [in Isaiah 57:16], 'For the spirit that would [enwrap itself] is from Me, and the souls which I have made.'"[155] No less famous a church theologian than Origen of Alexandria believed in the preexistence of the soul.[156] The Apostle James speaks of the preexistence of the soul when he says,

---

[151] See also *Allegorical Interpretations* 1:33ff.

[152] Tatian, *Address to the Greeks* 13b (Coxe).

[153] *Wisdom of Solomon* 8:19–20; 14:8; Josephus, *The Wars of the Jews* 2:154. Cf. b.*Shabbat* 32a, "I designated you the first; wherefore I commanded you concerning the first. The soul which I placed in you is called a lamp, wherefore I commanded you concerning the lamp. If ye fulfill them, 'tis well; but if not, I will take your souls." For an in-depth study on this concept in early Judaism, see Frank Chamberlin Porter, "The Pre-Existence of the Soul in the Book of Wisdom and in the Rabbinical Writings," *The American Journal of Theology* 12:53 (January 1908): 53–115.

[154] Ecclesiastes 12:7.

[155] b.*Yevamot* 63b quoting a literal reading of Isaiah 57:16. The "repository of souls" is called the *guf* (literally "body," גוף). According to Jewish mysticism, it is the place in which all the unborn souls reside waiting to be sent to earth. According to the *Talmud,* the redemption will not occur until all unborn souls will have entered this world. Cf. 2 Baruch 30:2–3. After the souls are returned from dwelling in their physical bodies the *Talmud* states that the "souls of the righteous are hidden under the Throne of Glory" (b.*Shabbat* 152b). Revelation 6:9 has a similar concept of souls being under the altar. Note also the words of 2 Enoch 23:4, [longer recension].

[156] *De Principiis,* 1:7:4. For a complete discussion of Origen's doctrine on the soul see Antiona Triipolitis, *The Doctrine of the Soul in the Thought of Plotinus and Origen* (Roslyn Heights, NY: Libra Publishers: 1978). See also *Clementine Recognitions* 1:28.

"Or do you think that the Scripture speaks to no purpose: 'He jealously desires the Spirit which He has made to dwell in us'?"[157]

While the soul dwells on earth, it yearns to return to its maker. Our godly soul beckons us to seek God and thus return to Him.

> For we know that if the earthly tent which is our house is torn down, we have a building from God, a house not made with hands, eternal in the heavens. For indeed in this *house* we groan, longing to be clothed with our dwelling from heaven, inasmuch as we, having put it on, will not be found naked. For indeed while we are in this tent, we groan, being burdened, because we do not want to be unclothed but to be clothed, so that what is mortal will be swallowed up by life. (2 Corinthians 5:1–4)[158]

The presence of the divine soul creates a hunger and thirst for godliness within us. This innate desire cannot be quenched by worldly pleasures and goods. We are to keep ourselves "unstained by the world."[159] Each impurity from the world that we allow into our life is like a blemish on the soul. This also further dims the light of godliness within us. When we dim this light, we in essence constrict the light of our soul and its cry for God. However, the more we put aside the impurities and desires of the world, the greater the light of our souls and the purer our connection to God.

Also James says:

---

[157] James 4:5. Note that the Greek here in James is ambiguous and there are other possible renderings into English which would negate this interpretation. For support of this translation of the Greek see Craig L. Bloomberg and Mariam J. Kamell, *Exegetical Commentary on the New Testament: James* (Grand Rapids: Zondervan, 2008), 190–192 and Dougals J. Moo, *The Letter of James* (Grand Rapids: Eerdmans, 2000), 190. See Luke 12:20 where it says, "This very night your soul is required of you" where it speaks in a manner of a lender requiring payment for an object that was on loan, i.e., the soul. This may also allude to the idea of a preexistent soul, for the verse is worded as if that which is entrusted to you must one day be returned. Also note the *Jewish Encyclopedia* cites several textual proofs that this concept is present in the New Testament: "In the New Testament the same view is expressed regarding the preexistence of persons and things forming part of the divine salvation. When Jesus, in John 8:58, says, 'Before Abraham was, I am,' allusion is made to the preexistence of the Messiah. So is the Kingdom—that is, the reward of paradise—'prepared for you [the righteous] from the foundation of the world' (Matthew 25:34; comp. m.*Avot* 3:16). From Matthew 13:35 it appears that the 'dark sayings of old' of Psalms 78:2 was understood to refer to Messianic secrets prepared from the foundation of the world. Similarly the names of the righteous are 'written in the book of life from the foundation of the world' (Revelation 17:8). But the blood of the martyr prophets was also believed to have been 'shed from the foundation of the world' (Luke 11:50); hence, also, that of the 'Lamb' (Revelation 13: 8; Hebrews 9:26). The apostles claimed to have been, with their master, 'chosen from the foundation of the world' (Ephesians 1:4; comp. John 17:24; 1 Peter 1:20; Hebrews 4:3)." See Kaufmann Kohler and Ludwig Blau, "Preexistence," *Jewish Encyclopedia* 8:182–184.

[158] See also 1 Corinthians 6:19.

[159] James 1:27.

But each one is tempted when he is carried away and enticed by his own lust. Then when lust has conceived, it gives birth to sin; and when sin is accomplished, it brings forth death. (James 1:14–15)[160]

When we resist the temptations of this world we are able to better feel the longing of our soul for its Creator. The early Church theologian Tertullian states:

Still there is a portion of good in the soul, of that original, divine, and genuine good, which is its proper nature. For that which is derived from God is rather obscured than extinguished ... Thus the divinity of the soul bursts forth in prophetic forecasts in consequence of its primeval good. (*A Treatise on the Soul* 41 [Coxe])

God desires that we should seek Him and return to Him. When our soul is returned to the Creator, we do not want it to be blemished from the stains of the world.[161] "Be diligent to be found by Him in peace, spotless and blameless, and regard the patience of our Lord as salvation."[162]

---

[160] Origen believed this: "Created in the image of God, man's rational soul is capable of attaining perfection or likeness to God ... However ... [the soul] became estranged from God and was clothed in a human body ... Ever since the time of the Incarnation, it is possible for man to recover his knowledge of and fellowship with the Logos. This can be accomplished by believing in Christ and by constant imitation of Him ... When the soul realizes its divine nature, and understands that the true reality lies within it, it recognizes that it must take up the struggle against sin and passion." (Triipolitis, *The Doctrine of the Soul*, 123–125). Similarly *Midrash Tanchuma, Pekudei* 3 sees the placement of souls into physical bodies as for their perfection.

[161] For examples of the descent-and-return theme in Apostolic Writings see Romans 1:36 and John 16:28. For the Jewish-Christian belief that Yeshua is the source of all souls see Elliot R. Wolfson, *Along the Path* (New York: State University of New York Press, 1995), 63–88. This is similar to the the Jewish concept of *neshama klalit* (נשמה כללית), a general soul that contains the souls of all Israel.

[162] 2 Peter 3:14–15.

2

THE LAW AND LOVE

THE WORD OF GOD

To the Chasid Scripture is full of spiritual truth, and even the Hebrew letters of the book are considered to be "vehicles which bring to the upper and lower worlds life from the divine centre." (43)

In chapter one of *Love and the Messianic Age*, Levertoff established that man's role in creation is to know and love HaShem. How can man fulfill his duty to know and love God unless he knows about God? "How then will they call on Him in whom they have not believed? How will they believe in Him whom they have not heard? And how will they hear without a preacher?"[1]

The path to knowing and loving God begins with the study of Scripture. The Chasid has the utmost reverence for the Scriptures. To him it is "spiritual truth" which connects the heavens with the earth. The study of Scripture allows the soul to ascend and descend, making a spiritual connection with God. Scripture connects "the upper and lower worlds"; herein is the mystery of the "Word of God," that "the Word became flesh."[2]

THE LIVING TORAH

The deepest longing, therefore, of the genuine Chasid is to become a "living Torah." (43)

The Chasid desires to become a "living Torah," that is, he desires to have his entire being—body and soul—given over to the will and wisdom of HaShem. He desires to completely nullify the self so as to allow godliness to fill his entire person.[3] The Torah is the means to reach this objective. In Chasidic teaching, it is said that the righteous person (tzaddik) "is the living incarnation of the

---

1   Romans 10:14.

2   John 1:14.

3   Cf. Galatians 2:20.

Torah."[4] Because the words of Torah are the embodiment of God's thoughts, studying the Torah is like studying God's mind. Obeying Torah gives action to His thoughts.

> R. Leib Sarah was wont to say that man's purpose is not just to *study* the Torah, but to *become* the Torah. This is what it means to be a "living Torah."[5]

> R. Schneur Zalman of Liad, too, said of his master, the Maggid of Mezhirech: Elsewhere one learns to master the Torah, i.e., how one is to study the Torah; in Mezhirech, however, one learns to let the Torah master you, i.e., how the Torah teaches man to become a Torah himself. [6]

Rabbi Menachem Nachum Twersky, disciple of the Baal Shem Tov, wrote:

> A human being is part of the Torah and each part of a whole is a microcosm of the whole. Thus every single Jew is a complete Torah in miniature and just as the Torah is called 'complete,' so must a Jew perfect himself in both his 'upper' and 'lower' half.[7]

The concept of the "living Torah" was present in the Talmudic era and the apostolic era. The disciples of Rabbi Eliezer referred to their teacher as "the Scroll of the Torah."[8] Likewise, in the early apostolic community, Yeshua was referred to as "The Torah."[9] This is part of the implication of "And the Word became flesh."[10]

SECRETS OF THE TORAH

🌿 *Great will be the joy when the divine mysteries hidden in the Law will be fully unfolded [by the Messiah]. (43)*

In this present age, man must observe the commandments in the Torah "without questioning." Israel declares, "All that the LORD has spoken we will do!"[11] Obedience to God should not be con-

---

[4]   Sholem, *Major Trends in Jewish Mysticism*, 344.

[5]   Jacob Immanuel Schochet, *The Mystical Dimension Volume Three: Chasidic Dimensions* (New York: Kehot Publication Society, 1995), 123.

[6]   Ibid, 123–124.

[7]   Rabbi Menachem Nachum Twersky, *Me'or Einyam* (trans. Rabbi Eugene J. Cohen; USA: Xlibris Corporation, 2003), 246.

[8]   b.*Sanhedrin* 101a.

[9]   Found in the second century *Preaching of Peter* as quoted in Clement of Alexandria, *Stromata* 1:29, 2:15.

[10]   John 1:14. Jacobus Schoneveld, "The Torah in the Flesh: A New Reading of the Prologue of the Gospel of John as a Contribution to a Christology without Anti-Judaism," *Immanuel* 24/25 (1990): 77–94. Cf. Elliot R. Wolfson, "Inscribed in the Book of the Living: *Gospel of Truth* and Jewish Christology," *Journal for the Study of Judaism* 38 (2007):234–271 and Elliot R. Wolfson, *Language, Eros, Being* (New York: Fordham University Press, 2005), 190–260.

[11]   Exodus 19:8.

tingent on receiving an explanation of a particular commandment. It is enough for a subject to be obedient to the king. He should not first insist on having to know the king's reason for an order.

However, the Messianic Age will bring the joy of knowing "the divine mysteries hidden in the Law." The deepest truths and mysteries behind every precept of the Torah will be revealed by the Messiah, for the Torah "will go forth from Zion and the word of the LORD from Jerusalem."[12]

> When he, about whom it is written [in Zechariah 9:9] "humble and mounted on a donkey" will come … he will explain for them the words of the Torah … and correct for them their misinterpretations. (*Genesis Rabbah* 98:9)

A medieval Jewish work called *Pesikta Hadta* depicts the Messianic Era as a time when the meanings of all the obscure laws of the Torah will be explained:

> When the Holy One, blessed be He, sees David and the Messiah … And the Holy One, blessed is He, sits and reveals the meanings of the Tora to [the righteous]: Why he prohibited us pork, and blood, and lard.[13]

The Master's teaching provides a foretaste of that day. He said to His disciples, "To you it has been granted to know the mysteries of the kingdom of heaven, but to them it has not been granted."[14]

> Blessed are your eyes, because they see; and your ears, because they hear. For truly I say to you that many prophets and righteous men desired to see what you see, and did not see it, and to hear what you hear, and did not hear it. (Matthew 13:16–17)

People who live their life with the goal of becoming a living Torah become a "letter of Messiah … written not with ink but with the Spirit of the living God."[15] Until that time, we continue to sow in tears, seeing all things "in a mirror dimly,"[16] thus only knowing in part. Nevertheless, one must not lose hope, for "those who sow in tears shall reap with joyful shouting."[17] Then we will see "face to face" and we will "know fully."[18]

The Chasidic teacher Levi Yitzhak of Berdichev imagined the Messianic Era as a great Torah study in the assembly of Messiah:

---

[12] Isaiah 2:3; Micah 4:2.

[13] Patai, *The Messiah Texts*, 253.

[14] Matthew 13:11. Chana Safrai sees the use of "mysteries" here by the Master as similar to the use of Mishnaic Hebrew word מסתורין ("mysteries") by the sages. In rabbinic literature it is sometimes used to refer to the Oral Torah. See Chana Safrai, "The Kingdom of Heaven and the Study of Torah," in *Jesus' Last Week* (ed. R. Steven Notley, Marc Turnage, and Brian Becker; Boston, MA: Brill, 2006), 175.

[15] 2 Corinthians 3:3.

[16] 1 Corinthians 13:12.

[17] Psalm 126:5.

[18] 1 Corinthians 13:12.

In the future to come, the name of God blessed be He, will reveal to us even the meaning of the blank spaces in the Torah scroll, so that we should understand the blank letters in our Torah. And this is the meaning of the passage in Isaiah 51:4 that says, "For a Torah shall go forth from me." That all Israel should understand even the letters which are blank in our Torah which was given to Moses. But at present those letters of whiteness are concealed from us, and when our Righteous Messiah comes, we shall understand also the blank spaces in the Torah, quickly in our days, Amen![19]

SALT OF THE SPIRIT

🌿 *However, it is possible "to keep all the commandments, and yet be far from God." (43)*

According to an axiom of the sages, it is possible to be an apostate with the permission of the Torah. That means it is possible to keep the external commandments and maintain religious appearances while one's heart remains unredeemed. This man becomes "a savor of death unto death"[20] and submits himself to "the law of sin and death,"[21] abiding only by the letter of the Torah, which kills[22] and leads to separation from HaShem, God forbid. Since this man becomes a part of "the ministry of death" and "the ministry of condemnation,"[23] the Torah has become to him a "deadly poison" (*sam mavet*, סם מות).[24] "This poison can be cured only by the 'salt' of the spirit of God." Our Master says, "Have salt in yourselves, and be at peace with one another."[25]

"But we know that the Law is good, if one uses it lawfully."[26] For when one lives out the Torah through the power of the Spirit, the Torah becomes "an elixir of life."[27]

If a man is worthy, the Torah becomes for him a medicine of life, but if he is not, it is a deadly poison. This is what Raba explained, "If he uses the Torah properly it is a medicine of life unto him, but for him who does not use it properly, it is a deadly poison." (b.*Yoma* 72b)

---

[19] Patai, *The Messiah Texts,* 257.

[20] 2 Corinthians 2:16 (KJV).

[21] Romans 8:2.

[22] Cf. 2 Corinthians 3:6.

[23] Cf. 2 Corinthians 3:7–9.

[24] Cf. e.g., *Deuteronomy Rabbah* 1:6, "Just as the bee reserves honey for its owner and for the stranger its sting, so to Israel the words of the Torah are the elixir of life, but to the other nations the poison of death" (Soncino). Cf. also b.*Taanit* 7a.

[25] Mark 9:50. Cf. Matthew 5:13.

[26] 1 Timothy 1:8.

[27] b.*Kiddushin* 30b.

A man who becomes "seasoned with salt"[28] becomes "an aroma of life to life."[29] His body and soul will then be in submission to the "Torah of the Spirit of life in Messiah Yeshua,"[30] and his mind will be "set on the Spirit [of God],"[31] enabling him to subject himself to the Torah of God. After being cured with such salt, he becomes a part of the "ministry of righteousness."[32] Such a man, having been cured with salt, now becomes able to unite "the spiritual with the material, the infinite with the finite."

DIVINE WISDOM DESCENDS

The Torah is the "descending of the divine wisdom from the highest heights and embodying itself in 'earthly' commandments." (44)

The commandments of the Torah contain the will and wisdom of God. Moreover, the commandments are really "one" with Him in that they are extensions and embodiments of His divine will and wisdom.

Every word of Torah is spoken from the mouth of HaShem. Our Master has taught us, "For the mouth speaks out of that which fills the heart."[33] Therefore, the words of Torah express the heart of HaShem. They are encapsulations of the divine nature. The *Tanya* discourses on this concept, and presents the Torah as a distillation and "incarnation," so to speak, of HaShem's own person—His will and wisdom:

> And although the Holy One, blessed be He, is called *En Sof* ("Infinite"), and "His greatness can never be fathomed," and "No thought can apprehend Him at all," and so are also His will and His wisdom, as it is written: "There is no searching of His understanding," and "Canst thou by searching find G-d?" and again: "For My thoughts are not your thoughts"—nevertheless, it is in this connection that it has been said [in b.*Megillah* 31a], "Where you find the greatness of the Holy One, blessed be He, there you also find His humility." For the Holy One, blessed be He, has compressed His will and wisdom within the 613 commandments of the Torah …

> Therefore, has the Torah been compared to water, for just as water descends from a higher to a lower level, so has the Torah descended from its place of glory, which is His blessed will and wisdom; [for] the Torah and the Holy One, blessed be He, are one and the same and no thought can apprehend Him at all. Thence [the Torah] has progressively descended … until it clothed itself in corporeal substances and

---

28 Colossians 4:6.

29 2 Corinthians 2:16.

30 Romans 8:2.

31 Romans 8:6.

32 2 Corinthians 3:9.

33 Matthew 12:34.

in things of this world, comprising almost all of the commandments of the Torah, their laws, and in the combinations of the material letters, written with ink in a book. (*Tanya* 4 [Kehot])

According to this concept, God's unknowable and divine will and wisdom (which are inseparable from His being) descended to be clothed in the corporeal substance of commandments of Torah and ink in a book. This is not to say that a Torah scroll is God, but that the Torah scroll is an earthly container for His will and wisdom. It is similar to the theological concept of the Shechinah (שכינה), the "Dwelling Presence of God." Just as the Shechinah took residence and filled the Tabernacle, the Spirit of God fills the words of the Torah.

This explains why Chasidic mysticism teaches that the one who commits himself to the study and application of Torah is able to unite "the Holy One, blessed be He, with His *Shechinah*."[34] He is able to find God in the Torah, for "the Lord—is—in the wisdom."

THE "REAL PRESENCE"

> 🌿 *It is not an exaggeration to speak of this conception of the Law as the Jewish doctrine of the "real Presence." (44)*

According to the above explanation, "the Torah and the Holy One, blessed be He, are one and the same."[35] Stated so succinctly, the concept is jarring and sounds idolatrous. Are the mystics teaching that the Torah is HaShem? Instead, they are teaching that the Torah is the divine expression of God's will and wisdom, placed within the physical limitations of this world and translated into terms comprehensible to human beings. However, God's will and wisdom cannot be separated from HaShem Himself. If the Torah contains HaShem's will and wisdom, then it contains something of HaShem Himself; they are "one and the same."

This explanation of how the infinite God clothed Himself in the finite and corporeal has important ramifications for the discussion of Christology. Levertoff notes the similarity. He compares the mystical explanation of how HaShem and the Torah are "one and the same" with the Christian theology of the "real Presence."

In Christian theology the term "real Presence" refers to the presence of Christ in the elements of the Eucharistic sacrament. Our Master took bread and wine at His last Seder and said, "This is my body; this is my blood." Far removed from the context of Passover and the simple symbolism of the Seder meal, Christian theologians asked, "How can the bread and wine be the body and blood of Christ?"

The theology of the "real Presence" asserts that Christ is really present in the bread and wine of the sacraments.[36] In Roman Catholicism the bread and wine are believed to actually, physically become the body and blood of Christ. This is called the doctrine of "transubstantiation." In some

---

[34] *Tanya* 41 (Kehot). This idea is often derived from Zechariah 14:9.

[35] *Tanya* 4 (Kehot).

[36] Günther Schnurr, "Eucharist," *The Encyclopedia of Christianity* 2:170–171.

Protestant denominations the bread and wine are regarded in their essence as the body and blood of Christ. This is called "consubstantiation." In the Anglican tradition, which is the tradition of Levertoff's confession, the question of how Christ can be present in the bread and the wine is left unresolved as a "holy mystery."[37]

Regardless of how the "real Presence" is interpreted, Levertoff sees a parallel between the Chassidic idea of Hashem's presence in the Torah and the Christian concept of Christ's incarnation in the Eucharist.

Another way of presenting the parallel is to say that just as the mystics and the *Tanya* teach that the Torah is God's will and wisdom made scroll, the apostles and the Gospel of John teach that Messiah is God's will and wisdom made flesh.

HASHEM IS IN THE WISDOM

Technically it is expressed in the words "The LORD is in the wisdom." (44)

As explained above, Levertoff's Chasidic sources taught that "the Torah and the Holy One, blessed be He, are one and the same."[38] In some inexplicable manner, God's Presence (through His will and wisdom) is in the Torah. Levertoff calls this "the Jewish doctrine of the 'real Presence.'" He cites Proverbs 3:19 as a proof text to support the idea that HaShem is in the Torah.

Proverbs 3:19 may be translated literally, "The LORD in wisdom founded the earth." Levertoff's sources interpret "wisdom" in this passage as another name for the Torah.[39] Thus the verse can be understood to say "HaShem is in the Wisdom," that is, "in the Torah."

---

[37] The Anglican theology of "real Presence" is expressed in the Church of England's Thirty-Nine Articles of Religion (1563). Levertoff would have had to declare his agreement with those thirty-nine articles prior to ordination as an Anglican priest. Article 28 reads as follows: "Of the Lord's Supper: The Supper of the Lord is not only a sign of the love that Christians ought to have among themselves one to another, but rather it is a Sacrament of our Redemption by Christ's death: insomuch that to such as rightly, worthily, and with faith, receive the same, the Bread which we break is a partaking of the Body of Christ; and likewise the Cup of Blessing is a partaking of the Blood of Christ. Transubstantiation (or the change of the substance of Bread and Wine) in the Supper of the Lord, cannot be proved by Holy Writ; but is repugnant to the plain words of Scripture, overthroweth the nature of a Sacrament, and hath given occasion to many superstitions. The Body of Christ is given, taken, and eaten, in the Supper, only after an heavenly and spiritual manner. And the mean whereby the Body of Christ is received and eaten in the Supper, is Faith. The Sacrament of the Lord's Supper was not by Christ's ordinance reserved, carried about, lifted up, or worshipped." (Thirty-Nine Articles of Religion [1563], Article 28).

[38] *Tanya* 4 (Kehot).

[39] See *Genesis Rabbah* 1:1 where the personification of Wisdom found in the Proverbs is identified with the Torah and depicted as assisting God in the creation of the world: "The Torah declares: 'I was the working tool of the Holy One, blessed be He.'" Also: "Thus God consulted the Torah and created the world, while the Torah declares, 'In the beginning God created,' the word 'beginning' refers to the Torah, as it says [in Proverbs 8:22], 'The LORD made me as the beginning of His way."

The early believers made similar equations when formulating apostolic-era Christology and even identified Messiah with the personification of Wisdom in the book of Proverbs.[40] For the early believers, God's Wisdom was not only the Torah, but it was also the person of Yeshua.

If it is possible to accept the notion that, through the expression of God's will and wisdom, "the Torah and the Holy One, blessed be He, are one and the same," then along the same line of thought, one might say, "The Messiah and the Holy One, blessed be He, are one and the same."

NOT BY BREAD ALONE

🌿 *The cloud which surrounded Moses emanated from God. (44)*

When Moses "remained on the mountain forty days and nights," he "neither ate bread nor drank water."[41] Instead, the cloud of God's Presence which surrounded him sustained him. This was to show that "man does not live by bread alone, but man lives by everything that proceeds out of the mouth of the LORD."[42] The "cloud which surrounded Moses," Levertoff says, "symbolizes the Law." Because the cloud enveloped Moses when he received the Torah, it was likened to a protective covering or garment,[43] and also a source of physical sustenance.

Like the cloud on Sinai, the Torah also emanates from God Himself and becomes Israel's spiritual food. Israel is sustained by this spiritual food "if they duly receive it."

Our Master alludes to a concept similar to this when He states, "I am the bread of life; he who comes to Me will not hunger, and he who believes in Me will never thirst."[44] He further says:

> I am the bread of life. Your fathers ate the manna in the wilderness, and they died. This is the bread which comes down out of heaven, so that one may eat of it and not die. I am the living bread that came down out of heaven; if anyone eats of this bread, he will live forever; and the bread also which I will give for the life of the world is My flesh. (John 6:48–51)

Unless a person takes in our Master's teachings to the extent that they become a part of his essence, he will not have life:

---

[40] Skarsaune states that "In early Christian writings, this idea of the mediatorship of Wisdom in creation is transferred, not to the Torah, but to God's Son. He is identified with *Sophia* as well as with the Sapiental *logos*: Col 1:15–16; Heb 1:2–3; John 1:1–3. The Jewish character of this Wisdom Christology shines through most clearly in Hermas, who directly identified God's Son with the Torah: 'This great tree that overshadows plains and mountains and the entire earth is the law of God that has been given to the world. And this law is the Son of God.' [Hermas Similitudes 8.3.2; Ehrman, Loeb Classic Library]" (Oskar Skarsaune, Reider Havalvik, eds., *Jewish Believers in Jesus: The Early Centuries* (Peabody, MA: Hendrickson Publishers, 2007), 403.

[41] Deuteronomy 9:9.

[42] Deuteronomy 8:3. Cf. Matthew 4:4.

[43] Cf. *Tanya* 4. Cf. *Igeret HaKodesh* 29. See also *Tzava'at Harivash* 111.

[44] John 6:35.

Truly, truly, I say to you, unless you eat the flesh of the Son of Man and drink His blood, you have no life in yourselves. He who eats My flesh and drinks My blood has eternal life, and I will raise him up on the last day. For My flesh is true food, and My blood is true drink. (John 6:53–55)

What does it mean to eat the flesh of Messiah and drink His blood? The *Midrash Rabbah* says that "All the references to eating and drinking in this book signify Torah and good deeds."[45] The bread that is the Messiah's flesh and the drink that is His blood is His teaching. His teaching is derived from the Torah, its teachings and its application in good deeds.

OIL FOR THE LAMP

> *Israel is symbolized by the seven-branched candlestick in the Tabernacle, the menorah, for through the possession of the Law they are destined to be "divine light-carriers." (44)*

If Israel receives the spiritual food of Torah and good deeds, "God's will embodies itself in their thoughts, words, and deeds." In Chasidic philosophy, thought, speech, and action make up the *sechel* ("intellect," שכל). One must purify each of them if he hopes to eliminate the hold the evil inclination has upon him.

In order for "the fire of God's holy love" to burn, it needs fuel; Torah is this fuel. Israel is the Menorah; they are the "divine light-carriers."[46] Those who submit to God's will become "the light of the world;"[47] this light shines before men as "a lamp shining in a dark place."[48] Note an elucidation of this idea as found in the *Tanya*:

> The Light of the *Shechinah* is compared to the flame of a lamp which produces no light nor clings to the wick without oil, and likewise the *Shechinah* does not rest on a man's body, which is likened to a wick, except through good deeds alone. (*Tanya* 35 [Kehot])

---

[45] *Ecclesiastes Rabbah* 2:28, 3:16, 5:23, and 8:16 (Soncino). Cf. b.*Sanhedrin* 98b. Note also b.*Sukkah* 52a which states that the *yetzer hara* ("the evil inclination," [יצר הרע] or the Satan, [השטן]) is called "the enemy," as stated in Proverbs 25:21–22. The *Talmud* goes on to quote this section from Proverbs to state that the enemy should be sated with food and drink—that is Torah study which is compared to bread and good deeds or words of Torah. In this same section of *Talmud*, Rashi cites in his commentary the passage from Isaiah 55:1: "Ho! Every one who thirsts, come to the waters." See also Romans 12:20–21. Cf. b.*Ta'anit* 7a which mentions that one should eat from a Torah scholar; and note the words of our Master: "Truly, truly, I say to you, unless you eat the flesh of the Son of Man and drink His blood, you have no life in yourselves" (John 6:53). See also b.*Chagigah* 14a. and b.*Sanhedrin* 98b.

[46] Cf. Revelation 2:5 which speaks of removing one's lampstand for failing to repent and to be a light to the world.

[47] Matthew 5:14; b.*Baba Batra* 4a; b.*Berachot* 28b.

[48] 2 Peter 1:19.

"The Supernal light that is kindled on one's head, namely, the *Shechinah*, requires oil," that is, to be clothed in wisdom, which is called "oil from the holy anointing," as is explained in the *Zohar*, that "these are the good deeds," namely, the 613 commandments, which derive from His blessed wisdom. Thereby the light of the *Shechinah* can cling to the wick, i.e. the vivifying soul in the body, which is metaphorically called a "wick." (*Tanya* 53 [Kehot])[49]

RIGHTEOUSNESS BY FAITH

Although the Torah is the revelation of God's will, yet His innermost secret is known only to His most intimate friends. (44)

God only reveals His most precious secrets and mysteries to those who are closest to Him. These are those who "through their perfect fellowship with Him, are the only true representatives of Israel." The innermost secrets are revealed to those who observe the Torah, not out of rote obedience, but rather, out of love for God. A mere observance of the Torah without love is "legalism." This is similar to Paul's words when he states: "For they are not all Israel who are descended from Israel; nor are they all children because they are Abraham's descendants."[50] This speaks of those who pursue a Torah of righteousness by works, pursuing the Torah without faith and out of loveless, mechanical obedience.[51]

The one who pursues a "righteousness which is by faith"[52] will attain righteousness "resulting in salvation."[53] Such a faith is manifest in works and good deeds. This is the man who seeks his praise from God; he is one who does not do his deeds to be seen by men; he therefore practices his righteousness in secret.[54] "He is not a Jew who is one outwardly, nor is circumcision that which is

---

[49] This is also the meaning of our Master's parable about the ten virgins (Matthew 25:1–12), five of which were foolish and did not bring sufficient oil, that is, good deeds. Note that in Christian mysticism the uncreated "light" is considered the way in which God reveals and transcends His unknowable self to His people. Gregory of Palamas (*The Triads* 2:3:9, 3:1:9–19) saw this concept expressed through Moses (Exodus 34:29), Yeshua (Matthew 17:1ff.), and Stephen (Acts 6:15) and saw that through Messiah, revelation of the uncreated light was available to all. St. Gregory of Thessalonica wrote: "He who participates in the divine energy … becomes himself, in a sense, Light; he is united to the Light and with the Light he sees in full consciousness all that remains hidden for those who have not this grace; he thus surpasses not only the corporal senses, but also all that can be known [by the mind] … for the pure of heart see God … who, being the Light, abides in them and reveals Himself to those who love Him, to His beloved ones" (See Lossky, *In the Image and Likeness of God*, 61). See also Lossky's entire discussion entitled "The Theology of Light in the Thought of St. Gregory" on pages 45–69. Cf. Matthew 13:43; John 1:9; 1 John 1:5. Note also the words of James: "Every good thing given and every perfect gift is from above, coming down from the Father of lights, with whom there is no variation or shifting shadow" (James 1:17).

[50] Romans 9:6–7.

[51] Cf. Romans 9:27–33.

[52] Romans 9:30.

[53] Romans 10:10.

[54] Cf. Matthew 6:1–18.

outward in the flesh. But he is a Jew who is one inwardly; and circumcision is that which is of the heart, by Spirit, not by letter; and his praise is not from men, but from God."[55]

BIRDS AND BEASTS

🌿 A "more excellent way" than legalism exists. (45)

By saying that a "more excellent way"[56] exists than "legalism," Levertoff means to say that there is a righteousness that transcends the simple, mechanical obedience to the Torah's list of rules. This can be seen "in some Chasidic writings" on the characterization of "different types of saintliness."[57] Levertoff says that some souls are "not bound by laws that govern those who must plod below." These souls are like birds, whose "movements are graceful, their flight easy, in the rare atmosphere above earthly things."

Others are different, being "like those angels, representatives of the cosmic forces, whom Ezekiel symbolizes as having the faces of oxen and lions." These are not the opposite of the aforementioned group but rather of a somewhat lower spiritual caliber than the first. Note the following from a discourse by Rabbi Schneur Zalman:

> For it is impossible to subdue and conquer the spirit of the animal soul and to place it under the domination of the G-dly soul without first contemplating the animal soul's "root," which is the holy *Chayot*-angels of the Divine chariot—the face of the lion and the face of the ox.[58]

The *Chayot*-angels (חיות) literally translates to the "Beasts-angels," thus the use of this term to describe the animalistic part (the flesh) of the soul. The second group possesses souls which are "naturally heavy, dull, or fierce, but by their close contact with God are enabled to overcome their original nature." Close contact with God allows these souls to soar; however their flight is only obtained through diligence and great effort.[59]

---

[55] Romans 2:28–29.

[56] 1 Corinthians 12:31.

[57] Levertoff's contrast between the naturally righteous, bird-like souls, and the somewhat lower, animal-like souls, is an obscure Chasidic concept. For an example, see Rabbi Mordechai Yosef, *Living Waters - The Mei HaShiloach: A Commentary on the Torah by Rabbi Mordechai Yosef of Isbitza* (trans. Betsalel Paul Edwards; Northvale: Jason Aronson, 2001), 49–50 in *parashat Vayeira*.

[58] Rabbi Schneur Zalman, *Transforming the Inner Self* (trans. Rabbi Chaim Zev Citron; Brooklyn: Kehot Publication Society, 2004), 26.

[59] The others who are characterized as "the majority [righteous] of Israel" are of the type of righteous ones that Rabbi Schneur Zalman labels in the *Tanya* the "*beinonim*." The *beinoni*, בינוני (pl. *beinonim*, בינונים) are "intermediates" whose evil inclination still resides within them but nevertheless has no control over them. The tzaddik has successfully eliminated his evil inclination from within, as stated in Psalms, "And my heart is a void within me" (Psalm 109:22 as cited in the *Tanya* 1 [Kehot]), a passage interpreted to mean that the heart is void of an evil inclination. The *beinoni*, however, though he still serves HaShem and does not sin in thought, speech, and action; nonetheless the evil inclination still resides in the left part of his heart. For the *beinoni* "the burning love of G-d is not in a revealed state in his heart, in the right part, but is only inwardly paved with hidden love, that is the natural adoration in the divine soul" (*Tanya* 12 [Kehot]).

OUR MOTHER SARAH

🌿 *To some few men because of their whole-hearted love for God, it becomes*
natural to live in harmony with the divine will, independent of the Law. (45)

There are some souls who fly effortlessly, while others plod below only through great diligence and effort. Regarding the latter, Levertoff says that the "majority of Israel can only attain this high spiritual experience by unceasing effort and unquestioning obedience to the Law," but some people exist whose natural piety is so great that it transcends the Torah. As an example, he cites a reference from the *Zohar*:

> Said R. Jose: "The problem is, why is the record of Sarah's years given with so much particularity, such as we find in the case of no other woman? Why, moreover, to Sarah alone of all the women of Scripture was a whole section of the Torah devoted? There is an esoteric reason, namely, that Sarah reached that grade on which depend all the years and the days of a son of man." (*Zohar* I, 122a [Soncino])

Sarah and the other *tzaddikim* (צדיקים, "righteous ones") of Scripture conducted lives of righteousness "independent of the Law." They lived independent of the Torah, in that it was so much a part of them that they naturally lived out its precepts without "unceasing effort." Fulfilling God's will and wisdom was naturally a part of their daily life. The righteous Sarah and all the patriarchs and matriarchs exemplify those who discovered the righteousness which is "apart from the Law" (Romans 3:21), but nevertheless fulfilled the Torah.[60]

THE LAW OF LOVE

🌿 *The law of love is derived from the love of God. (45)*

Levertoff says that a "more excellent way" than legalism exists. "Love" is the more excellent way. The observance of the Torah must be accompanied by love. Paul speaks of the "more excellent way" in 1 Corinthians 13, saying, "But now faith, hope, love, abide these three; but the greatest of these is love."[61]

Our Master states the two greatest commandments are love of God and love of fellow:

> "You shall love the Lord your God with all your heart, and with all your soul, and with all your mind." This is the great and foremost commandment. The second is like it, "You shall love your neighbor as yourself." On these two commandments depend the whole Torah and the Prophets. (Matthew 22:37–40)[62]

---

[60] Genesis 26:5.

[61] 1 Corinthians 13:13.

[62] Cf. Mark 12:28–34.

Thus the Torah depends on love. The Torah is rooted in love; and the Torah is "derived from the love of God." The Baal Shem Tov taught that the greater our love for God the greater our love for men will be:

> Love for Israel is love of G-d. "You are children of G-d, your G-d;" he who loves the Father also loves the children! The precept of "Love your fellow like yourself" is an interpretation and exposition of the precept [in Deuteronomy 6:5] "Love G-d, your G-d." He who loves an Israelite loves G-d. For every Israelite contains within himself a portion of G-d Above. Thus loving him, i.e., his inner self, is love of G-d.[63]

Therefore "let us love one another, for love is from God; and everyone who loves is born of God and knows God. The one who does not love does not know God, for God is love."[64] "Love the Lord through all your life, and one another with a true heart."[65]

LOVING THE UNLOVABLE

Love is not the same as natural kindliness … love means something more … loving even him who is unlovable, having mercy upon those who seem to us to be unworthy, bringing down the grace of God to sinners and to Gentiles. (45–46)

Our Master further commands: "A new commandment I give to you, that you love one another, even as I have loved you, that you also love one another. By this all men will know that you are My disciples, if you have love for one another."[66]

This love, however, goes beyond "natural kindliness." This love includes "loving even him who is unlovable"; as our Master states, "But I say to you, love your enemies and pray for those who persecute you, so that you may be sons of your Father who is in heaven,"[67] and, "If you love those who love you, what reward do you have? Do not even the tax collectors do the same?"[68] This love must be extended to "even the greatest sinner," for "Messiah Yeshua came into the world to save sinners;"[69] and "he who turns a sinner from the error of his way will save his soul from death and will cover a multitude of sins."[70]

> One should accustom himself to love his fellow men in his heart—even the wicked, as if they were his brothers. Moreover, [he should pursue this quality] until love for

---

63 *Keter Shem Tov, Hosafot*: par. 141:18, quoted in Schochet, *The Mystical Dimension Volume Three: Chasidic Dimensions*, 52–53.

64 1 John 4:7–8.

65 *Testament of the Twelve Patriarchs, Testament of Dan* 5 (Charles).

66 John 13:34–35.

67 Matthew 5:44–45.

68 Matthew 5:46.

69 1 Timothy 1:15.

70 James 5:20.

all people is fixed in his heart. He should even love the wicked in his heart, saying, "I only wish they were righteous, returning in repentance …"And how should he love them? By recalling in his thoughts the good qualities that are present in them and concealing their flaws, and refusing to see their defects; rather [he should look only for] the good qualities … "Why should I hate he whom the Holy One, Blessed is He, loves?"[71]

"Above all, keep fervent in your love for one another, because love covers a multitude of sins."[72] "Love covers all transgressions."[73]

LOVING THE WHOLE BODY

> *So must we love not only the learned and the pious, but also the ignorant and the unspiritual, in order that the body may be whole and active. (46)*

Levertoff's sources compare the spiritual community to a body composed of many parts: "Metaphorically speaking, all souls are regarded as limbs of the Shechinah."[74] Similarly, the apostles spoke of the assembly of believers as the "body of Messiah." "Israel is the 'measure of the Godhead'" inasmuch as "all Israel are related to each other, being that all [their] souls are united, and each contains a part of all others."[75] "We, who are many, are one body in Messiah, and individually members one of another,"[76] "holding fast to the head, from whom the entire body, being supplied and held together by the joints and ligaments, grows with a growth which is from God."[77]

Those members that seem to be unlovable are likened to the "feet in a body" and have "the advantage over the head because they carry the whole body, the head included." Therefore, we must love even those who seem to us to be unworthy of love, for they too are members of the body. The Apostle Paul uses the same metaphor:

> For the body is not one member, but many. If the foot says, "Because I am not a hand, I am not a part of the body," it is not for this reason any the less a part of the body. And if the ear says, "Because I am not an eye, I am not a part of the body," it is not for this reason any the less a part of the body. If the whole body were an eye, where would the hearing be? If the whole were hearing, where would the sense of smell be? But now God has placed the members, each one of them, in the body, just as He desired. (1 Corinthians 12:14–18)

---

[71] *Tomer Devorah* 2 (Fink and Finkelman).

[72] 1 Peter 4:8.

[73] Proverbs 10:12.

[74] *Igeret HaKodesh* 31 (Kehot).

[75] *Tomer Devorah* 1:4 (Fink and Finkelman).

[76] Romans 12:5.

[77] Colossians 2:19.

THE ROYAL TORAH

❧ Our relation to all men should be one of friendship. (46)

The beloved Apostle John taught us that "the one who says he is in the Light and yet hates his brother is in the darkness until now. The one who loves his brother abides in the Light and there is no cause for stumbling in him."[78] Levertoff says that our "love for man is more [significant] to God than the outward keeping of the whole Law." This type of love fulfills the Scriptures; as James states: "If, however, you are fulfilling the royal Torah according to Scripture, 'You shall love your neighbor as yourself,' you are doing well."[79] The *Tanya* elaborates on this theme:

> For love is the root of all the 248 positive commands, all originating in it and having no true foundation without it, inasmuch as he who fulfills them in truth, truly loves the name of G-d and desires to cleave to Him in truth; for one cannot truly cleave to Him except through the fulfillment of the 248 commandments which are the 248 "Organs of the King." (*Tanya* 4 [Kehot])[80]

Levertoff's sources say that when we display love towards others, then we become "an organ of the Shechinah," thus uniting ourselves with the spiritual world and causing the grace of God to come into the world. "Our love should not be measured," for "love is patient."[81] We should not "pay back evil for evil to anyone"[82] but should instead "forgive our enemies."

> [HaShem] does not withhold His goodness from man; rather, He tolerates the 'insult' [of sin and continues to] bestow power and to benefit man with his benevolence. Behold, [sin] is [an immeasurable] degree of insult and [HaShem's] tolerance [of sin] is immeasurable … Thus, this attribute of being tolerant, is one that man should emulate. Even when he is insulted to such a degree, he should still not withdraw his benevolence from the recipient. (*Tomer Devorah* 1:1 [Fink and Finkelman])

> I say to you, love your enemies and pray for those who persecute you, so that you may be sons of your Father who is in heaven; for He causes His sun to rise on the evil and the good, and sends rain on the righteous and the unrighteous. (Matthew 5:44–45)

---

[78] 1 John 2:9–10.

[79] James 2:8.

[80] The *Tanya* notes: "They are called 'organs' of the King, as a figure of speech, for just as the organs of the human body are a garment for its soul and are completely and utterly surrendered to it … so by way of example, is the life-force animating the performance of the commandments and their fulfillment completely surrendered to the Supreme Will which is clothed therein, becoming in relation to it like a body to a soul" (*Tanya* 23 [Kehot]).

[81] 1 Corinthians 13:4.

[82] Romans 12:17.

This love will bring "a sinner from the error of his way,"[83] thus bringing him "back to the 'wings of the Shechinah.'"

THE WEDDING

🖋 *The Law was given through Moses in order to bring forth a union between God and Israel, as between bridegroom and bride, but not as between husband and wife. (47)*

Levertoff contrasts the revelation of Torah in this age and the revelation that awaits us in the Messianic Era by contrasting the relationship between bride and bridegroom and the relationship between a husband and wife. A similar concept is represented by the words of our Master concerning John the Immerser: "For all the prophets and the Torah prophesied until John."[84] Levertoff explains this, saying in his commentary on the Gospel of Matthew, as meaning, "All that went before pointed to this."[85] The Torah prepares the bride for the bridegroom; it teaches what is expected of the bride to prepare herself for the bridegroom. John the Immerser was the one of whom the Torah and the Prophets spoke, predicting that he who would draw the bride to His bridegroom: "And if you are willing to accept it, John himself is Elijah who was to come."[86]

John himself declared, "He who has the bride is the bridegroom; but the friend of the bridegroom, who stands and hears him, rejoices greatly because of the bridegroom's voice. So this joy of mine has been made full."[87] John's efforts in helping prepare the bride by calling her to repentance were successful. John rejoiced knowing that the wedding between bride and bridegroom was soon to take place.

Levertoff says, "In the Messianic Age the perfect union will be established." This union began after the imprisonment of John, with our Master taking up the call of the gospel, preaching repentance to all men. "For the Law was given through Moses; grace and truth were realized through Yeshua Messiah."[88] In Levertoff's Chasidic sources, the Messianic revelation is often described as *chesed dikshot* ("the grace of truth," חסד דקשוט).

Through the Torah, Moses taught the bride to prepare herself for the bridegroom. Once the marriage is consummated, the bride's joy, experiencing intimacy and comfort in the presence of the bridegroom, is made full. In this present age, we are in the betrothal stage. Betrothal is a legally binding agreement. We are beautifying ourselves for the bridegroom. When the marriage occurs we will hear the shout, "Let us rejoice and be glad and give the glory to Him, for the marriage of the Lamb has come, and His bride had made herself ready."[89]

---

83 James 5:20.
84 Matthew 11:13.
85 Levertoff, *St. Matthew*, 35.
86 Matthew 11:14. Cf. Malachi 4:4–6.
87 John 3:29.
88 John 1:17.
89 Revelation 19:7.

THE PERMEATING LIGHT

🕊️ *In the days of the Messiah the inner nature of God will be revealed, and His light will permeate man. (47–48)*

In the Messianic Age, God's inner nature will be revealed to all mankind. The prophets teach that, in that time, everyone will know God. Jeremiah says, "They will not teach again, each man his neighbor and each man his brother, saying, 'Know the LORD,' for they will all know Me, from the least of them to the greatest of them."[90] So too, we read in the Revelation of John, "I saw no temple in it, for the Lord God the Almighty and the Lamb are its temple. And the city has no need of the sun or of the moon to shine on it, for the glory of God has illumined it, and its lamp is the Lamb."[91] This is the meaning of the petition from the siddur when we pray, "Cause a new light to shine upon Zion, and may we all be quickly privileged to see its light. Blessed are You, O LORD, who forms the luminaries."[92]

Levertoff cites the Chasidic description of this Messianic revelation as *chesed dikshot* ("the grace of truth," חסד דקשוט), a concept expounded upon in *Likkutei Torah*:

> The vessel for this [Higher Wisdom] is the attribute of "deeds of *chesed* ('loving-kindness')" and "The Torah which Moses commanded us, etc." (Deuteronomy 34:4). Corresponding to this it says twice in *Parshat Tzitzit* (Numbers 15:37–41) "I am the LORD your God" (*Ani Hashem Elohechem*). The first refers to the vessel and the second to what will be revealed in the future age, i.e., the attribute of *chesed dikshot* ("the grace of truth") and the Torah of God (Higher Wisdom). (*Likkutei Torah*, Numbers, 101d)

Chassidus believes in two Torahs: one revealed and one hidden. This is based on a midrashic exegesis of Psalm 1:2 which mentions "the law of the LORD" and "his law," i.e. man's Torah. The revealed Torah is the law given at Mount Sinai, but the hidden Torah contains God's supreme wisdom to be revealed in the age to come. *Likkutei Torah* says the hidden Torah will be revealed in the World to Come clothed in the vessel of *chesed dikshot* ("the grace of truth").

Similarly, the Gospel of John describes a revealed Torah given through Moses and "grace and truth" revealed through Messiah.[93] Paul also describes the revelation of the gospel as understanding "the grace of God in truth."[94]

---

[90] Jeremiah 31:34.

[91] Revelation 21:22–23.

[92] *Yotser Or* blessing (First Fruits of Zion translation).

[93] John 1:14, 17.

[94] Colossians 1:6.

3

FEAR AND LOVE

FEAR OF HASHEM

 *The rabbis often discuss the relationship between fear of God and love of God. (49)*

The Torah commands us to love HaShem, but it also commands us to fear Him. On the one hand it says, "You shall love the LORD your God with all your heart and with all your soul and with all your might."[1] On the other hand it says, "You shall fear the LORD your God."[2] On the surface, this might seem like a contradiction. How can you feel both love and fear for someone at the same time? The answer requires a proper understanding of the "Fear of HaShem."

To fear HaShem means to believe that God punishes sin and rewards good. It is the belief that God is watching us and holds us accountable for all of our deeds. Our Master tells us not to fear those who can destroy the body. Rather we must fear "Him who is able to destroy both soul and body in hell."[3] Without such fear, the awe and greatness of God is diminished in a man's sight.

One might say that there are two reasons for serving HaShem and obeying His commands. On the one hand, a person might fear punishment from Heaven. This man serves God in fear. On the other hand, a person might serve God simply out of love, with no thought to reward or punishment. Levertoff cites a story from the *Mishnah* to illustrate the tension between fear and love in the service of God:

> Rabbi Yehoshua ben Hyrkanos taught as follows: "Job served the Holy One, blessed is He, only out of love, as it is written [in Job 13:15], "Though He slay me, I will hope in Him." … Rabbi Joshua complained [to Yehoshua's teacher, Rabbi Yochanan ben Zakkai], "Who will remove the dirt from your eyes Rabban Yochanan ben Zakkai? For your entire life you have taught that Job served the Almighty only out of fear, as it is written [in Job 1:8], 'A blameless and upright man, fearing God and turning

---

[1] Deuteronomy 6:5.

[2] Deuteronomy 10:20.

[3] Matthew 10:28.

away from evil.' And now your disciple Yehoshua has taught the opposite: that Job served God out of love." (m.*Sotah* 5:5)

Rabbi Yochanan taught that Job served out of fear because the text explicitly says so. His disciple, Rabbi Yehoshua, taught that Job served only out of love because he had no fear of death or punishment from HaShem.

Chasidic philosophy explains that "fear and love dwell together" in the human heart, and both are necessary in the service of God.

> King David said, "I, in this world, what am I? What is there to say of myself except that my awe of God arises from my joy in Him, and my joy in Him arises from my awe in Him (paraphrase of Psalm 2:11). But my love of Him is stronger than both." (*Seder Eliyahu Rabbah* 3)[4]

THE BEGINNING OF WISDOM

> *In the deepest recesses of our hearts fear and love dwell together; they reveal themselves in joy. (49)*

Fear of HaShem is by no means a contradiction of love. Instead, such fear should come as a result of our love for God. If a man truly loves the King, he will accord him the reverence and awe a king deserves. The *Wisdom of Ben Sira* contains several passages which display the balance of fear and love towards God:

> The fear of the Lord is honour, and glory, and gladness, and a crown of rejoicing. The fear of the Lord maketh a merry heart, and giveth joy, and gladness, and long life. Whoso feareth the Lord, it shall go well with him at the last, and he shall find favour in the day of his death. To fear the Lord is the beginning of wisdom: and it was created with the faithful in the womb. (*Wisdom of Ben Sira* 1:11–14 [Brenton])

> They that fear the Lord are a sure seed, and they that love him an honourable plant: they that regard not the law are a dishonourable seed; they that transgress the commandments are a deceivable seed. Among brethren he that is chief is honourable; so are they that fear the Lord in his eyes. Whether he be rich, noble or poor, their glory is the fear of the Lord. (*Wisdom of Ben Sira* 10:19–22 [Brenton])

> O how great is he that findeth wisdom! Yet there is none above him that feareth the Lord. But the love of the Lord passeth all things for illumination: he that holdeth it, whereto shall he be likened? (*Wisdom of Ben Sira* 25:10–11 [Brenton])

---

4   *Tanna Debe Eliyahu* (trans. William G. Braude and Israel J. Krapstein; Philadelphia, PA: Jewish Publication Society, 1981), 29.

The relationship between wisdom and the fear of HaShem is found throughout the Scriptures. The Psalms state, "The beginning of wisdom is fear of the Lord; sound wisdom for all who practice it—his praise endures forever."[5] Note also the Proverbs: "The fear of the LORD is the beginning of knowledge; fools despise wisdom and instruction."[6] "The fear of the LORD is the beginning of wisdom, and the knowledge of the Holy One is understanding."[7] "The fear of the LORD prolongs life, but the years of the wicked will be shortened."[8]

The fear and love of God are revealed in joy, the joy that comes through submission to the will and wisdom of God—the Torah.

FEAR AND REPENTANCE

We rejoice in the consciousness of God's love and nearness but tremble at the same time because of the awfulness of His presence. (49)

God loves us. He draws near to us in a personal way. A man can speak to God in prayer as if he was speaking to his friend. In this regard, HaShem is intimate and familiar. Levertoff reminds us that, despite the joy of such familiarity, we should also "tremble at the same time because of the awfulness of His presence."

Levertoff draws our attention to Psalm 2:11, "Serve the LORD with fear, and rejoice with trembling."[9] We rejoice with trembling knowing that HaShem passes over our misdeeds when we seek Him with repentance. Though we deserve to be punished for our sins, "Often He restrained His anger and did not arouse all His wrath."[10] He is patient in that He does not execute judgment but rather allows His attribute of mercy to override His attribute of justice. *Eliyahu Rabbah* states: "He chooses to see the good and chooses not to see the evil."[11] The same source further states:

> In His wisdom and with His understanding God created His world and set it on its foundation. He then created Adam and had him lie prone before Him. As He scrutinized him till the end of all the generations that would come from him, He foresaw that his descendants would provoke His wrath. Hence He said: If I hold mankind to account for its successive misdeeds, the world will not endure; I must therefore have its successive misdeeds pass out of mind. And He had them do so.
> (*Eliyahu Rabbah* 3 [Braude and Kapstein])

---

5 Psalm 111:10. Yosef B. Marcus, *Sefer Tehillim: Ohel Yosef Yitzchak* (Brooklyn: Kehot Publication Society, 2004), 140. According to this translation, the praise of the one who practices wisdom will endure forever, a sentiment similar to the expression in *Wisdom of Ben Sira* 10:19–22.

6 Proverbs 1:7.

7 Proverbs 9:10.

8 Proverbs 10:27.

9 KJV.

10 Psalm 78:38.

11 *Eliyahu Rabbah* 3 (Braude and Kapstein).

Just as Abraham and Isaac represent love and fear respectively,[12] so too their Seed, the Messiah, represents both love and fear. He taught us to love God with all our heart as well as to fear the One who can destroy both body and soul.

TO FEAR EVIL

🌿 *To the Chasid everything that has even an appearance of evil becomes a thick wall of partition between him and God, and his soul is consequently full of fear and trembling before Him. (49)*

The Chasid distances himself from anything that has the appearance of evil, for he realizes that even the appearance of evil can bring a separation between him and HaShem, God forbid. The *Tosefta* in *Chullin* states that Rabbi Eliezer was arrested on account of heresy. After being cleared of the charges he states, "So I was arrested on account of matters of [heresy], for I transgressed the teachings of the Torah: Keep your way far from her and do not go near the door of her house."[13] One should therefore seek to distance himself from even the appearance of evil lest he be tempted and succumb to sin. Paul says, "Abstain from all appearance of evil."[14]

Levertoff teaches, "Such a fear is considered to be an original endowment of every Israelite." According to the *Tanya*, "It is the nature of all Jewish souls not to rebel against the blessed Holy King"[15] and "fear and love … are latent in the heart of all Jews."[16]

However, fear of sin must be surpassed by fear of God. The highest form of fear simply results from a proper knowledge of God's love. Even a wicked sinner would turn away from sin if he truly comprehended the depth of God's love for him. Experiencing God's love is the greatest and truest deterrent for sin, because the man who knows God's love will "pause in fear before he sins" and betrays that love.

TWO KINDS OF HOLY FEAR

🌿 *Only in the days of the Messiah will everyone experience such a fear. (50)*

Psalm 33:8 says, "Fear ye before HaShem," but Psalm 34:9 simply says, "Fear ye HaShem." What is the difference?

Levertoff explains that to fear "before HaShem" is to fear God because of His awesome power and holiness revealed in nature. One who fears "before HaShem" fears God outside of relationship

---

[12] "Abraham, my *beloved*" (Isaiah 41:8, italics added for emphasis). "The *Fear* of Isaac" (Genesis 31:42, italics added for empahsis).

[13] t.*Chullin* 2:24 (Neusner).

[14] 1 Thessalonians 5:22, KJV.

[15] *Tanya* 41 (Kehot).

[16] *Tanya* 39 (Kehot). See also *Tanya* 41–43.

with Him. He fears Him as a man might fear a stroke of lightning. Such fear "only intensifies the sense of our absolute remoteness from Him."

To "fear HaShem" directly is to fear God as the transcendent, omnipresent God, revealed in the Torah. This fear is based on knowledge of God. The man who fears God on this level does so because he realizes that HaShem is the source and the end of all things, and there is ultimately nothing beside Him. Levertoff says that in the days of Messiah, everyone will experience this type of fear, as it says, "They will not teach again, each man his neighbor and each man his brother, saying, 'Know the LORD,' for they will all know Me, from the least of them to the greatest of them."[17]

BEYOND REWARD AND PUNISHMENT

Our love for God must be pure, untainted by hope of reward or fear of punishment. (50)

Depending upon our relationship with God, we will experience different types of fear of Him. On its simplest level, fearing God means fearing punishment. The person who does not have a relationship with the king fears his wrath. He is filled with a guilty fear and flees the presence of the king. "But the King's friends rejoice." Rather than flee from God, their fear of God inspires them to dance before Him with joy. Thus, there is a fear of God that transcends concern for reward or punishment.

Levertoff's sources teach that "our love for God must be pure, untainted by hope of reward or fear of punishment." He notes *Pirkei Avot* which says, "Do not be like servants who serve their master for the sake of receiving a reward; instead be like servants who serve their master without concern for reward [or punishment]; and let the fear of Heaven be upon you."[18]

The Apostle John teaches a similar thought when he says that our love for God overpowers our fear of God. Because we have confidence in our salvation, we are not subject to the "guilty fear" of the sinner who flees from God. Instead, "love is perfected with us, so that we may have confidence in the day of judgment; because as He is, so also are we in this world. There is no fear in love; but perfect love casts out fear."[19] This is the love which causes men "to dance before Him with joy."

Men who flee from the Holy One due to a guilty fear are compared to tempestuous water which moves to and fro. Men who stand before the King and rejoice may be likened to a mountain that stands its ground and remains in its place. These two are compared to the sea and the mountains in the following Psalm: "The sea saw it, and fled … the mountains skipped like rams."[20]

> When the sea saw God, it fled, as it says, "The sea looked and fled" (Psalm 114:3).
> What did it see? The sea beheld God's right hand in the authority of Moses, and it
> dared not tarry, but fled at once. Moses asked of the sea, "What ails you, O sea, that

---

[17] Jeremiah 31:34.

[18] m.*Avot* 1:3 (Hertz). Cf. the words of Rabbi Yochanan ben Zakkai in b.*Berachot* 28b (Soncino), "May it be God's will."

[19] 1 John 4:17–18.

[20] Psalm 114:3–4 (KJV).

you flee?" (Psalm 114:5). The sea replied, "'Before the God of Jacob' (Psalm 114:7), for fear of the Holy One, blessed be He." (*Exodus Rabbah* 21:6)

SUFFERING FOR LOVE

We should love Him above all things and suffer sorrow gladly for His sake. (50)

Man fears God because he hopes to receive favor and to avoid suffering. However, love transcends such a simple fear because love does not hesitate to suffer on behalf of another. Levertoff says that our love for God should take precedence over all things and "we should suffer sorrow gladly for His sake." Our Master teaches us, "If anyone wishes to come after Me, he must deny himself, and take up his cross and follow Me. For whoever wishes to save his life will lose it; but whoever loses his life for My sake will find it."[21] Such words of endurance are found elsewhere. James states, "Consider it all joy, my brethren, when you encounter various trials, knowing that the testing of your faith produces endurance."[22] For as Paul writes, "If indeed we suffer with Him … we may also be glorified with Him"[23] and "if we endure, we will also reign with Him."[24] And Peter adds, "He who has suffered in the flesh has ceased from sin, so as to live the rest of the time in the flesh no longer for the lusts of men, but for the will of God."[25]

> For this finds favor, if for the sake of conscience toward God a person bears up under sorrows when suffering unjustly. For what credit is there if, when you sin and are harshly treated, you endure it with patience? But if when you do what is right and suffer for it you patiently endure it, this finds favor with God. (1 Peter 2:19–20)

> Now I rejoice in my sufferings for your sake, and in my flesh I am filling up what is lacking in Messiah's afflictions for the sake of his body, that is, the church. (Colossians 1:24)

DUTIES OF LOVE

Our love for God should not be less than our duty towards our fellow men. (50)

Since man was created in the image of HaShem, we truly love HaShem when we love those made in His image. However, our love for man should not exceed our love for God. Levertoff goes on to cite four acts which demonstrate love for fellow man: strengthening the weak, showing hospitality to guests, preparing the dead for burial, and making matches to bring about marriages. By per-

---

21 Matthew 16:24–25. Cf. Mark 8:34–38; Luke 9:23–26.
22 James 1:2–3.
23 Romans 8:17.
24 2 Timothy 2:12.
25 1 Peter 4:1–2.

forming acts of kindness like this, we demonstrate our love and concern for others. But a person should demonstrate no less love and concern for God Himself. Levertoff now goes on to explain how these duties may be performed for God.[26]

STRENGTHENING THE SHECHINAH

❧ *We are obliged to strengthen the weak in order that the whole body may benefit, "so we must strengthen the Shechinah, which is sick from love" and which "for our sakes has borne our griefs and carried our sorrows." (50–51)*

One of our obligations to our fellows is "to strengthen the weak, in order that the whole body may benefit." For "if one member suffers, all the members suffer with it; if one member is honored, all the members rejoice with it"[27] remembering that "you yourselves also are in the body."[28] However, "our love for God should not be less than our duty towards our fellow men." Just as we are obliged to strengthen the weak, "so we must strengthen the *Shechinah,* which is sick from love."

In what way is the Shechinah sick with love? Levertoff's sources quote Song of Solomon 5:8 which says, "I adjure you, O daughters of Jerusalem, if you find my beloved, as to what you will tell him: for I am lovesick." In the Chasidic treatise *Tomer Devorah,* this verse is applied to the Shechinah, the Dwelling Presence of God, who endures the suffering in exile along with Israel.[29] The Shechinah is "sick with love" because God longs for the final redemption and the end of the exile when His people and His Divine Presence will be reunited. Levertoff's mystical sources also identify the suffering servant "who has borne our griefs and carried our sorrows" as HaShem's suffering over the Shechinah, who suffers along with Israel through the exile:

> He too is ill because of our transgressions, crushed willingly because of our iniquities. The healing of both [HaShem and His Divine Presence] is in our hands. Therefore it is proper to visit Them [as one would visit the sick] and prepare for Their needs by studying Torah and performing *mitzvos.* (*Tomer Devorah* 5 [Fink and Finkelman])

We can strengthen the Shechinah, so to speak, by laboring to hasten the day of redemption; as it says in the Epistle of 2 Peter, "What sort of people ought you to be in holy conduct and godliness, looking for and hastening the coming of the day of God."[30]

---

26 Levertoff's ensuing exposition on performing acts of loving-kindness for HaShem is based upon *Tomer Devorah* 5.

27 1 Corinthians 12:26.

28 Hebrews 13:3.

29 *Tomer Devorah* 5 (Fink and Finkelman).

30 2 Peter 3:11–12.

THE SUFFERING MESSIAH

🌿 *Borne our griefs and carried our sorrows. (51)*

Levertoff's sources speak of the Shechinah of HaShem undergoing the suffering of exile along with and on behalf of the people of Israel, and he identifies the Shechinah with Isaiah's suffering servant "who has borne our griefs and carried our sorrows." [31]

According to Levertoff, Messiah is identical with the Shechinah. [32] He suffered on our behalf; as it says, "He was oppressed and He was afflicted," [33] and "the LORD was pleased to crush Him." [34] Nonetheless, our Master received these sufferings with unspeakable joy, for "He did not open His mouth." [35] "For the joy set before Him, [He] endured the cross." [36]

Paul speaks of rejoicing in his sufferings; as it says in the letter to the Colossians, "Now I rejoice in my sufferings for your sake, and in my flesh I do share on behalf of His body." [37] When we suffer in like manner it is for our benefit. In Hebrews we find: "Consider Him who has endured such hostility by sinners against Himself, so that you will not grow weary and lose heart." [38]

HOSPITALITY FOR HASHEM

🌿 *As it is our duty to be hospitable to wayfarers and to receive them as our guests, so should we receive God into our hearts. (51)*

Hospitality (*hakhnasat orchim,* חכנסת אורחים, i.e. "bringing in guests") is an important part of Jewish life. Genesis 18 describes how Abraham received guests with magnanimous hospitality. Just as Abraham was hospitable to his guests, "it is our duty to be hospitable to wayfarers and to receive them as our guests." The hospitality of Abraham is famous in Jewish sources. In the *Midrash Rabbah* it is stated:

> Abraham used to host travelers, and after they had eaten he would say to them, "Give the benediction." "What shall we say?" they asked. "Blessed be the God of the Universe of Whose bounty we have eaten," he answered. Then the Holy One, blessed be He, said to Abraham, "My Name was not known among My creatures, but you have made it known." (*Genesis Rabbah* 43:7)

---

[31] Isaiah 53 is often applied to the suffering Shechinah.

[32] See Levertoff's commentary of Matthew on Matthew 28:20, quoted earlier. See also Levertoff, "The Shechinah Motif."

[33] Isaiah 53:7.

[34] Isaiah 53:10.

[35] Isaiah 53:7.

[36] Hebrews 12:2.

[37] Colossians 1:24.

[38] Hebrews 12:3.

However, "our love for God should not be less than our duty towards our fellow men." Just as we are obliged to show hospitality to wayfarers, we should do no less for HaShem. We should "receive God into our hearts" as a person receives a guest into his home. The host does everything in his power to insure that the guest is comfortable. He devotes his attention to his guest, ministers to his needs, and does not hesitate to inconvenience himself on account of his guest. So too, we should regard the Spirit of God within us as our exalted guest. "Or do you not know that your body is a temple of the Holy Spirit who is in you, whom you have from God, and that you are not your own?"[39]

TAHARAH FOR THE SHECHINAH

> *As the Jews honor the dead by washing their bodies and clothing them in white garments, so should they wash off the spots with which their sins have stained the Shechinah, "and help Her to ascend from the depths into the heights." (51)*

Jewish burial custom requires us to ritually wash the dead and clothe them in white garments for burial. Nicodemus and Joseph of Arimathea performed this duty for our Master, and the women prepared spices to complete the burial ritual.[40] Likewise, we read that after Tabitha, the disciple of the Master died, "when they had washed her body, they laid it in an upper room."[41] Ritually washing and dressing the body for burial is called *taharah* (טהרה, "purification"). Proper burial is considered a basic duty of love for one's fellow. The ritual washing is performed in anticipation of the resurrection. It symbolizes the ascent of the soul to Paradise.[42]

However, "our love for God should not be less than our duty towards our fellow men." If our love for our fellow obligates us to wash a human corpse in anticipation of resurrection and the ascent of the soul, then we should do no less for the Shechinah, washing off the spots with which our sins have stained God's Divine Presence, "and help Her to ascend from the depths into the heights." We do this when we "draw near with a sincere heart in full assurance of faith, having our hearts sprinkled clean from an evil conscience and our bodies washed with pure water."[43] We must be diligent to keep such stains clear from our soul, for we were washed, sanctified, and justified "in the name of our Lord Yeshua Messiah and in the Spirit of our God."[44] We must cleanse the garment with which the Shechinah is enwrapped—the Torah. According to the *Tanya,* the dwelling of the Shechinah inside the human soul is strengthened by virtue of good deeds, that is, obedience to the Torah. If we stain our soul—committing lawlessness—then the garment of the Shechinah becomes stained. She is no longer fit to rise before the King, and as a result Her exile is prolonged.[45]

---

[39] 1 Corinthians 6:19.

[40] Mark 16:1.

[41] Acts 9:37.

[42] Cf. 1 Corinthians 15:29 for a reference to the ritual of *taharah.*

[43] Hebrews 10:22.

[44] 1 Corinthians 6:11.

[45] *Tanya* 52 (Kehot). Cf. *Tanya* 35.

"Do not grieve the Holy Spirit of God."[46] When we fail to live godly lives, the *Shechinah* cannot "ascend from the depths into the heights."

DIVINE MATCHMAKING

🍃 *As it is the duty to help to bring about pure marriages among the people, so should we, through our true love for God, further "the union of the divine bridegroom with His bride Israel." (51)*

In Judaism, matchmaking is considered to be an obligation of love for one's fellow. Every person is responsible for helping to put together successful matches and godly marriages. However, "our love for God should not be less than our duty towards our fellow men."

Through our love for HaShem we should strive to bring about "the union of the divine bridegroom with His bride Israel." "For the husband is the head of the wife, as Messiah also is the head of the assembly, He Himself being the Savior of the body."[47]

> Messiah also loved the assembly and gave Himself up for her, so that He might sanctify her, having cleansed her by the washing of water with the word, that He might present to Himself the assembly in all her glory, having no spot or wrinkle or any such thing; but that she would be holy and blameless. (Ephesians 5:25–27)

WINGS OF THE SOUL

🍃 *Fear and love are wings by which the soul is carried to heaven. (51)*

A bird needs two wings to fly. Fear of HaShem and love for HaShem are like the wings of the soul. The bird with a broken wing cannot fly. Neither can the soul ascend to cleave to God unless it possesses both the fear of HaShem and the love of HaShem.

Every commandment of the Torah is an expression of God's will. When a person obeys one of God's commandments, he is literally living out God's will on earth—uniting Himself with HaShem and partnering with Him on earth.

Levertoff draws this concept from the *Tanya* which teaches that keeping the commandments of the Torah unites us with God's will if the commandments are performed with fear of and love for HaShem: "Although fear and love also form part of the 613 commandments, nevertheless they are called 'wings.'"[48]

The Torah commands us to fear HaShem, and it commands us to love HaShem along with the other 611 commandments. Yet these two commandments are as wings to the others, because none

---

46 Ephesians 4:30.

47 Ephesians 5:23.

48 *Tanya* 40 (Kehot).

of the other commandments of the Torah can be properly performed without both fear and love. The concept is also explained in *Torah Or* as follows:

> It is taught that the love and fear of G-d that motivated a person while studying Torah and performing *mitzvos* [commandments] are like "wings" that serve to elevate and carry heavenward the Torah and the *mitzvos* themselves … [The] *mitzvos* literally connect us with G-d Himself. (*Torah Or*, Genesis, 16 [Wagshul])

THE LEAPING FLAME

🖋 *There is a natural inborn love of the soul for its native home as the flame by nature leaps upwards. (51)*

The cry of the soul is a yearning desire to ascend to its heavenly origin and original abode. Levertoff cites the example from the *Tanya* of a flame and its desire to separate from the wick "in order to enter into its own more aerial element." The *Tanya*, commenting on the verse "The candle of G-d is the soul (*neshamah*) of man,"[49] states that these souls are called "man," "by way of illustration, like the flame of the candle, whose nature it is always to scintillate upwards, for the flame of the fire intrinsically seeks to be parted from the wick in order to unite with its source above, in the universal element of fire."[50] Similarly does the soul of man "naturally desire and yearn to separate itself and depart from the body in order to unite with its origin and source in G-d, the fountain-head of all life, blessed be He."[51] For the body houses the soul and contains it, thus keeping the soul from leaving the body. "For indeed while we are in this tent, we groan."[52] Throughout man's life, the soul cries and longs to be reunited with its Creator, longing to return to its illustrious origin, "a house not made with hands, eternal in the heavens."[53]

THE SOUL'S LOVE FOR HASHEM

🖋 *The accumulation of good works, through the keeping of the Law, is nothing in comparison with this natural love of the soul for God. (51–52)*

Levertoff states, "All the riches of the world are as nothing in comparison with the love that we have for our own life." Note what our Master says, "For what will it profit a man if he gains the whole world and forfeits his soul? Or what will a man give in exchange for his soul?"[54] The same concept applies to "the accumulation of good works, through the keeping of the Law." All the *mitzvot* that

---

49   Proverbs 20:27 as quoted in the English translation of the *Tanya* 19 (Kehot).

50   *Tanya* 19 (Kehot).

51   *Tanya* 19 (Kehot).

52   2 Corinthians 5:4.

53   2 Corinthians 5:1.

54   Matthew 16:26.

we perform are "nothing in comparison with this natural love of the soul for God." The greatest act one can perform is to give up one's life on behalf of another; as our Master states, "Greater love has no one than this, that one lay down his life for his friends."[55] Yet, even Paul states, "And if I surrender my body to be burned, but do not have love, it profits me nothing."[56]

Fellowship with HaShem comes from a love that is "all-pervading, and leads to a self-surrender so complete, that the result is joy ineffable." Paul speaks of such a self-surrender when he states that "while we are at home in the body we are absent from the Lord—for we walk by faith, not by sight—we are of good courage, I say, and prefer rather to be absent from the body and to be at home with the Lord."[57] Paul expresses the cry of the soul elsewhere when he further states, "For to me, to live is Messiah and to die is gain … having the desire to depart and be with Messiah, for that is very much better."[58] Levertoff describes a depth of love for HaShem that cannot "endure the limitations of the body; the heart cannot contain it."

THE MENORAH

🌿 *God desires that the flame of their love should ascend to heaven. (52)*

Numbers 8 says that when HaShem gave Moses the instructions for the Tabernacle, He showed him a pattern which he was to copy when making the menorah:

> Now this was the workmanship of the [menorah], hammered work of gold; from its base to its flowers it was hammered work; according to the pattern which the LORD had showed Moses, so he made the [menorah]. (Numbers 8:4)

Similarly, the apostles teach that the Temple and its furnishings are "a copy and shadow of the heavenly things. For when Moses was about to erect the tent, he was instructed by God, saying, 'See that you make everything according to the pattern that was shown you on the mountain.'"[59]

Levertoff's sources interpret Numbers 8 to mean that Israel is "the divine pattern of the Menorah."[60] The connection between the nation of Israel and the pattern of the menorah is alluded to in the *Midrash Rabbah*:

> This is why it is written [in Numbers 8:4], "According to the pattern which the LORD had showed Moses, so he made the menorah." This verse does not say, "So Moses made the menorah." Instead, it says, "So he made the menorah." Who made it? The Holy One, blessed be He, made the menorah. This is why the Holy One, blessed be He, said to Moses: "If you, O Israel, will keep the lighting of lamps before Me, I will

---

55 John 15:13.

56 1 Corinthians 13:3.

57 2 Corinthians 5:6–8. That the body is a house or garment is an idea found throughout the *Tanya*.

58 Philippians 1:21, 23. Cf. *Tanya* 19.

59 Hebrews 8:5.

60 Cf. *Tanya* 35 (Kehot).

keep your souls from all evil things." For souls are compared to lamps; as it says [in Proverbs 20:27], "The spirit of man is the lamp of the LORD." (*Numbers Rabbah* 15:4)

Israel's love for HaShem is compared to the flames of the menorah. Levertoff explains that "God desires that the flame of [Israel's] love should ascend to Heaven."

Just as the menorah had seven branches and seven lamps, the prophet Micah says that Israel has seven shepherds: "Then we will raise against him seven shepherds and eight leaders of men."[61] The shepherds and leaders of men are those tzaddikim ("righteous ones") who throughout history aided Israel in her service of God. They are likened to shepherds who guide the flock towards the intended destination and away from harm. Such illustrious individuals may also be compared to pillars or princes who support Israel.[62]

Jewish tradition sometimes identifies the "seven shepherds" as heavenly representatives or mediators of Israel.[63] The book of Revelation speaks of "seven lamps of fire burning before the throne, which are the seven Spirits of God,"[64] which in turn correspond to the seven churches:

> As for the mystery of the seven stars which you saw in My right hand, and the seven golden lampstands: the seven stars are the angels of the seven churches, and the seven lampstands are the seven churches. (Revelation 1:20)

Levertoff's sources speak of the seven shepherds as mediators of Israel's love for God, fueling it and directing it heavenward. The greatest of the seven shepherds is "the prototype of the High Priest Aaron."[65] The Epistle to the Hebrews speaks similarly of a prototypical priest in the heavenly temple who is "according to the likeness of Melchizedek."[66]

---

[61] Micah 5:5. Cf. John 10.

[62] Based on the *Zohar* (III, 103b–104a) the seven shepherds of Israel (*ushpizin*, אושפיזין), "Abraham and five righteous ones and David with them," are greeted and honored in the sukkah on each night of Sukkot. This finds a parallel in Luke 9:28–36 where two shepherds of Israel, Moses and Elijah, appear with the Master at the Transfiguration, and Peter offers to build them booths (*sukkot*, סוכות).

[63] Cf. *Song of Songs Rabbah* 8:13. In the Soncino edition of the *Midrash Rabbah* the following names for the seven shepherds given: David, Adam, Seth, Methuselah, Abraham, Jacob, and Moses. In the same source, the eight princes are identified as Jesse, Saul, Samuel, Amos, Zephaniah, Hezekiah, Elijah, and the Messiah. However, Levertoff's sources employ a different tradition. In his source material, the prototype of Aaron the priest (who is not included in the *Midrash Rabbah*'s list) is the greatest among the seven shepherds. In the Jewish-Christian work *Clementine Homilies* (18:13–14) the seven shepherds are called the "seven pillars" based on Proverbs 9:1 (cf. b.*Chaggigah* 12b) and listed as Adam, Noah, Enoch, Abraham, Isaac, Jacob, and Moses. The idea here presented in the *Homilies* is that the Messiah was continually present with all these great prophets. See *Recognitions of Clement* 1:52 and also Irenaeus, *Fragments from Lost Writings* 53–54. For a detailed study of these Clementine passages see Charles A. Gieschen, "The Seven Pillars of the World: Ideal Figure Lists in the Christology of the Pseudo-Clementines," *Journal for the Study of the Pseudepigrapha* 12 (1994): 47–82.

[64] Revelation 4:5.

[65] See also *Apostolic Constitutions* 8:5 where Abel, Seth, Enosh, Enoch, Noah, Melchizedek, and Job are labeled as "high priests."

[66] Hebrews 7:15.

We have such a high priest, who has taken His seat at the right hand of the throne of the Majesty in the heavens, a minister in the sanctuary and in the true tabernacle, which the Lord pitched, not man. (Hebrews 8:1–2)

FRIENDS OF THE BRIDEGROOM AND BRIDE

🌿 *Moses, the friend of the Bridegroom, brings the infinite Light of God to Israel; and Aaron, the friend of the bride, leads Israel to her Bridegroom. (52)*

The Bible often employs the marriage metaphor when speaking of HaShem's relationship to His people. God is the bridegroom and Israel is the bride. In this extended metaphor, Moses is sometimes depicted as the groom's best man, the "friend of the Bridegroom" for the wedding of Israel and HaShem.[67] In this role, it was his job to bring Israel before HaShem at Mount Sinai and to draft the marriage document (*ketubah*, כתבה), i.e., the Torah. Levertoff's mystical sources take that tradition a step further by representing Aaron the priest in the role of the "friend of the bride."

Just as Moses and Aaron—descendants of Levi—are friends of the bridal chamber, so too, is John the Immerser, also from the line of Levi, a friend of the bridal chamber as he himself states, "but the friend of the bridegroom, who stands and hears him, rejoices greatly because of the bridegroom's voice. So this joy of mine has been made full."[68] Moses brought "the infinite Light of God to Israel"; so too John: "He came as a witness, to testify about the Light, so that all might believe through him. He was not the Light, but he came to testify about the Light."[69]

LOVE'S SLUMBER

🌿 *In the heart of the sinner this love for God is in a state of slumber. (52)*

Chasidic philosophy teaches that every soul has an innate love for God, but this love may exist only as an unrealized potential. Levertoff calls this a "state of slumber." Most people go through life oblivious to God. Their soul slumbers. For this reason Paul commands us, "Awake, sleeper, and arise from the dead, and Messiah will shine on you."[70]

Oftentimes it takes a crisis or personal tragedy to rouse the soul. When a man is faced with a crisis which is utterly beyond his control and without remedy, he has no one to turn to for assistance except God. Though he has never prayed before, he finds himself praying:

This love of the divine soul, whose desire and wish is to unite with G-d, the blessed fountain-head of all life, is called "hidden love," for it is hidden and veiled, in the

---

[67] For examples, *Exodus Rabbah* 43:7; *Numbers Rabbah* 21:2; *Deuteronomy Rabbah* 1:2, 3:12; *Lamentations Rabbah* 1:1; *Pirke de Rabbi Eliezer* 41.

[68] John 3:29.

[69] John 1:7–8.

[70] Ephesians 5:14.

case of transgressors of Israel … Nevertheless, when they are confronted with a test in a matter of faith … at such time it is aroused from its sleep and it exerts its influence by virtue of the Divine force that is clothed in it, as it is written, "Then the Lord awakened as one out of sleep. (*Tanya* 19 [Kehot])

THE ANGELIC FLAME OF LOVE

Man is a microcosm, in whom are to be found the elements of the whole cosmos, even the characteristics of the manifold celestial beings. (52)

Since man is the pinnacle of creation, it stands to reason that within his entire being are characteristics and elements of the whole of creation—not just the physical elements, but also the spiritual elements. Rabbi Moshe Codovero writes:

Behold, in its creation man integrates all that which is found, from the primeval point until the finality of creation, formation and action, as it is said, "I have created him, I have formed him, yea, I have made him" (Isaiah 43:7). (*Pardes Rimonim* 10 [Getz])

Therefore, human beings possess characteristics similar to the angelic beings. For example, Levertoff says, "There are some men in whom the seraphic fire is always burning brightly." These men are the leaders of each generation who guide others into the service of God. The soul of such men is constantly aglow and ever close to HaShem, thus constantly praising their Creator. However, in other men, "the fire glows faintly" and their "spark must be blown into a flame." Those in whom the flame burns low must attach themselves to a tzaddik ("righteous person") who can draw them closer to HaShem. This is similar to a small flame being brought into union with a larger flame so as to increase the light of the smaller.

We must attach ourselves to the seraphic flame of the true Tzaddik, our Master Yeshua, that He might draw us into union with the Father. To this end He prayed, "For those also who believe in Me … that they may all be one; even as You, Father, are in Me and I in You, that they also may be in Us."[71]

FIRE AND WATER

As there is a love like fire, so there is a love like water. (52)

Levertoff contrasts two types of love for HaShem. On the one hand is the fierce and passionate love of the soul for HaShem. Levertoff compares it to fire and to the passionate (erotic) love between a bridegroom and bride. On the other hand is the smooth and continuous love of the soul for HaShem. Levertoff compares it to water and to the calm, unwavering love between a father and son. Passionate, fiery, erotic love waxes and wanes. At times it bursts into hot flame of desire, and

---

[71] John 17:20–21. For more on this see *Appendix One: The Exalted Rebbe.*

at other times, it cools and even disappears: "It is impetuous." Unlike the highs and lows of passionate *eros* (ερως), "the mutual love of father and child is like a smooth-flowing river."

Both types of love are legitimate expressions, and they correspond to our experience of HaShem's love for us. When we experience His condescending love "which comes down even to the abode of sin" in order to lay claim on us, our souls respond with the passion of bride to bridegroom. When we experience His father-like affection, our souls respond with the love of a son for his father.

Therefore, a person should not be concerned when the passionate feelings of spirituality are absent. Such "feelings" come and go, even as in a marriage, there are times appointed for intimacy and times for separation. But the love between father and son is unwavering.

GEVURAH AND CHESED

> *This latter, condescending love of God is an act of His will, for it is supra-rational (humanly speaking), yet it is the highest wisdom of God.* (53)

In Jewish mysticism fire is likened to *gevurah* ("might" or "severity," גבורה) and water is likened to *chesed* ("kindness," חסד). A brief explanation of this concept will suffice.

Water by nature descends from a higher place to a lower one. Fire on the other hand rises from a lower place to a higher one. Note the following from *Igeret HaKodesh*:

> "[The angel] Michael is the prince of water and [the angel] Gabriel is the prince of fire, yet they do not extinguish one another." That is, Michael is the prince of *chesed*—which is called water because it descends from a high place to a low place, i.e., the aspects of the effusion and extension of vivification from the upper to the lower worlds. The aspect of fire [the nature of which is to soar upwards] is the category of *gevurah*, of a withdrawal of the effusion of vivification [from below upwards]. (*Igeret HaKodesh* 12 [Kehot])

The love from above flows downward to man; this love occurs when man contemplates the nearness and close relationship of HaShem to man. Water descends from an upper level and is drawn to a certain point below. The love like fire, however, is a love that rises from below to above and comes as a result of the contemplation of the transcendence and exalted nature of HaShem, that is, the distance of such a holy God from His creation. Of this type of love, Schneur Zalman says, "There is, however, yet another distinction of love which excels them all, and this is a love like fiery coals."[72] He goes on to explain the "fiery coals" concept as follows:

> Through contemplation on the greatness of the blessed *Ein Sof*, before Whom everything is truly accounted as nought, the soul is kindled and flares up towards the glory of the splendour of His greatness, in order to gaze on the glory of the King, like glowing coals of a mighty flame which surges upwards, striving to be parted from the wick and the wood on which it has taken hold. (*Tanya* 50 [Kehot])

---

[72] *Tanya* 50 (Kehot).

These two types of love seem opposite: How can severity and kindness co-exist? With God, these are not opposites but rather two sides of the same coin. Behold our Master, whose "eyes were like a flame of fire" and whose voice was "like the sound of many waters."[73] These two types of love merge when we ponder "the Divine fire that is in the soul."[74] Then our soul thirsts for the love of God. As a result, God pours down His love from above.

CHILDREN OF GOD

To him who has such a love to God "is given the name 'son of God' and all power over the treasures and mysteries of God." (53)

The children of Israel are called "the children of God"; as it is written, "When Israel was a youth I loved him, and out of Egypt I called My son."[75] Likewise, "Sons I have reared and brought up."[76] "Surely, they are My people, sons who will not deal falsely."[77]

The children of God are those who serve Him with joy. "For all who are being led by the Spirit of God, these are sons of God."[78] The Messiah, who is the Son of God, grants "a spirit of adoption"[79] "to those who believe in His name, who were born, not of blood nor of the will of the flesh nor of the will of man, but of God."[80] This is noted in the words of our Master to the Twelve, "To you it has been granted to know the mysteries of the kingdom of heaven,"[81] and in the words of Paul, "Let a man regard us in this manner, as servants of Messiah and stewards of the mysteries of God."[82] Levertoff describes the children of God as those individuals that "take on themselves the yoke of the Law joyously." Such describes Paul, who said, "For I joyfully concur with the Torah of God in the inner man,"[83] and "be imitators of me, just as I also am of Messiah."[84] Yet the children of God are also to be characterized as "humble, gentle, and forgiving."

---

[73] Revelation 1:14–15.

[74] Schneur Zalman, *Journey of the Soul*, 40–48..

[75] Hosea 11:1.

[76] Isaiah 1:2.

[77] Isaiah 63:8.

[78] Romans 8:14.

[79] Romans 8:15.

[80] John 1:12–13. See also Galatians 3–4.

[81] Matthew 13:11.

[82] 1 Corinthians 4:1.

[83] Romans 7:22

[84] 1 Corinthians 11:1.

4

JOY AND LOVE

JOY OF THE CHASIDIM

Joy is the keynote of Chasidic piety. (55)

The Chasidic approach to God is summarized by the word "joy." Rebbe Nachman said, "It's a great mitzvah to be happy at all times."[1] Rabbi Hanoch of Aleksandrow derived the importance of joy directly from the Torah:

> Do you wish to know how important it is to be full of joy at all times? Moses enumerated a long series of curses (Deuteronomy 28) and then remarked in verse 47, "because you did not serve the Lord your God with joyfulness, and with gladness of heart."[2]

For the Chasid, sadness is a barrier between one's self and God; happiness and joy draw a person closer to God. The Baal Shem Tov, the founder of the Chasidic movement, is purported to have said, "Sadness is not a sin, yet it may lead to consequences which the worst sin could not."[3] He further taught that a Chasid should regard depression as a deliberate transgression of Torah and joy as a mitzvah of the Torah.[4]

Despondency and depression is connected with self-centeredness. They arise from a sense of being wronged or from personal disappointments and frustrations which thwarted one's ambitions. The person depressed in such a manner is consumed with himself and his own sorrows. Therefore, the Chasid seeks to serve God in a spirit of joy and to always conduct himself cheerfully. Note the words of Paul in Philippians 4:4, "Rejoice in the Lord always; again I will say, rejoice!" As Levertoff comments, this verse has "a genuine Chasidic sound."

---

[1] Rabbi Nathan, *Likutey Etzot: Advice of Rebbe Nachman* (trans. Avraham Greenbaum; Monsey, NY: Breslov Research Institute, 1983), 254.

[2] Lou H. Silberman, "Joy," *Encyclopedia Judaica* (Second Edition) 11:470–471.

[3] Rabbi Aaron of Karlin. See Shochet, *The Mystical Dimension Volume Three: Chassidic Dimensions*, 129.

[4] Ibid. 132, quoting *Keter Shem Tov, Hossafot* par. 169.

Joy is important, not only as the antithesis of depression, but as a fundamental element of our Divine service in its own right. Just as the love of G-d and the fear of G-d are necessary for our Divine service to be complete, so too, joy is essential to our spiritual development. All the *mitzvos* that a person performs, and everything that he does as an expression of his connection to G-d, should be inspired with joy.[5]

Just as joy characterizes the life of the Chasid, so too, joy should characterize the life of the believer. For the kingdom of God is "righteousness and peace and joy in the Holy Spirit."[6]

CIRCUMSTANTIAL JOY

The joy which is experienced on special occasions, for instance during prayer, and the joy which is always potentially present. (55)

There is a type of joy that depends upon one's circumstances, and a type of joy that remains constant despite circumstances. This can be illustrated on a very simple level. A man finds joy in his wife and in his children. When he is away from them, he is saddened, but he still has joy in the knowledge that he will soon be reunited with them. Thus he is sad and joyful simultaneously.

We might contrast these two states of joy as "happiness" and "joy." The man's happiness is dependent upon his current circumstance, but his joy is undiminished by circumstance.

This explains how a man may have joy even when he finds himself in unhappy circumstances. The joy of a man whose faith is rooted in HaShem cannot be toppled or washed away by the storms of life. Such joy is "always potentially present."

The Chasid continually rejoices in God. His joy is combined with the happiness of his circumstance when he has the opportunity to pray or perform a mitzvah or keep an appointed time like the Sabbath or festivals. At such a time, the Chasid can rejoice in the nearness of HaShem and be happy in the circumstance of serving Him.

The man who experiences true spiritual joy is lit up by such joy from within. It shines through him, fills his personality, and transfigures him, as it were, into a glowing visage.

JOY OF THE COMMANDMENTS

The joy which results from the study of God's Word and from keeping the commandments does not reveal itself equally at all times. (55)

The Chasidim teach that every commandment should be executed with joy and that the keeping of the commandments is a source of spiritual joy. Our Master Yeshua says that if we keep the commandments as He has kept them, we will experience His joy:

---

[5]   Rabbi Shloma Majeski, *The Chassidic Approach to Joy* (Brooklyn, NY: Sichos in English, 1995), chapter 11.

[6]   Romans 14:17.

If you keep My commandments, you will abide in My love; just as I have kept My Father's commandments and abide in His love. These things I have spoken to you so that My joy may be in you, and that your joy may be made full. (John 15:10–11)

For the present time our joy is not fully manifest, because of our Master's physical absence from us; as He says, "Truly, truly, I say to you, that you will weep and lament … and you grieve … Therefore you too have grief now."[7] This grief, however, is temporary, for He is absent only for "a little while."[8]

Even though our Master left this present world to be with the Father—although it was for our benefit (see John 16:7), He gave us words of comfort: "I am with you always, even to the end of the age."[9] He says "I will see you again, and your heart will rejoice, and no one will take your joy away from you."[10] In that day the Messiah will dwell among us once again, and "we will see Him just as He is."[11]

FEAST OF TABERNACLES

Of all the feasts, that of Tabernacles is the most joyous. (55)

The only feast that is explicitly mentioned in connection with the Messianic Age is that of *Sukkot*, the Feast of Tabernacles. All "will go up from year to year to worship the King, the LORD of hosts, and to celebrate the Feast of Booths."[12] During the Feast of Tabernacles it is a commandment to rejoice: "And you shall rejoice in your feast."[13]

In the days of the Holy Temple, the priesthood honored the Feast of Tabernacles by pouring out a libation of water over the altar. Ordinarily, only wine was used for libations. Levertoff's sources explain that ordinarily the priests poured out wine over the altar because wine symbolizes joy. However, at the Feast of Tabernacles, when joy was actually being experienced, it would have been redundant to only pour out wine which only symbolized joy. Therefore the priests poured out water to illustrate that joy was already present. In connection with this concept, consider our Master's transformation of water into wine.

At the Feast of Tabernacles in the Messianic Era, we will ascend to Jerusalem and see King Messiah in His glory. When we see our righteous Messiah face to face, our joy will be complete. In that day, "no one will take your joy away from you."[14]

---

[7] John 16:20, 22.

[8] John 16:16.

[9] Matthew 28:20.

[10] John 16:22.

[11] 1 John 3:2. Cf. Revelation 21:3.

[12] Zechariah 14:16.

[13] Deuteronomy 16:14.

[14] John 16:22.

VINE AND BRANCHES

🌿 *The vine is a symbol of Israel, the grapes being individual Israelites. (55)*

In rabbinic literature, Israel is often compared to a vine. As the quintessential Israelite and king of Israel, the Messiah declared, "I am the true vine"[15] and the grapes (which are connected to the vine by means of the branches) are those who follow the will of the Messiah; as He says, "you are the branches."[16] Levertoff explains, "As the wine is hidden in the grapes, so is the joy of the love of God hidden in the soul." This joy is displayed to the world through our love for one another. "By this all men will know that you are My disciples, if you have love for one another."[17]

CRUSHING THE GRAPES

🌿 *The grapes must be trodden and the skins left behind in the winepress in order that the good wine should gush forth. (56)*

In his analogy, Levertoff compares Israel to a vine and the individual members of Israel to grapes on the vine. He compares the wine within the grapes to the "joy of the love of God hidden in the soul." Just as salt without saltiness is worthless and just as one does not "light a lamp and put it under a basket,"[18] neither is wine left within the skin of the grapes of any use to anyone. "The grapes must be trodden and the skins left behind in the winepress in order that the good wine should gush forth; so does pure joyous love towards God pour forth from our hearts only when it is trodden out humbly in God's winepress and the skin of our self-righteousness left behind." The good wine found within our hearts can only pour forth through the result of tribulations sent to us by God in order to strengthen our true self. "Consider it all joy, my brethren, when you encounter various trials, knowing that the testing of your faith produces endurance."[19] "For it is better, if God should will it so, that you suffer for doing what is right rather than for doing what is wrong."[20] Also, if one suffers "as a Christian, he is not to be ashamed, but is to glorify God in this name."[21] "Therefore, those also who suffer according to the will of God shall entrust their souls to a faithful Creator in doing what is right."[22]

---

[15]   John 15:1. Cf. John 15:5. For more on this see *Appendix One: The Exalted Rebbe.*

[16]   John 15:5.

[17]   John 13:35.

[18]   Matthew 5:15.

[19]   James 1:2–3.

[20]   1 Peter 3:17.

[21]   1 Peter 4:16.

[22]   1 Peter 4:19.

EXILE OF THE SHECHINAH

Self-righteousness is idolatry and prolongs the exile of Israel and of the Shechinah. (56)

Self-righteousness is the sin of pride and the rejection of God's grace. So long as we allow self-righteousness to obstruct "God's winepress" and refuse to repent, we are prolonging the time until redemption, when the Messiah will come and HaShem's Dwelling Presence (Shechinah) will return to Zion. Therefore, we prolong the exile in which we now reside as well as that of the Shechinah.

> From where do we learn that the *Shechinah* went along with Israel in exile? Because it says [in Isaiah 43:14], "For your sake I was sent to Babylon," and also [in Ezekiel 1:3, it says], "The word of the LORD came expressly to Ezekiel the priest, son of Buzi, in the land of the Chaldeans." (*Exodus Rabbah* 23:5)

That the Shechinah accompanied us into exile is also seen in the Gospel of Matthew: "I am with you always, even to the end of the age."[23]

To eliminate self-righteousness and hence shorten the exile, we must have the same attitude in us as which was displayed in John the Immerser: "He must increase, but I must decrease."[24] Peter admonishes us as follows, "What sort of people ought you to be in holy conduct and godliness, looking for and hastening the coming of the day of God."[25]

THE GIFT OF GOD

It is supposed that the best wine comes from grapes which are nearest the soil; so real joy in God is said to be found only where there is humility. This humility is a gift of God. (56)

Humility is a gift from HaShem. Serving HaShem with humility is a theme often repeated throughout the Scriptures. Note the following: "Seek the LORD, all you humble of the earth who have carried out His ordinances; seek righteousness, seek humility."[26] "And all of you, clothe yourselves with humility toward one another, for God is opposed to the proud, but gives grace to the humble."[27]

From where does one acquire humility? Levertoff says, "Without the awakening and inspiration from above, we see neither God nor ourselves in the true light." If we are granted a true revelation of HaShem, we will be humbled, as was the case with Job who said, "Behold, I am insignificant;

---

23 Matthew 28:20.
24 John 3:30.
25 2 Peter 3:11–12.
26 Zephaniah 2:3. Note Proverbs 18:12 and 22:4.
27 1 Peter 5:5. Cf. Ephesians 4:2; Philippians 2:3; Colossians 3:12; and James 1:21.

what can I reply to You? I lay my hand on my mouth. Once I have spoken, and I will not answer; even twice, and I will add nothing more."[28]

The words of our Master in the Gospel of John may relate to this idea: "No one can come to Me unless the Father who sent Me draws him; and I will raise him up on the last day."[29] Unless God stirs our heart to seek Him, we are only running without aim or beating the air. Paul says in his letter to the Corinthians, "Therefore I run in such a way, as not without aim; I box in such a way, as not beating the air; but I discipline my body and make it my slave, so that, after I have preached to others, I myself will not be disqualified."[30]

PHARAOH, MOSES, AND MESSIAH

❧ *Moses was great because he was humble. (56)*

Everything depends upon God's help. Man can accomplish nothing without God's help except sin and rebellion against God. Levertoff says, "The only thing we can do without His aid is to fight against Him." This is illustrated by the story of Moses and Pharaoh and their respective relationships to God. Pharaoh failed to humble himself before HaShem, and as a result his heart was hardened. In his Epistle to the Romans, the Apostle Paul says, "What shall we say then? There is no injustice with God, is there? May it never be! For He says to Moses, 'I will have mercy on whom I have mercy, and I will have compassion on whom I have compassion."[31] Of Moses, however, it is said, "Now the man Moses was very humble, more than any man who was on the face of the earth."[32] The Torah describes Moses in lofty terms when it says, "Since that time no prophet has risen in Israel like Moses, whom the LORD knew face to face."[33]

> Yet he, though thus greatly honored, did not adopt lofty language, but said, when the divine oracle came to him out of the bush, "Who am I, that Thou sendest me? I am a man of a feeble voice and a slow tongue." And again he said, "I am but as the smoke of a pot." (1 Clement 17:5–6)

Levertoff quotes *Torah Or* 95 as saying that Moses' soul came "from the Light of the Father Himself." Even higher appellations are applied to our Master. Concerning Him who "has been counted worthy of more glory than Moses,"[34] He is the very Light of the Father; as it says in the Gospel of John, "There was the true Light which, coming into the world, enlightens every man."[35]

---

[28] Job 40:4–5.

[29] John 6:44.

[30] 1 Corinthians 9:26–27.

[31] Romans 9:14–15. Cf. *Exodus Rabbah* 7:3.

[32] Numbers 12:3.

[33] Deuteronomy 34:10.

[34] Hebrews 3:3.

[35] John 1:9.

FRIEND, MOVE UP HIGHER

🍃 *When we know how far we are from God, just then He is near us. But when we think that we are near Him, then He is afar off. (56)*

Rebbe Nachman of Breslov said, "When a person begins to realize how far he is from God, even if he feels he is at the farthest extreme from God, this should not be a reason for despair. On the contrary, it should be his consolation; through this he can be revived."[36]

Levertoff says, "In our relationship to God we should be like servants who walk *behind* and follow their master, in order that we may be found worthy to reach the state of disciples, who walk *with* their master, later on." Our Master Himself teaches us in the parable of the wedding feast, "But when you are invited, go and recline at the last place, so that when the one who has invited you comes, he may say to you, 'Friend, move up higher'; then you will have honor in the sight of all who are at the table with you."[37] Note the words of the prophet Micah: "He has told you, O man, what is good; and what does the LORD require of you but to do justice, to love kindness, and to walk humbly with your God?"[38]

MORE HOPE FOR THE SINNER

🍃 *There is more hope for the greatest sinner than for the righteous who knows not his sinfulness. (56)*

The person who believes himself to be unworthy and therefore distant from HaShem is actually closer to Him than the person who believes himself to be worthy and near to HaShem. There is hope for the sinner because he knows that he is a sinner. Repentance remains an option for him. There is no hope for the self-righteous, because he does not perceive the need to repent.

This is well illustrated by the Master's teachings. In the parable of the two sons, the son who at first refused to do his father's bidding but later repented was the one who "did the will of his father."[39] In the parable of the Pharisee and the tax collector, only the tax collector who acknowledged his unworthiness "went to his house justified ... for everyone who exalts himself will be humbled, but he who humbles himself will be exalted."[40]

---

[36] Rabbi Nachman, *Restore My Soul,* (trans. Avraham Greenbaum and Aryeh Kaplan; New York: Breslov Research Institute, 1980), 32.

[37] Luke 14:10.

[38] Micah 6:8.

[39] Matthew 21:31.

[40] Luke 18:14.

BROKEN VESSELS

🌿 *God can only dwell in broken vessels. (56)*

A person does not try to store water in a cracked jar. Only an unbroken jar is able to contain a liquid. With HaShem, however, it is just the opposite. In order for God to dwell inside of us, we must be as broken vessels. The following midrash elaborates on the "frequently used phrase" that "God can only dwell in broken vessels":

> If an ordinary person tries to use broken vessels, he [fails and] is disgraced, but when the Holy One, blessed be He, uses vessels, he deliberately chooses broken ones, as it is said [in Psalm 34:18], "The LORD is near to the brokenhearted," [and in Psalm 147:3], "He heals the broken hearted," [and in Isaiah 57:15], "I dwell on a high and holy place, And also with the contrite and lowly of spirit," [and in Psalm 51:17], "The sacrifices of God are a broken spirit; A broken and a contrite heart, O God, You will not despise." (*Leviticus Rabbah* 7:2)[41]

BITTUL HAYESH

🌿 *The aim of all Creation is bittul hayesh; that is, ceasing from being something apart from God; to die, in order to be raised to life again. (56)*

Among Judaism's esoteric approaches to Torah, there is a teaching which contrasts humility to pride in a person's relationship with HaShem. A self-important person is called a "*yesh*" (יש), that is a "somebody" or a "something." The word *yesh* literally means, "there is." The *yesh*-person is like a container filled with the essence of himself. He has no room for God within him. He cannot acknowledge the unlimited God, because he is so certain of his own self and his own person.

On the opposite side is the "*bittul*" (בטול). The word "*bittul*" means "cancellation" or "negation." In Levertoff's sources, a *bittul*-person is a man of such total humility that he is like a container with nothing inside of it. Since the container is empty, it can be filled with God. "*Bittul hayesh*" (ביטול היש) means "abnegation of being." A person of self-abnegation is transparent, allowing the essence of God to fill him and flow through him. A person of pride is opaque. A person of total humility is one through whom a full expression of godliness could be demonstrated.[42] Such is our Righteous Messiah, who "emptied Himself"[43] and "humbled Himself by becoming obedient to the point of death, even death on a cross. For this reason also, God highly exalted Him, and bestowed on Him the Name which is above every name."[44]

---

[41] Cf. also *Zohar* III, 113b and II, 86b where it is the poor who are the broken vessels of God and that if anyone mistreats the poor, he is in effect mistreating the Shechinah; this is similar to Matthew 5:3, 11–12. Note also *Zohar* II, 218a.

[42] Explanation of *bittul* and *yesh* from *Torah Club Volume Five*'s comments on *parashat Behaalatecha*.

[43] Philippians 2:7.

[44] Philippians 2:8–9.

Levertoff says that *bittul hayesh*, "abnegation of being," is the aim of all creation. Apart from God, nothing exists. "Any thing whose reality is not completely nullified in Him, the light of G-d does not abide nor manifest itself therein, even if one be a perfect tzaddik who cleaves to Him with abundant love."[45] John the Immerser says, "He must increase, but I must decrease."[46] Our Master teaches us, "Whoever wishes to become great among you shall be your servant, and whoever wishes to be first among you shall be your slave; just as the Son of Man did not come to be served, but to serve, and to give His life a ransom for many."[47]

DEAD TO SELF

🖋 *To die, in order to be raised to life again. (56)*

Levertoff's sources teach that *bittul hayesh* ("abnegation of being") is a process of dying in order to live. This is identical to our Master's words on denying the self: "If anyone wishes to come after Me, he must deny himself, and take up his cross and follow Me. For whoever wishes to save his life will lose it; but whoever loses his life for My sake will find it."[48] Paul expanded on the Master's words in several of his epistles with his teachings about dying to the flesh. Like the concept of *bittul hayesh*, Paul taught that identification with Yeshua's death requires a death to the self, and therefore a death to sin. He asks, "How shall we who died to sin still live in it? Or do you not know that all of us who have been baptized into the Messiah Yeshua have been baptized into His death?"[49] Moreover, he says, "One died for all, therefore all died; and He died for all, so that they who live might no longer live for themselves, but for Him who died and rose again on their behalf."[50] "For you have died and your life is hidden with Messiah in God. When Messiah, who is our life, is revealed, then you also will be revealed with Him in glory. Therefore consider the members of your earthly body as dead to immorality, impurity, passion, evil desire, and greed, which amounts to idolatry."[51] Levertoff says that the ultimate purpose of *bittul hayesh* is "to die, in order to be raised to life again." Similarly, Paul says, "For if we have become united with Him in the likeness of His death, certainly we shall also be in the likeness of His resurrection … Now if we have died with Messiah, we believe that we shall also live with Him."[52]

---

45 *Tanya* 35 (Kehot).

46 John 3:30.

47 Matthew 20:26–28. See 2 Corinthians 8:9 and Philippians 2:3–11.

48 Matthew 16:24–25.

49 Romans 6:2–3.

50 2 Corinthians 5:14–15.

51 Colossians 3:3–5.

52 Romans 6:5–8.

REJOICING IN HIM ALWAYS

🌿 *If we have no joy in our hearts, we deny the love of God. (57)*

Every commandment of the Torah provides us with an opportunity to serve the King, but "the keeping of the Law does not profit us unless it is done joyfully." When serving in the presence of HaShem, the priests in the Tabernacle were not allowed to mourn.[53] So too, in our service of HaShem, "We must believe in the light of the countenance of the living King."

> "In the light of the King's countenance there is life," Proverbs 16:15, and, conclusively, "Strength and gladness are in His place," [1 Chronicles 16:27], because He is but good all the time. (*Igeret HaKodesh* 11 [Kehot])

> Though you have not seen Him, you love Him, and though you do not see Him now, but believe in Him, you greatly rejoice with joy inexpressible and full of glory, obtaining as the outcome of your faith the salvation of your souls. (1 Peter 1:8–9)

Levertoff notes that the maxim, "Let us therefore rejoice in Him always," is repeated often in Chasidic sources. The apostles had the same expectation of all believers:

> Rejoice in the Lord. (Philippians 3:1)

> Rejoice always. (1 Thessalonians 5:16)

> Rejoice in the Lord always; again I will say, rejoice! (Philippians 4:4)

"If we have no joy in our hearts, we deny the love of God," Levertoff says while citing the teaching of Schneur Zalman:

> Therefore, first of all, man ought to be happy and joyous at all times, and truly live by his faith in the Lord who animates him and is benignant with him every moment. But he who is grieved and laments makes himself appear as if he has it somewhat bad, and is suffering, and lacking some goodness; he is like a heretic, Heaven forfend. (*Igeret HaKodesh* 11 [Kehot])

THWARTING SATAN'S TAUNT

🌿 *We should not say, "Our heart is a dwelling place of lust, jealousy, anger; there is no hope for us." (57)*

When a person attempts to serve HaShem with joy, the adversary taunts him and says, "Who are you to serve God? What of the uncleanness of your hands and the uncleanness of your heart?" A

---

[53] Leviticus 10:6; 21.

person should not allow this taunting to rob him of joy. Neither should a person berate himself, saying, "I am an unworthy sinner; there is not hope for me." Instead, he should shove away such thoughts with both hands, so to speak, and remember that he is a new creature in Messiah, and God's grace is sufficiently abundant. "Therefore if anyone is in Messiah, he is a new creature; the old things have passed away; behold, new things have come."[54] "Therefore you are no longer a slave, but a son; and if a son, then an heir through God."[55]

Rather than regarding himself as a vessel of sin and shame, a person should think of himself as a vessel filled with God's Spirit. Levertoff says, "Let us realize that we have another guest in us who desires to give us life and joy, notwithstanding our sin." Paul writes, "Do you not know that you are a temple of God and that the Spirit of God dwells in you?"[56] Therefore, "guard, through the Holy Spirit who dwells in us, the treasure which has been entrusted to you."[57]

OVERCOMING EVIL THOUGHTS

Even if we are disturbed by worldly thoughts during our most intimate converse with God, we should not lose courage and joy. (57)

Satan tries to distract a man from prayer and from the service of HaShem by stirring up within a man uncleanness of heart. "For from within, out of the heart of men, proceed the evil thoughts, fornications, thefts, murders, adulteries, deeds of coveting and wickedness, as well as deceit, sensuality, envy, slander, pride and foolishness. All these evil things proceed from within and defile the man."[58] But "even if there occur to him lustful imaginations or other extraneous thoughts *during* Divine Service, in Torah or in devout prayer, he must not let his heart dwell on them but must immediately avert his mind from them,"[59] and "he should draw fresh strength and intensify [his] effort with all his power to concentrate on the prayer with increased joy and gladness."[60] For "we are taking every thought captive to the obedience of Messiah."[61]

It only proves the reality of our fellowship with God, if Satan tries to disturb it. When a person is distracted by worldly, lustful, or carnal thoughts, even if it happens in the midst of prayer, he should not be discouraged. "For the joy set before him,"[62] his attitude should be:

> As if he neither knows nor hears the thoughts that have befallen him; he must remove them from his mind and strengthen still more the power of his concentration. However, if he finds it hard to dismiss them from his mind, because they

---

[54] 2 Corinthians 5:17.

[55] Galatians 4:7.

[56] 1 Corinthians 3:16.

[57] 2 Timothy 1:14.

[58] Mark 7:21–23.

[59] *Tanya* 28 (Kehot).

[60] Ibid.

[61] 2 Corinthians 10:5.

[62] Hebrews 12:2.

distract his mind with great intensity, then he should humble his spirit before G-d and supplicate Him in his thoughts to have compassion upon him in His abundant mercies. (*Tanya* 28 [Kehot])

THE SOUL IN FLIGHT

🌿 *This joy is the revelation of the inner life of God in us. It is not what the world calls joy. (57)*

As noted above, worldly joy is circumstantial. Pleasures and happy occasions bring joy; pain and struggle bring sorrow. Godly joy transcends circumstance and is not dependent upon fortune, good or bad. "It is not what the world calls joy." Godly joy is watered by "the peace of God, which surpasses all comprehension;"[63] "content in whatever circumstances" [64] should come. Godly joy is rooted in the world of the soul, and therefore it is like air. Just as a bird's bones are hollow, enabling it to lift its body into flight, so too the joy of God fills the soul, enabling the human being to transcend the limitations of circumstance and simple materialism.

JOY AND DELIGHT

🌿 *There is a subtle difference between joy and delight. (57)*

Levertoff distinguishes between joy and delight. Joy anticipates. Delight realizes. With joy a bride anticipates her wedding. With delight she receives the groom into her chamber. With joy a man considers a treasure he has hidden in a field. With delight, he digs it up and brings it forth. The Torah is a source of joy because it is like the promise of the bridal chamber and the secret of the hidden treasure. The Torah's "deepest spiritual meaning is as yet not made perfectly clear to us."

In the Messianic Era, the Torah will pass from the realm of joy and into the realm of delight. No longer will it be promises only, but promises fulfilled. "The divine mysteries of the Law will be unfolded by the Messiah, and we shall see God face to face. Then our souls will be filled with *delight*."

> An especially sublime level of Divine revelation which, according to Jewish tradition was hidden away by G-d at the beginning of time for the enjoyment of the righteous in the Messianic future to come … The revelation of this "goodness" in the future to come will be even greater than the revelations experienced by our forefathers. (*Torah Or*, Genesis, 13 [Wagshul])

"For as many as are the promises of God, in Him they are yes; therefore also through Him is our Amen to the glory of God through us."[65]

---

[63] Philippians 4:7.
[64] Philippians 4:11.
[65] 2 Corinthians 1:20.

5

PRAYER AND LOVE

SERVICE OF THE HEART

That prayer should take a central position in Chasidic piety is only what is to be expected. (59)

The Chasidic life is a life of prayer. The Chasidim are renowned for their intense, ecstatic, and fervent prayer lives. To the Chasid, prayer is communication with the Divine and the means by which one draws near to HaShem. "It is for the soul what food is for the body."[1] In Jewish tradition, prayer is called *avodat halev* (עבודת הלב) which means "service of the heart."

> It has been taught: What does it mean, "To love the LORD your God and to serve Him with all your heart" [Deuteronomy 11:13]? What is service of heart? You must say that it is prayer. (b. *Ta'anit* 2a)[2]

The Chasidim use this Talmudic axiom to "emphasize the true character of worship." Real prayer must come forth from the heart; as our Master says, "For the mouth speaks out of that which fills the heart" (Matthew 12:34).

KAVANAH

Prayer without intention is like a body without a soul. (59)

It is possible to pray without paying any attention to the words one is praying. It is possible to stand in prayer without ever directing one's heart toward HaShem. While praying, one's mind is busy with other thoughts. According to the Chasidim, mindless prayer is not prayer at all.

---

[1] Rabbi Judah HaLevi, *Kuzari* 3:5 as quoted in Jacob Schochet, *The Mystical Dimension Volume Two: Deep Calling Unto Deep* (New York: Kehot Publication Society, 1995), 23.

[2] Cf. *Sifre* Deuteronomy 42 (on Deuteronomy 11:13). See also *Tanya* 29.

Instead, the Chasidim teach that one must pray with *kavanah* (כונה), "intention." *Kavanah* refers to one's cognitive and spiritual focus during the course of prayer.[3] "*Kavanah* means proper thoughts and devotion, proper intention and attention, 'to clear the heart (mind) of all thoughts and visualize oneself as standing in the presence of the *Shechinah.*'"[4]

"Prayer or other benediction [recited] without *kavanah* is like a body without a *neshamah* [i.e., a soul]."[5] Just as a body cannot exist and remain alive without a *neshamah* (נשמה), "a soul," so too prayer without proper intention is dead. "Like a body without a soul, a husk without a kernel … one may as well be digging holes in the ground or chopping wood in a forest. That kind of prayer is no different than the mindless chirping of birds."[6]

Neither the rote recitation of liturgy nor the plodding, perfunctory forms of artless, spontaneous prayer hold merit, one over the other, for both are simply inanimate and lifeless unless they be infused with simple, heartfelt intention. Chasidic sources quote various passages from the prophets as evidence that prayer without intention is useless:

> This people draw near with their words and honor Me with their lip service, but they remove their hearts far from Me. (Isaiah 29:13)

> You are near to their lips but far from their mind. (Jeremiah 12:2)

> When you come to appear before Me, who requires of you this trampling of My courts? Bring your worthless offerings no longer, incense is an abomination to Me. New moon and sabbath, the calling of assemblies—I cannot endure iniquity and the solemn assembly. I hate your new moon festivals and your appointed feasts, they have become a burden to Me; I am weary of bearing them. So when you spread out your hands in prayer, I will hide My eyes from you; Yes, even though you multiply prayers, I will not listen. (Isaiah 1:12–15)

Our Master taught us to pray privately and with singular intention. "Pray to your Father who is in secret, and your Father who sees what is done in secret will reward you. And when you are praying, do not use meaningless repetition as the Gentiles do, for they suppose that they will be heard for their many words."[7] The apostles experienced such intense *kavanah* in prayer that they were at times swept into a trance (*ekstasis* [εκστασις], "a state of ecstasy").[8]

---

3   For a historical study of *kavanah* see Joseph Weiss, "The Kavvanoth of Prayer in early Hasidism," in *Studies in Eastern Jewish Mysticism* (ed. David Goldstein; New York: Oxford University Press, 1985), 95–125.

4   Rambam, *Hilchot Tefilah* 4:15–16, as quoted in Schochet, *The Mystical Dimension Volume Two: Deep Calling Unto Deep*, 33.

5   *Tanya* 38 (Kehot). The *Tanya* quotes this axiom from the *Shnei Luchot HaBerit* vol. 1, 249b. Note also the words of the *Tanya*: "It is also His blessed will that one should cleave to Him with one's intelligence, thought and intention in the active commandments, and with intention during the recital of Shema, prayer and other benedictions." (*Tanya* 38 [Kehot]).

6   *Chovot HaLevovot, The Gate of Self Accounting* 9; *Moreh Nevushim* 3:51; *Akeidat Yitzchak, Tzav, Sha'ar* 58 as quoted in Schochet, *The Mystical Dimension Volume Two: Deep Calling Unto Deep*, 33.

7   Matthew 6:6–7.

8   See Acts 10:9–10, 22:17.

If a person finds that his mind wanders while he prays, let him remember the One before whom he stands. Then his mind will focus and his heart will lift each word toward heaven in fear and love.

The sixth-century Christian monk John Climacus encourages:

> Make every effort to raise up, or rather, to enclose your mind within the words of your prayer; and if, like a child, it gets tired and falters, raise it up again. The mind, after all, is naturally unstable, but the God who can do everything can also give it firm endurance … Spirit cannot be bound, but where He is found everything yields to the creator of spirit. (*Ladder of Divine Ascent* 28 [Luibheid and Russell])

HITLAHAVUT

❧ *It means the concentration of the whole mind on God. (59)*

Not only should a person have proper *kavanah* in prayer, he should also have *hitlahavut* (התלה־בות), which means "enthusiasm."[9] *Hitlahavut* refers to one's attitude during prayer. The Chasidim are known for their enthusiasm in prayer and their ecstatic experiences which might be expressed in sudden, contagious melody, a bout of weeping, a joyous dance, or a sad and soulful *niggun* ("wordless song," נגון).

King David says, "I will offer in His tent sacrifices with shouts of joy; I will sing, yes, I will sing praises to the LORD."[10] When our Master prayed, He "offered up both prayers and supplications with loud crying and tears."[11]

Prayer should not feel rote or meaningless. If a person finds that he feels listless and disinterested while he prays, let him strengthen his soul; let him remember the privilege of speaking to the King; and let his love for his Father in heaven well up into a spring of joy and enthusiasm.

THE IDEAL PRAYER

❧ *The ideal prayer is not asking God for this or for that, but the desire that He may, so to speak, concentrate His whole mind upon us. (59)*

The popular idea of prayer is one of petition. An effective prayer is a petition granted. In Chasidic ideology, though, "The ideal prayer is not asking God for this or for that, but the desire that He may, so to speak, concentrate His whole mind upon us."[12] When commenting elsewhere on this

---

9   See *Tzava'at Harivash* 111 (Schochet).

10   Psalm 27:6.

11   Hebrews 5:7.

12   See also *Tzava'at Harivash* 73 (Schochet).

concept, Levertoff pointed to the words of Madame Acarie, "He asks too much to whom God is not sufficient."[13]

The Chasid does not pray in order to have his petition granted; he prays for the simple delight of conversing with the love of his soul: the Holy One, Blessed is He. In the words of the Christian monk John Climacus, "Prayer is by nature a dialog and a union of man with God."[14]

To illustrate this concept, Levertoff tells a parable originally told by the Baal Shem Tov, in which all the king's subjects petition him for one thing or another, but one man asks him nothing other than the "privilege of seeing the king each day and speaking to him personally."[15]

The conversation between a benefactor and a beneficiary is not like the conversation between friends. With the benefactor and beneficiary, the one thinks, "What does he want," and the other thinks, "What will he give me?" Friends ask nothing of one another, but they delight to be together. Nevertheless, friends are quick to inquire of one another's needs and to meet those needs as best they can. Such is the man who desired only "to have the privilege of seeing the king each day and speaking to him personally."

This is comparable to the words of our Master: "But seek first His kingdom and His righteousness, and all these things will be added to you."[16] These words make no mention of imploring first and foremost for our material needs, but rather seeking first a nearness to God. Only afterwards is there mention of our material needs.

This type of prayer is also seen in the model of prayer employed by the Master, where we first praise God by asking that His name will be hallowed, His kingdom will come, and His will be done. Only after drawing near to God through our praises do we ask for our daily bread. When we draw near to God by praising Him, He in turn concentrates His mind on us.

PRAYER AND CHARITY

If we concentrate all our mental and spiritual faculties on Him, He will come down and concentrate His infinite creative power and love on us. (60)

In Chasidic thought, the performance of *tzedakah* (צדקה), "charity" or, more literally, "righteousness," is a vehicle through which we draw down the grace of God and cause Him to concentrate His mind upon us:

> "Rabbi Eliezer gave a coin unto a poor person, and then prayed; as it is written: through *tzedek* [righteousness/charity] I will see Your face." This means that the manifestation of His blessed Divinity, which becomes revealed in the thought of

---

[13] Madame Acarie was the sixteenth century founder of the French Carmelites. "Some Jewish Thoughts on Prayer," *Church and the Jews* 79 (April 1929): 14.

[14] *The Ladder of Divine Ascent* 28 (Luibheid and Russell).

[15] *Keter Shem Tov* 97 as found in Schochet, *The Mystical Dimension Volume Two: Deep Calling Unto Deep*, 29–30.

[16] Matthew 6:33. Levertoff, in his commentary to Matthew, notes the following: "Righteousness here means both the coming manifestations of God's power, and the moral goodness demanded of the Christian" (Levertoff, *St. Matthew*, 19).

man and in his devotion during prayer, each according to his own measure, is by way of the charity and the "*Chesed* [kindness/devotion] of the Lord eternally upon those who fear Him." (*Igeret HaKodesh* 8 [Kehot])[17]

The idea that God concentrates His mind on us through our righteous deeds is seen in the teaching of our Master when He says, "Beware of practicing your righteousness before men."[18] Rather our deeds are to be "in secret; and your Father who sees what is done in secret will reward you."[19] A similar thought is found in the book of Job: "The LORD said to Satan, 'Have you considered My servant Job? For there is no one like him on earth, a blameless and upright man, fearing God and turning away from evil.'"[20] That prayer and charity are measured together is evidenced by the angelic word spoken to Cornelius: "Your prayers and your alms have ascended as a memorial before God."[21]

TWO FLAMES—WITHIN THE FLAME

> *In a candle flame there are two parts: the outward yellow flame and the inner blue one. (60)*

The flame of a candle appears in two colors. The outer part of the flame is yellow; the inner part is hot blue. "Similarly is it with the human soul, which is divided in two— intellect (*sechel*, שכל) and emotional attributes (*middot*, מדות)."[22] Thus, the intellect is likened to the outer yellow flame which does not burn as intensely as the inner blue flame. This outer flame is limited to each person's own intellectual knowledge and is therefore neither equal nor the same for every individual. However, the burning desire within the depth of each person's heart (likened to the inner blue flame) is something that, once awakened, can elevate the soul to a deep union with the Creator. When we pray, we should pray with both parts of the soul—the intellect and inner soul. The Apostle Paul taught a similar concept when he distinguished between praying with the spirit and praying with the mind.[23] He seems to allude to the verse that says "the spirit (i.e. the *neshamah*) of man is the candle of the LORD,"[24] when he describes of the Spirit of God assisting us in prayer by searching the inner heart:

> In the same way the Spirit also helps our weakness; for we do not know how to pray as we should, but the Spirit Himself intercedes for us with groaning too deep

---

[17] St. Augustin ascribes the fourth-century theologian Pelagius as having a similar view regarding prayer and righteous deeds. E.g., St. Augustin, *On Nature and Grace* 20; *On the Proceedings of Pelagius* 42.

[18] Matthew 6:1.

[19] Matthew 6:4.

[20] Job 1:8.

[21] Acts 10:4.

[22] *Tanya* 3 (Kehot).

[23] 1 Corinthians 14:14.

[24] Proverbs 20:27 (KJV).

for words; and He who searches the hearts knows what the mind of the Spirit is, because He intercedes for the saints according to the will of God. (Romans 8:26–27)

CANDLE OF HASHEM

🌿 *The inner flame is at the centre and depth of our heart. The love burning there is of a higher quality than that love which arises only from the knowledge of God's power. (60)*

Commenting on the verse, "The spirit of man is the candle of the LORD,"[25] the *Tanya* says that the souls of men are "like the flame of the candle, whose nature it is always to scintillate upwards, for the flame of fire intrinsically seeks to be parted from the wick in order to unite with its source above."[26] In like manner, the soul of man desires to separate from the body and be united with its original source, its Creator. Paul expresses a similar idea in his second Epistle to the Corinthians:

> For indeed in this house we groan, longing to be clothed with our dwelling from heaven, inasmuch as we, having put it on, will not be found naked. For indeed while we are in this tent, we groan, being burdened, because we do not want to be unclothed but to be clothed, so that what is mortal will be swallowed up by life. (2 Corinthians 5:2–4)

Paul also says, "But I am hard-pressed from both directions, having the desire to depart and be with Messiah, for that is much better."[27]

Prayer is an opportunity for the soul to reconnect with HaShem while remaining clothed in the mortal body. This is why fervent prayer "frees the imprisoned Divine spark that flickers in each, and makes it burst forth into a fiery flame consuming the obstacles of the body and animal soul, and to generate a state of ardent love and desire to become attached to—verily, united with—the Source of Life."[28]

THE DIVINE SPARK WITHIN

🌿 *From this life and light proceeds the divine "spark" which is hidden in every soul. (60)*

Levertoff describes the inner flame that burns inside the heart of man as "the divine 'spark' which is hidden in every soul." The spark is the divine soul that dwells inside each of us; it is this spark that cries out longing for HaShem. Levertoff says that "Not all men succeed in rising to this close

---

[25] Ibid.

[26] *Tanya* 19 (Kehot).

[27] Philippians 1:23.

[28] *Torah Or*, Exodus, 51b as quoted in Schochet, *The Mystical Dimension Volume Two: Deep Calling Unto Deep*, 33.

union with God at prayer, because this spark is *imprisoned* in them." That is to say that everyone has within them the potential of experiencing an intimate, spiritual relationship with God, but not everyone does. The unredeemed heart is like a prison to the potential of an immortal soul which HaShem has planted within every human being.

A similar idea is found in Paul's Epistle to the Romans when he says, "And not only this, but also we ourselves, having the first fruits of the Spirit, even we ourselves groan within ourselves, waiting eagerly for our adoption as sons, the redemption of our body."[29] Levertoff quotes the *Tanya* to suggest that the divine spark is actually the presence of "the Shechinah in our souls."[30]

The concept of the Shechinah dwelling within the soul is also a fundament of apostolic theology. The apostolic writers testify that HaShem quickens the believer's soul by placing His Holy Spirit within our hearts: "God has sent forth the Spirit of His Son into our hearts."[31] "The love of God has been poured out within our hearts through the Holy Spirit who was given to us."[32] God "also sealed us and gave us the Spirit in our hearts as a pledge."[33]

INGATHERING OF SPARKS

ꛒ *Only through true prayer can the wall of partition between man and God be removed; only then can He use it for the gathering of these "sparks." (60–61)*

Although every man has the divine potential of a godly soul planted within him, this is not a guarantee that every man will enter into a relationship with HaShem or even that every soul will be redeemed. Instead, the soul is separated from God by a wall of partition—sin and guilt. HaShem removes the wall of partition between man and Himself through the work of the Messiah. When the wall is removed, then the soul can connect with HaShem. Then He can "use it for the gathering of these 'sparks.'"

The culmination of the gathering of the sparks of God's Presence will not occur "until the period of restoration of all things about which God spoke by the mouth of His holy prophets from ancient time."[34] "For it was the Father's good pleasure for all the fullness to dwell in Him, and through Him

---

[29] Romans 8:23.

[30] The early Church writer Tatian speaks of the inner spark: "Now, in the beginning the spirit was a constant companion of the soul, but the spirit forsook it because it was not willing to follow. Yet, retaining as it were a spark of its power, though unable by reason of the separation to discern the perfect" (Tatian, *Address to the Greeks* 13 [Coxe]). Similarly, "The reason that not every person merits this rank [of the service of the heart from the depth of the heart in a state of *pnimiyut*] is because this aspect is with him in a state of exile and captivity. And this is actually the state of the exile of the Shechinah, for this precisely is the aspect of the spark of the Divinity that is in his divine soul" (*Igeret HaKodesh* 4 [Kehot]). A similar idea may be expressed in John 1:9. For a historical study of this concept see Louis Jacobs, "The Doctrine of the 'Divine Spark' in Man in Jewish Sources," in *Studies in Rationalism, Judaism and Universalism* (ed. l Loewe; London: Routledge and Kegan Paul, 1966), 87–114.

[31] Galatians 4:6.

[32] Romans 5:5.

[33] 2 Corinthians 1:22.

[34] Acts 3:21. Cf. Ezekiel 16:53.

to reconcile all things to Himself, having made peace through the blood of His cross; through Him, *I say*, whether things on earth or things in heaven."[35]

RESTORATION OF THE SACRIFICES

🌿 *The coming of the Messiah, and with it the restoration of sacrifices, will mean also the restoration of all things, the ascending of all beings, through the Redeemer. (61)*

Chasidic mysticism teaches that every element in creation houses a divine spark, so to speak.[36] All things originated with HaShem. All things have an intrinsic godly potential and are intended for His service. This is symbolized by the sacrificial system. The animals that the Torah designates for sacrifice have within them the potential to serve HaShem by sacrificing their bodies completely to Him. This potential for complete surrender to HaShem is the "divine spark" within those animals, and it symbolizes the godly potential contained within every aspect of the creation. So long as the Temple is in ruins, there can be no sacrifice, and the divine potential for the sacrificial animals to fulfill HaShem's will is thwarted. This is a microcosm of the frustration of the entire universe. Until the final redemption when the upper is united with the lower (as symbolized by the Temple), HaShem's creation cannot fulfill its intended purpose. "For we know that the whole creation groans and suffers the pains of childbirth together until now."[37]

Levertoff says, "The coming of the Messiah, and with it the restoration of sacrifices, will mean also the restoration of all things, the ascending of all beings, through the Redeemer." Then the divine potential contained within the animals offered on the altar will be realized, symbolizing the restoration of creation. Then "the creation itself also will be set free from its slavery to corruption into the freedom of the glory of the children of God."[38] Commenting on the restoration of the sacrificial services in the Messianic Era,[39] Levertoff says in another place, "But prayer worth the name has even in the present dispensation a sacrificial character. If only Israel would pray 'out of the depths' they would hasten Messiah's coming."[40]

---

[35] Colossians 1:19–20.
[36] Cf. John 1:9.
[37] Romans 8:22.
[38] Romans 8:21.
[39] For example, see Jeremiah 33:14–18.
[40] "Some Jewish Thoughts on Prayer," *Church and the Jews* 79 (April 1929): 15.

MESSIAH NOW

🕊️ *If Israel would only pray in the true spirit, the Messiah would reveal Himself in all His glory now. (61)*

Talmudic and medieval rabbinic literature often states that if all Israel would pray "in the true spirit," their prayers would usher in the Messianic redemption immediately. Then "the Messiah would reveal Himself in all His glory now." But for those who have eyes to see and ears to hear, the Messiah has revealed Himself in glory: "He who was revealed in the flesh, was vindicated in the Spirit, seen by angels, proclaimed among the nations, believed on in the world, taken up in glory."[41] Yet we still wait for His glorious coming when He "will be revealed from heaven with His mighty angels in flaming fire."[42] Therefore, "with all prayer and petition pray at all times in the Spirit,"[43] and "live sensibly, righteously and godly in the present age, looking for the blessed hope and appearing of the glory of our great God and Savior: Messiah Yeshua."[44]

THE BATTLE WITHIN

🕊️ *The divine soul is longing to unite itself with its source as indeed, as we have seen, it is a part of God Himself. But the natural soul strives more and more to descend into its material surroundings. (61)*

The divine soul (*neshamah*) within us seeks to be united with HaShem, just as the flame of a candle always reaches upward. The animal soul (*nefesh*), however, is attached to the material world. Thus the heart of man is polarized, desiring to ascend to heaven and drawn to earth simultaneously:

> For I joyfully concur with the law of God in the inner man, but I see a different law in the members of my body, waging war against the law of my mind and making me a prisoner of the law of sin which is in my members. (Romans 7:22–23)

We should "make no provision for the flesh in regard to its lusts,"[45] for "the mind set on the flesh is death, but the mind set on the Spirit is life and peace, because the mind set on the flesh is hostile toward God; for it does not subject itself to the law of God, for it is not even able to do so, and those who are in the flesh cannot please God."[46] Obeying the flesh separates one from God; as it says, "But your iniquities have made a separation between you and your God, and your sins have hidden His face from you so that He does not hear."[47] Those who obey God's voice "are not in

---

[41] 1 Timothy 3:16.

[42] 2 Thessalonians 1:7.

[43] Ephesians 6:18.

[44] Titus 2:12–13.

[45] Romans 13:14. Cf. Romans 6:12–14.

[46] Romans 8:6–8.

[47] Isaiah 59:2.

the flesh but in the Spirit."[48] Therefore, "We are under obligation, not to the flesh, to live according to the flesh—for if you are living according to the flesh, you must die; but if by the Spirit you are putting to death the deeds of the body, you will live. For all who are being led by the Spirit of God, these are sons of God."[49]

THE STRUGGLE BEGINS

 They cannot possibly be at one any more than fire and water. But sometimes they must come to close grips; for instance, at prayer. Then a struggle between them begins. (61)

Although there is a struggle between the flesh and the spirit, there are things that neither one can do alone. For example, true prayer can only occur when flesh and spirit cooperate together. Levertoff says, "Then a struggle between them begins."

The struggle of the spirit and the natural affections (i.e., the flesh) is described by Paul when he says, "For what I am doing, I do not understand; for I am not practicing what I would like to do, but I am doing the very thing I hate."[50] Due to the intense desire of the Spirit (the divine soul), one's entire being can be carried "into higher spheres and spiritualize all his natural affections." At such times, the flesh is brought into the service of HaShem.

There are times when this struggle is not manifest and "the spirit of man is drawn, without any struggle, towards God, as the light of the candle in the daytime ceases to have individuality or as the soul in Paradise is at home with God." This can occur during the "ideal Sabbath worship," for "on every Sabbath the edifice is completed *if we do the will of God*." The Sabbath foreshadows the Messianic Era, when the mortal inclination will be defeated and HaShem's Torah will be written upon our hearts. Keeping the Sabbath is a foretaste of that coming time of peace. "For the one who has entered His rest has himself also rested from his works, as God did His. Therefore let us be diligent to enter that rest, so that no one will fall, through following the same example of disobedience."[51]

PENTECOST TRANSFORMATION

 The seven weeks between Passover and Pentecost represent the struggle between the two souls. (62)

Levertoff says that the seven-week period of counting the omer between Passover and Pentecost is a time of intense struggle between the divine soul and the mortal inclination. At Passover, everyone is responsible to eliminate all the leaven and leavened things (*chametz*, חמץ) from their possession. By doing so, we emulate the Holy Temple where leaven and *chametz* is always prohibited.

---

[48] Romans 8:9.
[49] Romans 8:12–14.
[50] Romans 7:15. See Romans 7:14–25.
[51] Hebrews 4:10–11.

Levertoff's sources interpret leaven as symbolizing pride and the natural, mortal inclination of the animal soul, i.e., the flesh. Levertoff notes the words of Philo:

> In another passage also He has ordained something similar to this, commanding that upon an altar upon which victims [i.e. animals] are offered in sacrifice leaven is not to be brought. He indicates through two necessary symbols that one should despise sensual pleasures, for leaven is a sweetener of food but not food (itself). And the other thing (indicated) is that one should not be uplifted in conceit by common belief. For both are impure and hateful, (namely) sensual pleasure and arrogance (or) foolish belief, (both being) the offspring of one mother, illusion. But the blood of the sacrificed victims is a sign of the souls which are consecrated to God. Moreover, it is not right to mix the unmixed. (*Fragment on Exodus 23:18* [Marcus])

However, on Pentecost, leaven and *chametz* is not only permitted but commanded in the Temple offering of the two loaves of leavened bread.[52] The festival of Pentecost, "therefore, symbolizes the spiritualization of natural life." At Pentecost, the struggle is over, the "natural" soul (flesh) is defeated by the "divine" (spirit). This is represented in the outpouring of the Spirit at Pentecost in the book of Acts. God poured out His Spirit upon the believers to demonstrate that He was beginning the work prophesied in the book of Ezekiel, where it says, "Moreover, I will give you a new heart and put a new spirit within you; and I will remove the heart of stone from your flesh and give you a heart of flesh. I will put My Spirit within you and cause you to walk in My statutes, and you will be careful to observe My ordinances."[53]

Normally leaven symbolizes pride and mortal corruption, but "at Pentecost, leaven symbolizes the sublime Spirit of God which penetrates even the natural life, and therefore it had to be used in sacrifices at that Feast."

The conclusion of the time between Passover and Pentecost symbolizes the transformation of the flesh and its desires and the conquering of the Spirit. Leaven, a symbol of pride and corruption, now becomes united with, and overpowered by, the Spirit. Pentecost looks forward to the time when "this perishable must put on the imperishable, and this mortal must put on immortality."[54]

THIEF OF PRAYER

🌿 *We may be disturbed during our most fervent prayers by alien powers which cling to us just when our spirit is in its closest approach to God. (62)*

When a person attempts to pray, his mind is sometimes flooded with ungodly thoughts. These alien thoughts are likened to a thief who desires to steal the richness we share in our communion with God. Therefore a person should not be surprised that his thoughts rebel against him when

---

52 Leviticus 23:17.

53 Ezekiel 36:26–27.

54 1 Corinthians 15:53.

he goes to pray. Instead, since he knows at what hour the thief will be coming, he should ready himself and not "allow his house to be broken into."[55]

Consider a thief who asks God to allow his ploy to be successful.[56] When the thief seeks God to assist him in sin, it shows that he believes in Divine Providence, but this belief does not persuade him to change his ways for the good. At such a time, the "evil in man gathers strength from the life of the spirit at prayer." The Apostle James says, "You ask and do not receive, because you ask with wrong motives, so that you may spend it on your pleasures."[57]

CLOSE CONTACT

🌿 *In the struggle between a saintly man and a godless one, something of the impurity of the latter must needs cleave to the former because of their close contact during the struggle. (62)*

During prayer, a struggle occurs between the natural-animal soul (*nefesh,* the flesh) and the divine soul (*neshamah*); each fights to dominate the person. The animal soul seeks to distract a person during his prayer, while the divine soul stirs one's soul to cleave to HaShem. Therefore a person should anticipate that his flesh will resist his attempts to pray. It may seem that prayer actually strengthens the flesh, and that our prayers are disqualified by contact with the corruption of the flesh.

> For it is known that the way of combatants, as of wrestlers, is that when one is gaining the upper hand the other likewise strives to prevail with all the resources of his strength. Therefore, when the divine soul exerts itself and summons its strength for prayer, the [outer-shell] also gathers strength at such time to confuse her and topple her by means of a foreign thought of its own. (*Tanya* 28 [Kehot])

Although the animal soul causes outside thoughts to enter the mind during prayer, we should not be discouraged. Instead, we should be encouraged that we are indeed connecting with HaShem and this is why our flesh so desperately desires to distract us.

Levertoff says, "After prayer, when the struggle has come to an end, the evil thoughts cannot derive any more nourishment from the divinely strengthened soul. They are separated and scattered." The soul, having been attached to HaShem in prayer, is now strengthened, and the animal soul is weakened. The exercise of prayer weakens the flesh "by crushing the passions and suppressing the *sitra achra* ["side of evil," סיטרא אחרא] so that 'all the workers of evil are dispersed.'"[58]

---

[55] Luke 12:39.

[56] See the *Ein Yaakov,* b.*Berachot* 63a.

[57] James 4:3.

[58] *Igeret HaKodesh* 26 (Kehot) quoting Psalm 92:9.

CONSCIOUS AND UNCONSCIOUS SOUL-LEVELS

🖎 *This struggle during prayer is carried on only by (to use a modern*
psychological term) the "conscious" souls, one of which is called in Chasidism
"the inner light in the vessel of limitation." (63)

There are aspects of the soul of which we are aware, and aspects of which we are not aware. Everyone possesses the character traits of intellect and emotion, that is, "conscious souls." However, the godly soul (*neshamah*) operates at a deeper level than simple consciousness.

When attempting to pray, a person may be aware of the struggle between his flesh and spirit. He desires to pray, but he does not desire to pray. He seeks to pray, but his mind is distracted. All of these struggles occur only on the conscious level.

The "inner light in the vessel of limitation" is the godly soul that is clothed within the animal soul. When the godly soul seeks HaShem, the animal soul surrounds it and attempts to constrict and limit it. But the child of God's "personality is also endowed with that very life of God, which cannot be contained in any 'vessel of limitation.'" This is because the "conscious souls" of the children of God are not only rational but also divine in nature.[59] This may at times be evidenced by the fact that even if we are distracted in prayer, "not mindful of the meaning of the words, there are certain passages or verses which are recited with inner warmth, a vitality permeating the supplicant's whole being."[60]

BEYOND THE STRUGGLE

🖎 *This life surrounds his personality as a radiance, only to be perceived*
by spiritual vision, just as God's immanence permeates the world in a
mysterious way. (63)

The child of God possesses a deeper level of spiritual being, a soul-level of which he is not conscious, "the mind of the Spirit," that "intercedes" in prayer.[61] This living spirit within "is not concerned in the struggle of the 'souls' during prayer; it cannot be approached by any alien power." Nothing can distract it because it is focused only on HaShem. Therefore, even when a person's prayers are distracted, he does well to pray, for the divine soul within him cleaves to its source.

The godly soul's love for HaShem is that of *chesed* (חסד), loving-kindness.

> For the Godly soul, '*Chesed* within *chesed*' is the revelation of this natural love, so
> that it is not limited to the heart. Herein lies the difference between loving God

---

[59] The godly intellect and emotion "are imbued with a spiritual force that enables them—via the rational intellect and emotion—to affect man's instinctive intellect and emotion, these being the intellect and emotion of the animal soul and [evil inclination] (the animal soul being intellect and the [evil inclination] emotion)" (Yosef Yitzchak Schneersohn, *Chassidic Discourses* [2 vols.; Sholom B. Wineberg trans.; Brooklyn: Kehot Publication Society, 1999], 1:210).

[60] Ibid., 1:106.

[61] Romans 8:27.

"with all your heart" and loving Him "with all your soul." In the latter instance, the love is not limited to the heart, but spreads throughout a person, affecting all his powers. This love enables an individual to reject physical delights and worldly wisdom.[62]

The child of God has his origin in the very essence of HaShem Himself. This allows him to remain continuously connected to HaShem at all times. Nothing can sever his bond with HaShem:

> For I am convinced that neither death, nor life, nor angels, nor principalities, nor things present, nor things to come, nor powers, nor height, nor depth, nor any other created thing, will be able to separate us from the love of God, which is in the Messiah Yeshua our Lord. (Romans 8:38–39)

---

[62] Schneersohn, *Chassidic Discourses*, 1:212.

6

REPENTANCE AND LOVE

CIRCUMCISE OUR HEARTS

Conversion in the Chasidic sense is therefore "circumcision of the heart." (65)

In Chasidic thought, the evil desires, "the lust of this world," are referred to as a foreskin over the heart. Such imagery is used throughout the Scriptures. Jeremiah 4:4 says, "Circumcise yourselves to the LORD and remove the foreskins of your heart."[1]

Chasidic teaching contrasts two seemingly contradictory verses. Deuteronomy 10:16 commands us to circumcise our own hearts, saying "Circumcise your heart, and stiffen your neck no longer." However, Deuteronomy 30:6 says that, in the final redemption, God will circumcise our hearts:

> Moreover the LORD your God will circumcise your heart and the heart of your descendants, to love the LORD your God with all your heart and with all your soul, so that you may live. (Deuteronomy 30:6)

What is the difference between a man circumcising his own heart and God circumcising his heart?

According to Levertoff's sources, man's circumcision of his own heart refers to his efforts to repent in this present age:

> If one has become so engrossed in worldliness that he or she has actually transgressed the Will of G-d (Heaven forbid); such a person must certainly strive to return to G-d by breaking through and casting aside the hardened covering of his or her heart and giving expression to the true nature of his or her soul … our circumcising the foreskin of our hearts refers to our sincere efforts to come close to G-d by fulfilling the Torah and *mitzvos*. In the merit of his repentance, we will be redeemed from exile. (*Torah Or,* Genesis, 13 [Wagshul])

---

[1] Cf. Leviticus 26:41 and Deuteronomy 10:16, 30:6.

Therefore, man's circumcision of his heart (i.e., repentance) is something he does on his own initiative in this present age. The circumcision of heart that comes from HaShem is an act of God in the Messianic Age. It is explained as "a revelation of G-dliness flowing from heaven above, downward, since it is reciprocation from G-d for our prior efforts to perceive spirituality. Whereas before the redemption, we had to try to remove the 'foreskin' that concealed G-d from our perception, after the redemption G-d will reveal Himself to us."[2]

COVERING OF THE HEART

🌿 *Now, in circumcision there are two operations. (65)*

Chasidic teaching carries the circumcision analogy a step further: "Now, in circumcision there are two operations; after the circumcision proper comes the uncovering of the corona, without which circumcision is not valid. First the thick skin is circumcised, and then the thinner skin is stripped away." The thick outer skin represents the obvious misdeeds and sins a man commits. The thinner skin represents the far more subtle condition of the heart. Unless both skins are removed, the circumcision is invalid: "Beware of the false circumcision. For we are the true circumcision, who worship in the Spirit of God and glory in the Messiah Yeshua."[3] Levertoff's sources teach that the second phase of circumcision can only be accomplished by God through the coming of the Messiah:

> Now, in circumcision there are two grades: *milah* and *peri'ah*, which (apply respectively to) the coarse prepuce and the thin membrane. With respect to the prepuce of the heart there are likewise coarse and delicate desires. These require *milah* and *peri'ah*, and "Having circumcised and not having uncovered is tantamount to not having circumcised," because, after all, the innermost point of the heart is still covered in a garment of thin sack-cloth: in a state of exile and captivity. Now, concerning the excision of the prepuce itself it is written: "And you shall excise the prepuce of your heart," i.e., *you*, by yourselves. But the removal of the thin membrane is a difficult matter for man, and of this it was said that with the coming of the Messiah "*the Lord, your G-d, will circumcise your heart ... to love the Lord your G-d with all your heart and all your soul, for the sake of your life*," i.e., because the Lord alone is literally your whole life. (*Igeret HaKodesh* 4 [Kehot])

This is in keeping with what the apostles taught about circumcision of the heart. Paul says that "circumcision is that which is of the heart, by the Spirit, not by the letter,"[4] and that in Messiah, "We were also circumcised with a circumcision made without hands, in the removal of the body of the flesh by the circumcision of Messiah."[5]

---

[2] *Torah Or,* Genesis, 13 (Wagshul).
[3] Philippians 3:2–3.
[4] Romans 2:29.
[5] Colossians 2:11.

THE PANGS OF HELL

🌿 *The motive for repentance should not be fear of the pangs of hell, but "the sorrow for our own soul which has fallen from its highest state to the depths of sin, from God's palace to the lower places of impurity." (65)*

A sinner who repents because he fears punishment from God is like a criminal who resists the temptation to rob his fellow only because he fears being arrested and put in jail. If it were not for the fear of prison, he would certainly rob his fellow.

When a person loves HaShem, he does not repent because he fears punishment. Instead, he understands that a sin is a blasphemy against his own soul which has its source in the Holy One, blessed is He. He feels anguish over the thought that his sin lowers his soul and separates him from the Most High. His love for HaShem draws him to repent, and fear of hell is hardly a thought at all.

ASCETICISM

🌿 *Fasting, although an outward expression of repentance, is not one of its essentials. (65)*

One might suppose that repentance requires severe treatment of the body and mortification of the flesh through ascetic disciplines like fasting. Disciples of our Master are expected to fast on occasion; as He Himself says, "Whenever you fast,"[6] and He says, "The days will come when the bridegroom is taken away from them, and then they will fast."[7] However, our path is not one of severe asceticism. Our Master was known to fast, but "the Son of Man came eating and drinking."[8] Note the following from *Tzava'at Harivash*: "It is preferable to serve God in joy, without self-mortifications, because the latter cause feelings of depression."[9]

Levertoff acknowledges that fasting does serve as an "outward expression of repentance," but he also points to the Talmudic passage that says, "We shall have to give account of everything in this world that we might have enjoyed and did not."[10]

> Fasting, self-mortification, may be means through which man expresses remorse. They may be acts of purification, of self-cleansing. But they do not constitute repentance … they do not touch sin itself. They do not tackle the root and source in the heart: ignorance, carelessness, neglect, wrong attitudes, egocentricity, self-justification.[11]

---

6   Matthew 6:16.

7   Matthew 9:15.

8   Matthew 11:19.

9   *Tzava'at Harivash* 56 (Schochet).

10   y.*Kiddushin* 66d.

11   Schochet, *The Mystical Dimension Volume Two*, 23. Cf. *Igeret HaTeshuvah* 1–3.

Paul warns against relying on ascetic practices: "These are matters which have, to be sure, the appearance of wisdom in self-made religion and self-abasement and severe treatment of the body, but are of no value against fleshly indulgence."[12] This is the meaning of the words, "Rend your heart and not your garments."[13]

SPARKS IN THE FOOD

🌿 *Food should not only strengthen us for God's service, but, by concentrating our minds on the giver of all good gifts, we should spiritualize the material. (66)*

Chasidic philosophy discourages fasting because fasting prevents us from releasing the godly sparks that are contained in the food. Like all things in the material world, food contains within it sparks of godly potential.

In what way does food contain sparks of godly potential? Food nourishes the body and therefore provides energy which the body can use to serve God. For example, the food eaten at breakfast fuels the body while the body engages in study of the Torah. When we use food to provide us with the necessary vitality to better serve God, we are using it for its intended purpose. We are then releasing its godly potential. In addition, food provides us with the occasion to bless God, thanking Him for provision, both before we eat and after we eat. In this way, the so-called sparks are released.

The apostles placed great emphasis on the importance of breaking bread together and the table fellowship of believers. They transformed meals into "love feasts"[14]; "they were continually devoting themselves … to fellowship, to the breaking of bread and to prayer."[15]

> Day by day continuing with one mind in the temple, and breaking bread from house to house, they were taking their meals together with gladness and sincerity of heart, praising God and having favor with all the people. (Acts 2:46–47)

Some Chasidim even regarded the meal as akin to the service in the Holy Temple:

> Once, Rabbi Monele Karliner entered the tish [table] of Rabbi Shmuel of Karlin and the Ratner Maggid was cutting the meat for him. His face was burning like a torch, and he took a piece of meat and put it in his mouth and said: I eat this with the same intent as the High Priest in the Holy Temple would eat the sin offering; then he took another piece and said, this one, as a burnt offering.[16]

---

[12] Colossians 2:23.

[13] Joel 2:13.

[14] Jude 1:12.

[15] Acts 2:42.

[16] Allan Nadler, "Holy Kugel: The Sanctification of Ashkenazic Ethnic Foods in Chasidism," in *Food and Judaism: A Special Issue of Studies in Jewish Civilization Volume 15* (ed. Leonard J. Greenspoon, Ronald A. Simkins, Gerald Shapiro; Omaha: Creighton University Press, 2005), 193–214. Nadler also sees similarities between Chasidic meals and the Last Supper in Christian thought.

In these ways, the apostles and the Chasidim elevated the otherwise animal-act of eating food to a spiritual level.[17] Likewise, we can "spiritualize the material and gather the 'soul sparks' which are contained in the food, and help them to ascend with our prayers to heaven." By serving God in this way, "we co-operate with God in this process of spiritualization" of the material world.

INGATHERING OF SPARKS

🌿 *When the Messiah comes, God will gather the scattered sparks again and unite them with Himself. (66)*

"The divine sparks of the soul are scattered through sin."[18] The Torah says that at the time of the final redemption, HaShem will gather the children of Israel together and return them to the land:

> If your outcasts are at the ends of the earth, from there the LORD your God will gather you, and from there He will bring you back. (Deuteronomy 30:4)

In a footnote on this concept, Levertoff comments on Deuteronomy 30:4 by citing a strange, mystical anecdote which speaks of the souls of unrepentant sinners unable to enter into heavenly mansions, suspended in the air and languishing in Gehenna.[19] In the anecdote, such souls cling to the prayers and to the soul of a true tzaddik ("righteous one") who, by merit of his righteousness, enables the souls of the sinners to ascend to paradise. Levertoff has in mind our righteous Messiah who "who gave Himself as a ransom for all,"[20] "descended into the lower parts of the earth,"[21] and "ascended far above all the heavens," leading a host of captives.[22]

Since the Messiah is the agent of the final redemption spoken of in Deuteronomy 30:4, He is responsible for the ingathering. This ingathering of sparks is in accord with the coming of the Son of Man: "He will send forth His angels with a great trumpet, and they will gather together His elect from the four winds, from one end of the sky to the other."[23] Levertoff's sources depict the time of the Messianic ingathering as a great regathering of the sparks of godliness which are scattered throughout the created universe. At that time, all that is wrong shall be righted, and all that is amiss shall be squared. All godly potential will be realized.

---

17 See also Louis Jacobs, "Eating as an Act of Worship in Hasidic Thought," in *Studies in Jewish Religious and Intellectual History* (ed. Siegfried Stein and Raphael Loewe; Alabama: The University of Alabama Press, 1979), 157–166. Cf. Joel Hecker, "The Blessing in the Belly: Mystical Satiation in Medieval Kabbalah," in *Food and Judaism: A Special Issue of Studies in Jewish Civilization Volume 15* (ed. Leonard J. Greenspoon, Ronald A. Simkins, Gerald Shapiro; Omaha: Creighton University Press, 2005), 257–279.

18 Paul P. Levertoff, "Jewish Mystical Thoughts on Repentance and Forgiveness," *Church and the Jews* 77 (October 1928): 10.

19 Levertoff also cites *Kav HaYasher* 1 in relating the traditional Jewish belief about Gehenna that it is a place of "tribulations and afflictions" which every soul that has sinned must go through for purification.

20 1 Timothy 2:6.

21 Ephesians 4:9.

22 Ephesians 4:10.

23 Matthew 24:31.

The day in which "God will gather the scattered sparks again and unite them with Himself" is seen in the following verse: "And the LORD will be king over all the earth. On that day the LORD will be one and His name one."[24]

PREPARE THE WAY OF HASHEM

🌿 *But we should prepare the way for Him by repenting daily and by helping others to repent. (66)*

The Torah describes the Messianic ingathering as a time of national repentance. All Israel is told: You will "return to the LORD your God and obey Him with all your heart and soul according to all that I command you today, you and your sons."[25] For this reason, Chasidic philosophy teaches that "we should prepare the way for Him by repenting daily and by helping others to repent."

> Therefore, when we have received forgiveness for our sins, we should not be self-ishly satisfied, but should pray for others, in order that we may help them on the wings of our prayers to a higher state. We should pray thus, "May it be Thy pleasure, O Lord our God, and God of our Fathers, to make an opening in the Throne of Thy Glory for the repentance of … and may all who break Thy commandments receive a new heart to do Thy Will with all their strength. For Thy Hand is stretched out to receive sinners who repent, and to bring them again to Thee. Blessed are Thou, O Lord, who has pleasure in repentance."[26]

The concept of repentance to prepare the way for Messiah is a constant theme in the Gospels and all the Apostolic Scriptures. John the Immerser came preaching repentance to prepare Israel to receive her King. "This is the one about whom it is written, 'Behold, I send My messenger ahead of you, who will prepare your way before you.'"[27] The message of the gospel was a call to repent in anticipation of the Messianic Age.

> From that time Yeshua began to preach and say, "Repent, for the kingdom of heaven is at hand." (Matthew 4:17)

"My brethren, if any among you strays from the truth and one turns him back, let him know that he who turns a sinner from the error of his way will save his soul from death and will cover

---

[24] Zechariah 14:9 (ESV).

[25] Deuteronomy 30:2.

[26] Paul P. Levertoff, "Jewish Mystical Thoughts on Repentance and Forgiveness," *Church and the Jews* 77 (October 1928): 11.

[27] Matthew 11:10, Malachi 3:1.

a multitude of sins."[28] For, "what sort of people ought you to be in holy conduct and godliness, looking for and hastening the coming of the day of God."[29]

THE POOR ONES

> *"The meek ones" are those whose joy in God increases through the keeping of the Law. But the "poor ones" are the repentant sinners, the spiritual beggars. (67)*

Isaiah 29:19 says, "The [meek] also will increase their gladness in the LORD, and the [poor ones] of mankind will rejoice in the Holy One of Israel." Levertoff's sources interpret this verse as referring to the righteous and to penitent sinners respectively. The "meek" are those who have accumulated some measure of merit through obedience to God. Their merit will be increased and rewarded as gladness in HaShem. The "poor ones of mankind" "are the repentant sinners, the spiritual beggars." They have no merit of their own to claim. They suffer from a poverty of righteousness.

One prominent sect of early Jewish believers identified themselves with the "poor ones" mentioned in Isaiah 29:19 and similar passages. The Hebrew for "poor ones" is *evyon* (אביון). Their sect identified themselves as the "Poor Ones," i.e., *Evyonim* (אביונים), also known as the "Ebionites." The name refers to one who completely throws Himself upon the mercy of God, claiming no personal merit before HaShem.

This is comparable to the words of our Master in Matthew 5:3: "Blessed are the poor in spirit, for theirs is the kingdom of heaven."[30] "Because they have no … good works, they have only *one* desire, God Himself. And He becomes their only joy."

THE GREATNESS OF REPENTANCE

> *The sinner, in whose soul the light of the divine fire has been quenched, is greater, when he repents, than the righteous who have no need for repentance. (67)*

We are commanded, "Do not quench the Spirit,"[31] but, "if anyone sins, we have an Advocate with the Father, Yeshua Messiah the righteous."[32] If we become guilty, we should not mourn and become depressed. Rather, we should immediately repent for the wrong we committed and strive to serve HaShem more diligently than before. "Better is one hour of repentance and good deeds in this world than the whole life of the world to come."[33] "I tell you that in the same way, there will

---

[28] James 5:19–20.

[29] 2 Peter 3:11–12.

[30] Cf. Levertoff in his commentary to Matthew. On Matthew 5:3 he says, "The words describe not just the poor in earthly goods, but the 'remnant' who wait for the Messiah" (Levertoff, *St. Matthew*, 11).

[31] 1 Thessalonians 5:19.

[32] 1 John 2:1.

[33] m.*Avot* 4:22 (Hertz).

be more joy in heaven over one sinner who repents than over ninety-nine righteous persons who need no repentance."[34]

Levertoff's sources say that the place of the penitent sinner is even greater than that of the righteous who does not need to repent, because the sinner "throws himself entirely into the arms of God." This was the cry of the penitent thief crucified with our Master, to whom Yeshua said, "Truly I say to you, today you shall be with Me in Paradise."[35]

> Happy are the penitent who in the space of one day, one hour, nay, one second, can draw near to the Holy One, as near as even the truly righteous in the space of many years ... the penitent immediately finds entrance, and is brought close to the Holy One, blessed be He. R. Jose said: "We have been taught that the place assigned to the penitent in the next world is one where even the wholly righteous are not permitted to enter, as the former are the nearest of all to the King; they are more devoted and strive more intently to draw near to the King. For there are many abodes prepared by the Holy One, blessed be He, for the righteous in the next world, each one according to his grade." (*Zohar* I, 129a–129b (Soncino])

For those who are forgiven much love much, but those who are forgiven little love little.[36] "How blessed is the one whom You choose and bring near to You to dwell in Your courts. We will be satisfied with the goodness of Your house, Your holy temple."[37]

STAND UPON THE ROCK

When Moses was to bring down the "forgiving love" of God to Israel, he had to stand upon a rock to receive it. (67)

Moses implored HaShem to be merciful and forgive Israel for the sin of the golden calf. "Then the LORD said, 'Behold, there is a place by Me, and you shall stand there on the rock.'"[38] This rock may be compared to the Messiah, about whom it is said, "Behold, I lay in Zion a stone of stumbling and a rock of offense, and he who believes in Him will not be disappointed."[39]

Levertoff says, "When a sinner is converted, he brings down the *hidden* fire of the Divine love. This 'forgiving love' of God passes all understanding." In another place, he elucidates upon the concept and compares the "forgiving love" of God to the "new light" that will be revealed in the Messianic Era:

---

[34] Luke 15:7.

[35] Luke 23:43.

[36] Cf. Luke 7:47.

[37] Psalm 65:4.

[38] Exodus 33:21.

[39] Romans 9:33.

This forgiving love of God is greater than the love which His reason causes Him to bear to us. Therefore Israel prays in the "days of repentance"—in the ten days between the New Year and the Day of Atonement—that God should send them a new light, namely, that the hidden, forgiving love of God should be revealed in that season in all its power.[40]

Believers in our Master Yeshua need not wait for the revelation of the Messianic Era to experience the "new light" of God's "forgiving love." When a sinner repents of his evil ways, he will be renewed "by the Holy Spirit, whom He poured out upon us richly through Yeshua Messiah our Savior,"[41] and "the peace of God, which surpasses all understanding, will guard your hearts and your minds"[42] in your righteous Messiah.

> [The truly penitent sinner's] premeditated sins become transmuted into veritable merits, which is achieved through "repentance out of love," coming from the depths of the heart, with great love and fervor, and from a soul passionately desiring for G-d like a parched desert soil. For inasmuch as his soul had been in a barren wilderness, and in the shadow of death, which is the *sitra achra* [the other side], and infinitely removed from the light of the Divine Countenance, his soul now thirsts [for G-d] even more than the souls of the righteous, as our Sages say: "In the place where penitents stand, not even the perfectly righteous can stand." It is concerning the repentance out of such great love that they have said: "The penitent's premeditated sins become, in his case, like virtues," since thereby he has attained to this great love. (*Tanya* 7, [Kehot])

> In the place where penitents stand even the wholly righteous cannot stand, as it says: Peace, peace to him that was far and to him that is near (Isaiah 57:19)—to him that was far first, and then to him that is near. (b.*Berachot* 34b)

TWO LOVES

✍ *The love of man to God which comes from the keeping of the Law is a love which proceeds from the "outer side" of the heart, but the love which the repentant sinner feels for God comes from within the heart. (67)*

Levertoff's sources contrast two types of love for HaShem. One is the love which inspires a man to live in obedience to God. This love proceeds from the "outer side" of a man's heart. The other is the love which man feels for God because he has not been obedient but has been forgiven nonetheless. This love proceeds from the innermost parts of a man's heart. This relates to the concept above

---

[40] Paul P. Levertoff, "Jewish Mystical Thoughts on Repentance and Forgiveness," *Church and the Jews* 77 (October 1928): 9.

[41] Titus 3:5–6.

[42] Philippians 4:7 (ESV).

which speaks of the candle and the differences between the outer yellow flame and the inner blue one. A man may observe the commandments of the Torah from mere knowledge of its contents. He may even do so without love. If so, he keeps the Torah from the outer side of the heart. Love for God and the desire to obey Him, which is inspired by the knowledge that God has pardoned a man's sin, proceeds from the inner heart. "For having lived without the means of grace, he has nothing to bring before God, and can only pour out his heart before Him."[43]

> The sinner repents to such an extent that his premeditated sins become transmuted into veritable merits, which is achieved through "repentance out of love," coming from the depths of the heart, with great love and fervour, and from a soul passionately desiring to cleave to the blessed G-d like a parched desert soil. (*Tanya* 7 [Kehot])

This concept is well elucidated by the story of the sinful woman who wept over our Master's feet[44] and our Master's parable of the two debtors:

> A moneylender had two debtors: one owed five hundred denarii, and the other fifty. When they were unable to repay, he graciously forgave them both. So which of them will love him more? (Luke 7:41–42)

WILL OF ALL WILLS

🌿 *This "will of all wills" will be perfectly manifested in the Messianic times. (68)*

We often speak of God's will and seek after His will. Our Master taught us to pray, "Your will be done, on earth as it is in heaven."[45] When He prayed in Gethsemane, He said, "Not My will, but Yours be done."[46] The mystics speak of God's will on two levels. On the one hand is the revelation of His will in Torah and in His providence in all things. On the other hand is a deeper level of God's will which emanates from His very innermost being—the unknowable *Ein Sof.* This can be illustrated with the following analogy:

In any situation, a person has choices set before him, and he demonstrates his will in the choices he makes. However, the limitation presented by the choices may not be the person's ultimate will. For example, imagine a situation in which a lifeguard sees two swimmers struggling in the water. He immediately realizes that he cannot save both of the swimmers, so he decides to rescue one of them but must let the other drown. He demonstrates his will by deciding which one to save. But his ultimate will would have been to save both.

---

43 Paul P. Levertoff, "Jewish Mystical Thoughts on Repentance and Forgiveness," *Church and the Jews* 77 (October 1928): 9.

44 Luke 7:36–39.

45 Matthew 6:10.

46 Luke 22:42.

The analogy is imperfect because a human's will and choices cannot be compared to Him whose thoughts and ways are higher than ours as the heavens are higher than the earth. However, it does illustrate the concept that beyond God's revealed will, He has a perfect and ultimate will. The mystics refer to this highest, perfect will of God as the "will of all wills," and the Crown (*keter*, כתר) of HaShem.[47]

The will of all wills is not a particular desire or choice focused upon some goal within the finite universe. It is HaShem's highest, original Supreme Will which preceded all of His attributes, manifestations, expressions, and revelation. As such, the will of all wills transcends even His will and wisdom as revealed within His holy Torah. Levertoff says that in the Messianic Era, the "'will of all wills' will be perfectly manifested," and that the will of wills is manifested in the "'sin-forgiving love' of God." The Apostle Paul alludes to this sin-forgiving love as an expression of the will of all wills when he speaks of "the mystery which for ages has been hidden in God who created all things."[48] This mystery is "made known through the assembly to the rulers and the authorities in heavenly places … in accordance with the eternal purpose which he carried out in the Messiah Yeshua our Lord."[49]

DAY OF ATONEMENT

When the high priest entered the holy of holies, the place where God dwells alone, in order to make atonement for the people, dressed in linen garments, he represented God's forgiveness as being something unique and independent of man's piety and his good works. (68)

Like the high priest on the Day of Atonement, the Messiah entered the true Temple in heaven; "through His own blood, He entered the holy place once for all, having obtained eternal redemption."[50] This was "independent of man's piety and his good works." "For the law having a shadow of good things to come, and not the very image of the things, can never with those sacrifices which they offered year by year continually make the comers thereunto perfect."[51] The perfection granted through the atonement made through the Messiah's own blood is seen in the symbolism in the garments of the high priest. In Chasidic symbolism, white symbolizes "the pure forgiveness of God which is independent of man's work." The priest's garments were linen, "because the flax has *one* flower on *one* stalk," displaying that there is only one sacrifice which is perfect and is offered only once.

---

[47] The Supreme Will (*Ratzon HaElyon*, רצון העליון).

[48] Ephesians 3:9.

[49] Ephesians 3:10–11. Cf. John 6:40.

[50] Hebrews 9:12.

[51] Hebrews 10:1 (KJV).

TRUE REPENTANCE

🌿 *True repentance consists in the longing that God should let His countenance shine upon us, that His relationship to us should be the relationship of one personality to another. (68)*

If a person does not turn to God out of true repentance and surrender himself completely, then God is unable to "let His countenance shine upon" him. The *Tanya* elaborates:

> However, that which does not surrender itself to G-d, but is a separate thing by itself, does not receive its vitality from the holiness of the Holy One, blessed be He, that is, from the very inner essence and substance of the holiness itself, but from "behind its back," as it were. (*Tanya* 6 [Kehot])

The true penitent desires that God's "forgiveness should come to us from the innermost part of His Will—not like that of a man who throws a gift behind his back to his enemy, in whose face he cannot look" because the giver of the gift does not have his heart into presenting of the gift to his enemy and thus cannot tolerate to face his enemy. Instead, regarding the true penitent, Levertoff says, "The Lord thy God will make His countenance to shine upon thee; the Lord will circumcise thy heart."[52]

The man who does not surrender himself in repentance says in his heart that he is a separate entity unto himself and is not subject to God. Concerning this man the *Talmud* says, "Every man in whom is haughtiness of spirit, the Holy One, blessed be He, declares, I and he cannot both dwell in the world."[53]

UNEXPECTED REPENTANCE

🌿 *Just as the Messiah comes unexpectedly, the awakening of the sinner towards repentance comes unexpectedly. (68)*

The Messiah comes unexpectedly. The *Talmud* says, "Three come unawares: Messiah, a found article, and a scorpion."[54] "Behold, I am coming like a thief. Blessed is the one who stays awake and keeps his clothes, so that he will not walk about naked and men will not see his shame."[55] "Therefore be on the alert, for you do not know which day your Lord is coming."[56] Like the unexpected coming of the Messiah so is the awakening of the sinner. Repentance is a gift from God. "Thanks

---

[52] "Jewish Mystical Thoughts on Repentance and Forgiveness," *Church and the Jews* 77 (October 1928): 11; *Tanya* 47.

[53] b.*Sotah* 5a.

[54] b.*Sanhedrin* 97a.

[55] Revelation 16:15.

[56] Matthew 24:42.

be to God for His indescribable gift!"[57] In the Messianic Era, this gift will be bestowed upon Israel as a whole:

> What happens in the future will happen to Israel as a whole, happens to the individual now when there is true repentance: the Divine spark is set free and ascends to Heaven to unite itself to God, its true life. [58]

THE PRODIGAL SON

When the wanderer returned, the father's delight over him was greater than the joy he had felt in the continuous presence of the son who had stayed at home. (69)

Levertoff presents two parables to illustrate HaShem's relationship with the penitent sinner. The first involves a father with a disobedient son. The father indicated his displeasure by hiding his face from his son for a time, but this withdrawal was born out of love, not spite. "This is in order that when [the father] again reveals himself to his son, he should call him 'Abba, Abba,' and the latter may realize afresh how much his father means to him."[59] When the son repented, the father turned his attention to him all "the more strongly."

The second involves a king who had two sons, one a rebel, the other obedient. When the rebellious son repented, the father's joy over him was even greater than his joy over the obedient son who had not strayed.

"I tell you that in the same way, there will be more joy in heaven over one sinner who repents than over ninety-nine righteous persons who need no repentance."[60] "We had to celebrate and rejoice, for this brother of yours was dead and has begun to live, and was lost and has been found."[61]

---

[57] 2 Corinthians 9:15.

[58] Paul P. Levertoff, "Jewish Mystical Thoughts on Repentance and Forgiveness," *Church and the Jews* 77 (October 1928): 11.

[59] Ibid., 8.

[60] Luke 15:7.

[61] Luke 15:32.

LOVE IN THE FOURTH GOSPEL

THE FELLOWSHIP OF BELIEVERS

The predominant and determining note of the life of the early church is [fellowship]. (73)

In the six chapters of *Love and the Messianic Age,* Levertoff presented a Chasidic discourse on the love between man and God in this age and in the Messianic Era. Throughout those chapters, he labored to display the concept of love and its relation to various aspects of the life of a Chasid. In so doing, he drew primarily from the literature of the mystical Chasidic world. In the epilogue, Levertoff turns his attention to the concept of love as taught in the Gospels and Epistles. The Gospel of John best shows the love of our Master for His disciples and how this love is a direct outpouring of the love that exists between our Master and His Father in heaven.

The epilogue sets out to prove the thesis with which Levertoff started this work, namely that the concept of love as found in the entirety of the apostles' writings (and especially in the Gospels) is no different than that espoused by Chasidic Judaism, except that among the apostles it was of higher quality and actual realization.[1] That is to say that the aspirations of Chasidic Judaism are realities in the gospel. This higher quality and realization occurs as a result of the Word of God dwelling within us; as it says, "And the Word became flesh and dwelt in us."[2]

In the opening statement of the epilogue, Levertoff notes that the early believers were characterized by fellowship. "And they devoted themselves to the apostles' teaching and fellowship, to the breaking of bread and the prayers."[3] The same emphasis on unity, known as *achdut* ("unity," אחדות), is found among the Chasidim. Levertoff quotes Acts 4:32: "The multitude of the believers were of one heart and of one soul," as an example of Chasidic *achdut.* Love for one another was the defining characteristic of the Messianic fellowship of early believers.

---

[1] See Levertoff's remarks in his Preface on page viii of *Love and the Messianic Age.*

[2] John 1:14 (author's literal translation).

[3] Acts 2:42 (ESV). Cf. also 1 John 1:3. Several texts from the Pauline corpus also speak of the fellowship that exists among the early believers.

THE SON OF GOD

🌿 *The love of God is concentrated in the Messiah, His Son, and only through Him He loves the world. (74)*

The Son is the firstborn, meaning that He receives first place in all things. In the biblical economy, a man's firstborn was his principal heir and the carrier of his name. Because of his position as Son of God, the Messiah is the inheritor of all humanity and the created universe. But the greatest gift the Son receives is that of the Spirit of the Father, a gift given beyond measure. "Through the Spirit the Father enables Him to participate in His creative and redemptive activities: 'He shows Him all that He doeth.'"

Genesis 1:2 says that "The Spirit of God was moving over the surface of the waters." The *Midrash Rabbah* explains, "This alludes to the spirit of Messiah, as you read [in Isaiah 11:2], "The Spirit of the LORD will rest on Him."[4] "All things came into being through Him, and apart from Him nothing came into being that has come into being."[5] The unity of the Father and the Son displays the depth of the Father's love towards the Son.

FOR GOD SO LOVED THE WORLD

🌿 *The Son is the organ of God's love, and the intensity of this love is shown in the gift. (74)*

The Son of God is the agent through whom God expresses His love for the creation. "For God so loved the world, that He gave His only begotten Son."[6] Through the Son, the Father extends His love to the world; He gave the Son to His creation in order for the creation to draw near to the Father. "There was the true Light which, coming into the world, enlightens every man."[7] "And we know that the Son of God has come, and has given us understanding so that we may know Him who is true; and we are in Him who is true, in His Son Yeshua Messiah. This is the true God and eternal life."[8]

KIDDUSH HASHEM

🌿 *God's love for His Son brings forth a corresponding love of the Son for Him. (74)*

God's love for the Son is reciprocated in the Son's love for the Father. The Son expresses His love for HaShem through glorifying Him and sanctifying His Name. In Judaism, the highest form of obedience, sacrifice, and even martyrdom for the sake of God is called *Kiddush HaShem* (קדוש השם),

---

4   *Genesis Rabbah* 2:4 (Soncino).

5   John 1:3.

6   John 3:16.

7   John 1:9.

8   1 John 5:20.

the sanctification of God's Name. Our Master lived a life of *Kiddush HaShem* and died a death of *Kiddush HaShem*. The Son says, "Now My soul has become troubled; and what shall I say, 'Father, save Me from this hour'? But for this purpose I came to this hour. Father, glorify Your name."[9] "Now is the Son of Man glorified, and God is glorified in Him; if God is glorified in Him, God will also glorify Him in Himself, and will glorify immediately."[10] Levertoff says that the Son "lives and dies for God's honour. His love is a conscious self-oblation to the will of God."

"I am the good shepherd; the good shepherd lays down His life for the sheep."[11] "Greater love has no one than this, that one lay down his life for his friends."[12]

IT IS FINISHED

His will is "to finish the work of Him who sent Him." (75)

The Son's will is to complete the work of the Father. "For the works which the Father has given Me to accomplish—the very works that I do—testify about Me, that the Father has sent Me."[13] Our Master says to His disciples, "We must work the works of Him who sent Me as long as it is day; night is coming when no one can work."[14] "It is His duty towards the Father, for through it He makes God's goodness visible." When the Son does the work of the Father, it brings glory and honor to the Father. The Father rewards Him for being a faithful Son through those He has given to Him. "I glorified You on the earth, having accomplished the work which You have given Me to do."[15] Concerning those whom the Father has given, the Son says, "I give eternal life to them, and they will never perish; and no one will snatch them out of My hand. My Father, who has given them to Me, is greater than all; and no one is able to snatch them out of the Father's hand."[16]

GROUNDED IN THE LOVE OF HASHEM

Thus, Jesus' love for men is grounded in the love of God. (75)

Just as HaShem loves the Son because the Son is obedient, so, too, does the Son love His disciples when they are obedient as well. He desires to be one with His disciples just as He is one with His Father. "If you keep My commandments, you will abide in My love; just as I have kept My Father's

---

9   John 12:27–28.
10 John 13:31–32.
11 John 10:11.
12 John 15:13.
13 John 5:36.
14 John 9:4.
15 John 17:4.
16 John 10:28–29.

commandments and abide in His love."[17] "The glory which You have given Me I have given to them, that they may be one, just as We are one."[18]

Levertoff says, "As His love for men has its source solely in God, men's desires do not move Him to action. The people could not force Him to do 'signs and wonders' against His will." "I can do nothing on My own initiative. As I hear, I judge; and My judgment is just, because I do not seek My own will, but the will of Him who sent Me."[19] The Son only desires to obey the Father and therefore "it is not mere caprice that rules Him." Those who come to the Son become a special treasure to Him; He guards them as a shepherd guards his sheep.

MIRACLES OF THE MASTER

His miracles are acts of His all-powerful love, revealing the will of the Father. (76)

The Master's miracles were not signs for the sake of signs, nor miracles for the sake of astounding the masses. Instead, they rose out of His compassion for human beings. "Seeing the people, He felt compassion for them, because they were distressed and dispirited like sheep without a shepherd."[20] "The compassion of Jesus for human suffering and need is in no instance a mere emotion, but is always translated into action. His miracles are acts of His all-powerful love, revealing the will of the Father." The miracles of the Master demonstrate that the Father wills an end to suffering and sorrow. The works done by the Son are not His own but rather those the Father sent Him to do.

Nevertheless, "All His works, although primarily deeds of love, are 'signs' intended to reveal His glory and to awaken men's faith in His Messiahship." "If I do not do the works of My Father, do not believe Me; but if I do them, though you do not believe Me, believe the works, so that you may know and understand that the Father is in Me, and I in the Father."[21] When questioned as to whether He was the Messiah, our Master responded, "I told you, and you do not believe; the works that I do in My Father's name, these testify of Me."[22]

The signs performed by our Master are all signs of His Messiahship. By providing wine at the wedding in Cana, He showed the people that the joy of the marriage between the Messiah and His bride is soon to take place. By providing bread for the multitude, He taught that He is the Last Redeemer, just as Moses, the First Redeemer, provided bread to the people of Israel in the desert. The Son also gives sight to the blind and brings the dead to life—all expectations of the coming Messiah. "His miracles are, in their immediate as well as in their ultimate purpose, a revelation of His love; for the awakening of faith is a higher proof of love than the healing of the sick and the feeding of the hungry."

---

[17] John 15:10.

[18] John 17:22.

[19] John 5:30. Cf. John 8:28–29.

[20] Matthew 9:36.

[21] John 10:37–38.

[22] John 10:25.

Though the miracles testified to His Messiahship, "He prefers the faith which is awakened by His *word* to that which is based on His *works*." Our Master spoke saying, "Unless you people see signs and wonders, you simply will not believe."[23] However, upon passing through the region of the Samaritans, they "believed because of His word."[24] Our Master prefers that people repent based upon His words as opposed to seeing signs to stir their repentance.

GRACE FOR GRACE

All that God has given to Him, He gives to them. (77)

He gives to the disciples His fullness. "For of His fullness we have all received, and grace upon grace,"[25] "which means, grace succeeding grace perpetually." He gives of His freedom, peace, joy, and glory. He even "declares unto them the Father's Name; i.e., His character, 'that the love wherewith Thou hast loved Me may be in them, and I in them.'" The Name of the Father, that is, His character, is Love; as it says, "We have come to know and have believed the love which God has for us. God is love, and the one who abides in love abides in God, and God abides in Him."[26] "He gives all this by giving Himself. He is the Way, the Truth, and the Life." "We know love by this, that He laid down His life for us,"[27] and "the Son of Man did not come to be served, but to serve, and to give His life a ransom for many."[28]

Levertoff says, "The consummation of His 'giving Himself' is His Death. It is not only the highest expression of His Love, it is its perfection." "Greater love has no one than this, that one lay down his life for his friends."[29] "But God demonstrates His own love toward us, in that while we were sinners, Messiah died for us."[30]

THE EXPECTATION OF LOVE

The whole messianic consciousness of Jesus is expressed in this expectation of love. (78)

By bestowing love upon us, the Master expects to stir up love within us which will be reciprocated toward Him, toward the Father, and toward our fellows. Similarly, by "awakening faith in Himself He awakens faith in God. Thus God Himself is either loved or hated in Him."

The *Mechilta* on Exodus 14:31 says:

---

23 John 4:48.
24 John 4:41.
25 John 1:16.
26 1 John 4:16.
27 1 John 3:16.
28 Matthew 20:28.
29 John 15:13.
30 Romans 5:8.

This teaches you that [for] anyone who has faith in the shepherd of Israel, it's as if he believed in He who spoke, and the world came into being.[31]

Levertoff sums up this quote by saying that the people "proved their faith in God by believing in Moses." Our Master says, "Believe in God, believe also in Me."[32]

"For if you believed Moses, you would believe Me, for he wrote about Me. But if you do not believe his writings, how will you believe My words?"[33] "The world hates Jesus because He reveals its sin."

> This is the judgment, that the Light has come into the world, and men loved the darkness rather than the Light, for their deeds were evil. For everyone who does evil hates the Light, and does not come to the Light for fear that his deeds will be exposed. But he who practices the truth comes to the Light, so that his deeds may be manifested as having been wrought in God. (John 3:19–21)

A FINE RETICENCE

While the apostles readily applied their expressions of endearment to one another, yet with a fine reticence they refrained from applying them to Him. (78)

Levertoff notes that the writings of the apostles do not contain terms of endearment for Yeshua. Though the apostolic community lavished fraternal love on one another, they did not apply the same expressions to the Master. Levertoff explains that their relationship with the Master transcended simple terms of affection and left them tongue-tied. "His love towards them was of such a kind as to leave them without a name for the extra-ordinary response it awakened in their own hearts."

The apostles are continually asking, "Who then is this?"[34] This is similar to the two men who met the risen Messiah on the road to Emmaus: "Then their eyes were opened and they recognized Him; and He vanished from their sight. They said to one another, 'Were not our hearts burning

---

[31] *Mechilta de Rabbi Shimon bar Yochai, BeShallach* 26 (JPS). This midrash is often used in rabbinic and Chasidic literature to promote the idea of connecting to God through a tzaddik, a completely righteous person. One was required to not only believe in HaShem but the *tzaddik* as well. Commenting on this, Rabbi Shloma Majeski writes, "Recognizing that G-d and the *tzaddik* share oneness of spirit means that one's faith in a *tzaddik* is an expression of one's faith in G-d; love for a *tzaddik* is an expression of one's love for G-d; and fear or awe of the *tzaddik* is an expression of one's fear or awe of G-d. This is what makes one's spiritual connection to a *tzaddik* such an undeniable imperative; the connection brings out a person's faith, love and awe for G-d in much greater measure than could otherwise exist" (Rabbi Shloma Majeski, *A Tzaddik and His Students* [Brooklyn, NY: Sichos in English, 2008], 93). Levertoff was familiar with the Chasidic concept and would have had this idea in mind while citing this midrash. For more on this see *Appendix One: The Exalted Rebbe.*

[32] John 14:1.

[33] John 5:46–47.

[34] Mark 4:41.

within us while He was speaking to us on the road, while He was explaining the Scriptures to us?,"[35] "They were 'but as vessels swept onwards to their haven by an irresistible tide of unfailing love.'"

THE LOVE TEST

The test of true love for Him is love for the brethren. (78)

"A new commandment I give you, that you love one another, even as I have loved you, that you also love one another. By this all men will know that you are My disciples, if you have love for one another."[36] By our love for one another we become as one, just as the Son and the Father are One. "It is a reciprocal giving and receiving. This unity of the disciples will be the best proof to the world that God has sent Him." "I in them and You in Me, that they may be perfected in unity, so that the world may know that You sent Me, and loved them, even as You have loved Me."[37]

The church father Jerome relates the following legend about the last days of the life of the Apostle John:

> The blessed evangelist John, when he delayed at Ephesus up to the highest old age and could scarcely be carried to congregation in the hands of disciples and was not able to put together a statement of several words, used to offer in different sayings nothing but: "Little children, love one another." At last the disciples and brethren who were present, tired of the fact that they always heard the same thing, said, "Teacher, why do you always say this?" John made a worthy response: "Because it was the Lord's precept, and if it alone is done, it is enough."[38]

I AND HE

All His gifts to them—"the name of God," His glory—have this end in view.
This mystical oneness of the church, this perfect achdut is founded on the
oneness of Jesus with the Father. (79)

At the Last Seder, Yeshua prayed, "I have manifested Your name to the men whom You gave Me out of the world,"[39] and, "Keep them in Your name, the name which You have given Me, that they may be one even as We are."[40]

---

[35] Luke 24:31–32.

[36] John 13:34–35. Cf. 1 John 4:7–21.

[37] John 17:23.

[38] Jerome in his commentary on Galatians 6:10; see R. Alan Culpepper, *John, the Son of Zebedee* (Columbia, SC: University of South Carolina Press, 1994), 165.

[39] John 17:6.

[40] John 17:11–12.

Levertoff cites these passages as evidence that God's name is one of the manifestations of the unity of the body. To Levertoff, the hidden name of God is not about pronunciations or phonetics or uttering the name of God as it is spelled, but rather it reveals the character of *achdut* ("unity," אחדות) within HaShem that protects His people.

In a footnote, Levertoff suggests that when the Master says He manifested God's Name to His disciples, "the name which you have given me," He was referring to "the hidden name of God" as found in Jewish mysticism, *Ani Vehu* (אני והו), that is "I and He."[41] One scholar has suggested that *Ani Vehu* might be the Hebrew behind the "I am He" (*ego ami*, εγω ειμι) statements of John 18:5, et al.[42]

The name itself has various interpretations. Rashi sees it as an abbreviated, coded reference to the seventy-two-letter name of God. Others see it as alluding to the first words of Ezekiel 1:1 and Jeremiah 40:1, passages which depict the Shechinah going into exile.[43] The Talmud links it to a homiletical reading of Exodus 15:2 that stresses man's imitation of the Creator.[44] A much later formulation in Jewish mystical literature describes the meaning of the name "I and He" as representing perfect unity with God:

> This is my God and I will glorify Him" (Exod. 15:2), [the word *we-'anvehu*, "I will glorify Him," can be read as] I and He (*'ani we-hu'*). When one cleaves to them [the sefirot], the divine Holy Spirit enters into him, in all his sensations and all his movements.[45]

Therefore the name *Ani Vehu*, the so-called secret name of God, reveals a man's closeness and unity with HaShem.

ABIDE IN ME

🌿 *The power to bring forth fruit—that is, to be active in love—rests on communion with Him. (79)*

For the Master's disciples, the aim is love. Love bears fruit in good works, but if we do not remain connected to the source of love, we will be unable to love or produce fruit. "Abide in Me, and I in you. As the branch cannot bear fruit of itself unless it abides in the vine, so neither can you unless

---

41 Based on its usage in rabbinic passages such as m.*Sukkah* 4:5, Rabbi Klein has suggested that this is the secret name of God mentioned in passages such as 1 Enoch 69:14 (See Rabbi G. Klein, *Der älteste christliche Katechismus und die jüdische Propaganda-Literatur* [Berlin: G. Reimer, 1909], 44–55, and Ethelbert Stauffer, *Jesus and His Story* [London: SCM Press, 1960], 149–159). It is found in the Hoshanot prayers of Sukkot vocalized as *Ani Vaho*.

42 See David Catchpole, "You Have Heard His Blasphemy," *Tyndale Bulletin* 16 (October 1965): 10–18.

43 See Rabbi Avie Gold, *Hoshanos: A New Translation with a Commentary Anthologized from Talmudic, Midrashic and Rabbbinic Sources* (Brooklyn, NY: ArtScroll Mesorah, 1980), 84–85.

44 b.*Shabbat* 133b.

45 Elliot Wolfson, *Through a Speculum that Shines: Vision and Imagination in Medieval Jewish Mysticism* (Princeton: Princeton University Press, 1994), 283. See also the discussion in 332–331.

you abide in Me. I am the vine, you are the branches; he who abides in Me and I in him, he bears much fruit, for apart from Me you can do nothing."[46] The Messiah lets His disciples participate in His creative power. "For we are His workmanship, created in Messiah Yeshua for good works, which God prepared beforehand so that we would walk in them."[47] "Every branch that beareth fruit, he purgeth it, that it may bring forth more fruit."[48] Levertoff explains, "The 'purging' means the freeing from sin; sin will be removed because it disturbs the growth of love. Love is thus the aim; freedom from sin only a means to an end."

"Just as the Father has loved Me, I have also loved you; abide in My love."[49] "From this reciprocal giving and receiving the fellowship's unity is derived." "Behold, how good and how pleasant it is for brothers to dwell together in unity!"[50] "Do not love the world nor the things in the world. If anyone loves the world, the love of the Father is not in him."[51]

HATRED

Hatred separates the church from the world. (80)

The Master says, "If the world hates you, you know that it has hated Me before it hated you."[52] Hatred is a characteristic of the world, but love is a characteristic—even the chief characteristic—of the fellowship of believers. "The one who loves his brother abides in the Light and there is no cause for stumbling in him. But the one who hates his brother is in the darkness and walks in the darkness, and does not know where he is going because the darkness has blinded his eyes."[53] "The proof of the immensity and the satanic character of this hatred is the cross of Christ." This is evidenced by the words of Cleopas as he traveled on the road to Emmaus, "And how the chief priests and our rulers delivered Him to the sentence of death, and crucified Him."[54] "They have both seen and hated Me and My Father as well. But they have done this to fulfill the word that is written in their Law, 'They hated me without a cause.'"[55] This hatred is extended to His disciples: "And you will be hated by all because of My name."[56] "They will deliver you to tribulation, and will kill you, and you will be hated by all nations because of My name."[57] "If the world hates you, you know that it has hated Me before it hated you."[58]

---

[46] John 15:4–5. See Chassidic parallel to this on page 155.
[47] Ephesians 2:10.
[48] John 15:2 (KJV).
[49] John 15:9.
[50] Psalm 133:1.
[51] 1 John 2:15.
[52] John 15:18.
[53] 1 John 2:10–11.
[54] Luke 24:20. Cf. Acts 2:22–24 and 3:13–16.
[55] John 15:24–25.
[56] Luke 21:17.
[57] Matthew 24:9.
[58] John 15:18.

COVENANT LOVE

🖋 *Between God and the world, and therefore also between the church and the world, between life and death, light and darkness, truth and falsehood, love and hatred, children of God and children of the devil, there are only absolute contrasts. (80)*

The holiness of God and the wickedness of the world are opposites. "No compromise can exist between them. There are no *nuances* and intermediate shades." "Do not love the world nor the things in the world. If anyone loves the world, the love of the Father is not in him."[59]

"The conception of love here is not a 'humanitarian' one, in the Hellenic sense, but is an Israelitish covenant relationship." Covenant love is demonstrated through fulfillment of covenant obligations. "He who has My commandments and keeps them is the one who loves Me; and he who loves Me will be loved by My Father, and I will love him and will disclose Myself to him."[60]

LOVE AND THE MESSIANIC AGE

🖋 *The love of God for the world remains to the world something outside itself. His love for the believers expresses itself in the fact that He gives them His spirit, as He does to the Son. (80)*

In its current, broken state, the world is unable to receive the love of God. God's love is a concept that remains outside of the world, and consequently, the world cannot receive His love nor can it receive His Holy Spirit. "For those who are according to the flesh set their minds on the things of the flesh, but those who are of the Spirit, the things of the Spirit. For the mind set on the flesh is death, but the mind set on the Spirit is life and peace."[61] For "we have received, not the spirit of the world, but the Spirit who is from God, so that we may know the things freely given to us by God."[62]

Because the love of God remains outside the world, the experience of love and the expectations of the Messianic Age remain inaccessible to the world. "The purpose of the Divine Love is not anything that might be selfishly appropriated and rejoiced in by its recipients, *but is for the sake of the world,* in order that the discipleship may be extended to all—'that the world might believe.'" "For God so loved the world, that He gave His only begotten Son, that whoever believes in Him shall not perish, but have eternal life. For God did not send the Son into the world to judge the world, but that the world might be saved through Him."[63]

Through the work of Messiah, the love of God is made manifest to us, and we receive the Holy Spirit. "The bestowal of His Spirit, the basis of the new covenant, brings forth a new birth; God in

---

59 1 John 2:15.

60 John 14:21.

61 Romans 8:5–6.

62 1 Corinthians 2:12.

63 John 3:15–16.

His Spirit makes the heart of the believer His habitation, and thus the highest expectation of the Messianic Age is fully realized."

The "highest expectation of the Messianic Age" is that "the tabernacle of God [will be] among men, and He will dwell among them, and they shall be His people, and God Himself will be among them."[64] Those who are in Messiah have already entered into Love and the Messianic Age.

> But blessed are your eyes, because they see; and your ears, because they hear. For truly I say to you that many prophets and righteous men desired to see what you see, and did not see it, and to hear what you hear, and did not hear it. (Matthew 13:16–17)

---

[64] Revelation 21:3.

APPENDIX 1
THE EXALTED REBBE

AN INTRODUCTION TO THE CONCEPT OF DEVEKUT
AND TZADDIKISM IN CHASIDIC THOUGHT

BY TOBY JANICKI

In *Love and the Messianic Age,* Paul Philip Levertoff compares the teaching of Chasidic Judaism with the apostolic-era teaching of faith in Yeshua of Nazareth, but he is strangely silent in regard to the Chasidic concept of "tzaddikism." Chasidic Judaism idealizes the righteous saint (tzaddik). Connection with the righteous saint (tzaddik) and devotion to him is at the center of Chasidic philosophy. A Chasid is, by definition, the disciple of a Chasidic saint. Levertoff's longer dissertation *Die religiöse Denkweise der Chasidim* develops the concept further. For purposes of rounding out this current study, we have included this brief essay.

The word *tzaddik* (צדיק) is derived from the Hebrew word for "righteousness" (*tzedek,* צדק). A true tzaddik is a sinless person. Tzaddik has the sense of "one whose conduct is found to be beyond reproach by the divine Judge."[1] According to the Apostolic Scriptures, there is no such person, "for all have sinned and fall short of the glory of God,"[2] the only exception being Yeshua of Nazareth, who was "tempted in all things as we are, yet without sin."[3] From apostolic reckoning and the perspective of Messianic faith, Yeshua is the only true tzaddik. However, Chasidic Judaism (which operates without the benefit of the New Testament Scriptures) supposes that there might be several such individuals who have completely subjugated their evil inclinations and live their lives as pure vessels for HaShem.[4]

---

[1] Nahum Sarna, *The JPS Torah Commentary: Genesis* (Philadelphia, PA: Jewish Publication Society, 1989), 50.

[2] Romans 3:23.

[3] Hebrews 4:15.

[4] In Chassidic thought there are different types of tzaddikim. Two special levels are the *tzaddik hador* ("the righteous one of the generation," צדיק הדור), who is the special tzaddik for a specific generation, and the *tzaddik yesod olam* ("the righteous one who is the foundation of the world," צדיק יסוד עולם), who is the ultimate tzaddik.

In Chasidic thought, the tzaddik is a miracle-worker. He is an intermediary between man and God. When he suffers, his suffering atones for the sins of his generation. He is a prophet and visionary who can give answers directly from heaven. He is a shepherd for his followers, and he cares for each individual Jew. He is a priest of sorts in that his prayers do not go unanswered: "The effective prayer of a righteous man (tzaddik) can accomplish much."[5] The tzaddik is therefore seen as an intercessor. The tzaddik is the foundation of the world.[6] He "draws everything to him, for the true *Tzaddik* is the foundation of the world and everything derives from him. All the other *Tzaddikim* are only branches of the true *Tzaddik*."[7]

The tzaddik is treated as a king in that his word is absolute and must be obeyed without hesitation or question. He draws disciples around him which form a spiritual type of royal court, and his children often follow in the tzaddik path, thereby establishing dynastic houses of tzaddikim.

Attachment to such a tzaddik elevates one's spiritual status and is the only means for attachment to HaShem himself. The way to reach HaShem is through connection and devotion to a tzaddik. A Chasid is the disciple of a tzaddik. However, the concept of attachment to a tzaddik did not begin with the Chasidic movement. Instead, it is a concept which reaches all the way back to the Talmudic era, and perhaps even to the apostolic era.[8]

ATTACHMENT TO HASHEM

Tzaddikism begins with a Torah command: the commandment of *devekut* (דבקות). *Devekut* is a Hebrew word that means "attachment," and it comes from the root word *davak* (דבק), which means "to cling, cleave, keep close." Yet the concept of *devekut* is not so much a physical action as it is a state of being. The commandment is found in the book of Deuteronomy:

> You shall fear the LORD your God; you shall serve Him and cling (*davak*) to Him, and you shall swear by His name. (Deuteronomy 10:20)

The sages saw that Deuteronomy 10:20 commands us to "cling," "hold fast," and "bind ourselves" to HaShem.[9] The Torah even says that it was *devekut* that preserved the Israelites in the wilderness.[10]

While on the surface it seems plausible that this command can be carried out, there is a problem with clinging to HaShem. Deuteronomy 4:24 says, "The LORD your God is a consuming fire." To the rabbis, the idea of literally clinging to the Holy One did not seem feasible. Human beings

---

[5]   James 5:16.

[6]   Proverbs 10:25.

[7]   Rabbi Nachman, *The Essential Rabbi Nachman* (trans. Avraham Greenbaum; Jerusalem, Israel: Azamra Institute, 2006), 280.

[8]   For a good scholarly study on the history of the tzaddik in Judaism see Aurthur Green, "The Ẓaddiq as *Axis Mundi* in Later Judaism," *Journal of the American Academy of Religion* 45:3 (1977): 327–347.

[9]   This commandment is found in Deuteronomy 11:22; 13:4, and is considered "positive commandment six" according *Rambam*.

[10] Deuteronomy 4:4.

are unholy. Just seeing God means death.[11] Literally approaching and laying hold of HaShem is impossible.

Therefore, the sages reasoned, the commandment of clinging to HaShem can only be fulfilled by clinging to a worthy representative of HaShem. They reinterpreted the commandment to mean that one must cling to a worthy sage or to his disciples, and this clinging would in turn be counted as clinging to the Almighty. Maimonides codifies the commandment of *devekut* this way in his *Book of the Commandments*:

> By this injunction we are commanded to mix and associate with wise men, to be always in their company, and to join with them in every possible manner of fellowship: in eating, drinking, and business affairs, to the end that we may succeed in becoming like them in respect of their actions and in acquiring true opinions from their words. (Rambam, *Sefer HaMitzvot*)[12]

In Hebrew thought, the closer a person is connected to HaShem's agent, whether that agent be a prophet, a sage, or a rabbi, the closer the person is connected with HaShem. A prototype of this can be seen in the life of Moses, who received the commandments and mediated between HaShem and Israel:

> I was standing between the LORD and you at that time, to declare to you the word of the LORD; for you were afraid because of the fire and did not go up the mountain. (Deuteronomy 5:5)[13]

The more carefully Israel clung to Moses and his teaching, the better they were clinging to HaShem. Thus a tzaddik becomes a *shevil* ("pathway," שביל) and a *tzinor* ("pipeline," צנור) to God.

ATTACHMENT TO THE MASTER

The same model applies to the apostolic understanding of our relationship with Yeshua. The concept of *devekut* sheds light on the "oneness" passages in the Gospel of John. For example:

> I am the way, and the truth, and the life; no one comes to the Father but through Me. If you had known Me, you would have known My Father also; from now on you know Him, and have seen Him. (John 14:6–7)

Read with the concept of *devekut* in mind, these words call us to communion with the Father through means of clinging to the Master. In a way similar to the rabbinic concept explained above,

---

[11]   b.*Ketubot* 111b.

[12]   Charles B. Chavel, *Maimonides the Commandments Volume One: Positive*, (New York, NY: Soncino Press, 1967), 9.

[13]   Also Exodus 14:31and Numbers 21:5. The *Mechilta* on Exodus 14:31 expounds on these passages as proof that faith in Moses was a demonstration of faith in HaShem. Another example of an intermediary in Torah is the priests and the Urim and Thumim in Exodus 28:30. Additionally, it was the issue of the need for an intermediary with which Korah and his followers challenged Moses (Numbers 16:3).

the Master reveals the Father to us, and the more we know Yeshua, the more we will know HaShem. From the Torah's perspective of clinging to HaShem, our intimate relationship and connection with Yeshua takes on the level of a mitzvah. By clinging to Him, we are fulfilling the commandment of Deuteronomy 10:20 "to cling" to God.

CLINGING TO THE TZADDIK

Devekut is understood as clinging to a righteous man (tzaddik) in order to cleave to God. The term tzaddik is used many times throughout the Scriptures and is even applied to several individuals in the Gospels: Joseph (the father of Yeshua), Zachariah and Elizabeth, John the Immerser, Simeon the Priest, and Joseph of Aramathea. In church literature it is recorded that James the brother of Yeshua was called James the Righteous and described as "the most just of men" (i.e., a tzaddik) by his contemporaries.[14] It is a term that is used sparingly and only given to people who lived their lives with utmost piety and dedication to the Torah. In these cases, though, the term is used in the figurative sense, not in the absolute theological sense. The New Testament does not mean to imply that these individuals were completely without sin.

In rabbinic literature, the tzaddik is sinless and, in many ways, superhuman. In the *Talmud*, HaShem is reputed to declare, "Who rules Me? It is the righteous."[15] According to this Talmudic passage, the tzaddik—much like Moses in the story of the Golden Calf—is said to have the ability to annul God's decrees of judgment.[16] The *Talmud* goes on to suggest that it is the righteous who are destined to resurrect the dead.[17] For Judaism to suggest that HaShem would allow the tzaddik to partner with Him in resurrecting the dead elevates the righteous to a very high level. In fact seeing a tzaddik was to behold the "very face of the Shechinah."[18] The tzaddik is said to be a mini-temple, a dwelling place for the God's presence here on earth:

> The Beit HaMidrash of Rabbi Eliezer was shaped like an arena, and there was in it a stone, which was reserved for him to sit on. Once Rabbi Joshua came in and began kissing the stone and saying, "This stone is like Mount Sinai, and he who sat on it is like the Ark of the Covenant." (*Song of Songs Rabbah* 1:20)[19]

---

[14] Eusebius, *Ecclesiastical History* 2:23. Additionally we find Simon Peter labeled as a tzaddik by Rabbi Yehudah in *Sefer Chassdim* 191 (see Avraham Ya'akov Finkel, *Sefer Chassidim: The Book of the Pious* [New Jersey: Jason Aronson, 1997], 85).

[15] b.*Moed Katan* 16b. See Joseph Weiss, "The Ṣaddick—Altering the Divine Will," in *Studies in Eastern Jewish Mysticism* (ed. David Goldstein; New York: Oxford University Press, 1985), 183–193.

[16] Commenting on Genesis 12:2, "And so you shall be a blessing," Rashi writes, "The blessings are put into your hands" (ArtScroll). Chasidus uses this to show proof for the power a tzaddik's prayers and blessings. See Majeski, *A Tzaddik and His Students*, 108–109.

[17] b.*Pesachim* 68b.

[18] *Zohar* II, 163b. See also *Zohar* I, 9a. Cf. *Zohar* II, 32a in its comments on Exodus 23:17 where Rabbi Shimon bar Yochai is called "the face of the Lord."

[19] Cf. b.*Rosh HaShannah* 18b; b.*Bava Batra* 4a.

In the eighteenth century, devout Chasidic Jews travelled to visit their teachers, men they believed to be tzaddikim, at the pilgrimage festivals: Passover, Pentecost, and Booths.[20] They made the pilgrimages to fulfill the Torah's command that the Israelites were to go up to the Temple for those festivals.[21] The Chasidic world believed that the tzaddik revealed God's presence here on earth just as the Temple once had.[22] The Chasidim taught that the tzaddik was able to do this through the process of *bittul* ("annulment"), in which he completely divested himself of his own interests so that his entire essence might be emptied and he might become a vessel for HaShem alone.[23] The last Chabad Rebbe, Menachem Schneerson, taught that through this process the tzaddik becomes "the essence and being of God placed in a body."[24] Commenting on Schneerson's words Rabbi Avraham Pevzner believed:

> "The essence and being of God placed in a body" means that a supremely righteous man literally annuls his own identity so that his entire essence becomes God.[25]

Chasidic thought regards the righteous as HaShem's lightning rods throughout the earth, ready to conduct His presence and draw it to the earth. Consider the words of Rebbe Nachman of Breslov:

> No matter what a person needs or is lacking in life—whether in livelihood, health or anything else—it can only be provided through the help of the true Tzaddik and Teacher he is attached to … The source of the spirit of life is the Torah, and therefore it can be received only from the Tzaddik, who is totally bound to the Torah … The Tzaddik hears the sighs of all who are attached to him, for he is the source of life for each one of them.[26]

The tzaddik is the fountainhead of Torah and godliness for his disciples. Rebbe Schneerson said of the previous Lubavitcher Rebbe known as the Rebbe Rayatz:

> Each and every one of us [must] know—i.e., must think deeply and affix his thought on this—that he is indeed the Nasi (prince of the generation) and the head; from him and by him are [directed] all the material and spiritual [Divine] influences in the world; and by being bound to him (and he already directed us in his letters

---

20 See b.*Sukkah* 27b where 2 Kings 4:23 is cited as a proof text for visiting one's teacher on the festivals. Also see *Mishneh Torah, Hilchot Talmud Torah* 5:7.

21 See Exodus 23:14–17, 34:18–23; Deuteronomy 16:16.

22 Even praying at the grave of the tzaddik is considered to be like praying at the Temple. See *Whispers Between Worlds* (trans. Rabbi Eliyahu Touger; Brooklyn, NY: Sichos in English, 2009), 11–17.

23 Cf. Philippians 2:7.

24 Menachem M. Schneersohn, *Likutei Sichos* (37 vols.; Brooklyn: Kehot, 2000), 2:510–511.

25 Avraham Baruch Pevzner, *Al HaTzaddikim* (Kfar Chabad: Beis Agudas Chassidei Chabad, 1991) as summarized by David Berger, *The Rebbe, the Messiah, and the Scandal of Orthodox Indifference* (Oxford: Littman Library of Jewish Civilization, 2001), 97. Rabbi Majeski sees a Torah allusion of this in the phrase "man of God" (*ish haElokim*, איש האלקים) in Deuteronomy 33:1 and Psalm 90:1. He also brings up, citing *Reishis Chochma* and the *Alshich*, that Exodus 25:8, "Let them construct a sanctuary for Me, that I may dwell among them," could be translated "that I may dwell *in* them." See Majeski, *A Tzaddik and His Students*, 30.

26 Rabbi Nathan, *Likutey Etzot: Advice of Rebbe Nachman*, 205.

how and in what way to bind ourselves [to him]) we are bound and united with the spiritual root, with the ultimate Supernal spiritual root. (*Igrot HaKodesh*, 3 Tammuz 5710, 3:331, 635)[27]

Rebbe Nachman believed that all service to HaShem was worthless unless done through attachment to a true tzaddik:

> If a person is not bound to a true Tzaddik, all his devotions are nothing but twisting and turning and pretending to be something he isn't—as if an ape were pretending to be a man. Service of God is nothing without the True Tzaddik.[28]

Rebbe Nachman also spoke of three levels of discipleship: "One in whose heart I am engraved, another who comes to hear my lessons, and third who comes to eat my left-overs."[29]

Chasidic teaching suggests that a tzaddik is often be rejected by his generation, particularly by the "scholars and leaders."[30] The Baal Shem Tov said that "the world does not recognize that they are great tzaddikim, and therefore maligns them."[31] At the same time, it is taught that the true tzaddik will not contest his critics.

This all sounds surprisingly similar to apostolic concepts about Yeshua.

ONENESS

In Chasidic Judaism, a tzaddik is typically known as a *rebbe* over a school of disciples. "Rebbe" is the affectionate Yiddish term for Rabbi. The relationship between a rebbe and his disciples was expressed in several different metaphors such as master and slave, teacher and pupil, king and subject, and even husband and wife.[32]

> You should love the Tzaddik with a perfect love until your soul is bound up with his and your love for him will replace the love for women: "Wonderful was thy love to me, passing the love of women" (II Samuel, 1:26)[33]

---

27   Special thanks to Nick Amik for translating this passage from Hebrew.

28   Ibid., 233. Rabbi Israel Dov Odesser said of Rebbe Nachaman, "Rabbeinu is the father, he is the mother, he is everything. He is the Torah, he is the faith, he is everything. Everything is Rabbeinu!" and that "Breslov is Truth and everyone needs to receive from Rabbeinu. If people oppose Rabbeinu, then they are false!" (*Israel Saba: Conversations of the Holy Rabbi Israel Dov Odesser* [Jerusalem, Israel: Keren Rabbi Israel Dov Odesser, 2007], 466, 472).

29   Rabbi Nathan, *Until Mashiach Comes: Rabbi Nachman's Biography* (trans. Aryeh Kaplan; Far Rockaway, NY: Breslov Research Institute, 1985), 82.

30   Schochet, *The Mystical Dimension Volume Three: Chasidic Dimensions*, 116–119.

31   Ibid., 117.

32   Rabbi Shloma Majeski, *Yechudis: The Essence of Chosid-Rebbe Relationship*, audiotape lectures (Brooklyn, NY: Sichos in English).

33   *Likutei Etzot*, Tzaddik 79 [Greenbaum].

In Chasidic thought the ultimate goal of the disciple of such a rebbe is to attain the status of *yechidut* (יחידות), which means "oneness." This oneness takes place when the *yechidah* ("singular soul," יחידה) of the disciple connects with the *yechidah* of his rebbe.

> The word *yechidah* refers to the highest rung of the soul, the innermost core, which is at one with G-d in constant and consummate unity. A *yechidus* with his Rebbe—a one-to-one encounter between the *yechidah* of the [disciple] and the *yechidah* of the Rebbe—charges the [disciple's] *yechidah* with dynamism, so that it vitalizes his day-to-day conduct.[34]

A spiritual union has taken place that is much like that of a marriage. The disciple would be so inspired by this intimate relationship with the tzaddik and so connected to him that the rebbe's being would permeate his entire life. The disciple's devotion to his tzaddik-rebbe was manifested through continual devotion and a willingness to lay down his entire life for the sake of his teacher.

The connection between the rebbe and his followers is felt so deeply that the devoted disciples believe they cannot pray without being "infused with the concept that the Rebbe is the one who is the 'connecting intermediary.'"[35] The tzaddik gives his disciple the connection to his Creator. In a sense, after this connection takes place one could say that his soul is born again.

The tzaddik thus becomes a head to a body and his disciples the limbs:

> Every tzaddik in every generation can be seen in terms of Moses, in terms of Shabbat—able to assemble and to join and to gather all of those who draw near to him, so that they are close to him like limbs to a body, and to connect them in the sense of the construction of the Tabernacle. Then they are made a complete edifice and a tabernacle and a dwelling place for the inspiration of holiness.[36]

> The matter is like this: The Rebbe with his chassidim are a *"koma shlema,* (lit. "one measure," קומה שלמה)," a complete body. The Rebbe is the brain, the mind, and the *chassidim* are the limbs, which draw their life force from the brain, every limb according to its level and its ability. And just like in the body there are limbs of various kinds—some limbs are pure, comely, and exposed, like the eyes, face, and hands, and some limbs are private, covered, and unsightly—in the same way there are *chassidim* of various kinds. There are *chassidim* who are pure, comely, and exposed, and there are, at times, those who are unsightly and covered.[37]

---

[34] Rabbi Eliyahu Touger, *To Know and To Care: An Anthology of Chassidic Stories about the Lubavitcher Rebbe* (3 vols.; Brooklyn, NY: Sichos in English, 1993), 1:87.

[35] Rabbi Sholom Charitonov, "Our Generation: What Makes Us Different," *Beis Moshiach* 320. Cited 27 January 2009. Online: http://www.beismoshiach.org/Moshiach/Moshiach320/moshiach320.htm.

[36] Rabbi Menachem Mendel of Kasover, *Sefer Ahavat Shalom* (Jerusalem: Ma'yan haHasidut, 1995), 161. Translation by Aaron Eby.

[37] Reb Naftoli of Ropshitz, *Der Sanzer Tzaddik* (Austria: 1930/31), 27.

BEYOND DEATH

The disciples' relationship with their rebbe is so strong that it actually transcends the death of the tzaddik. Rabbi Schneerson makes this point while commenting on a Talmudic story in which a dying rabbi makes a request for his sons [to be understood as his disciples] to draw near.

> It would have been reasonable to assume that he would no longer have any connection with us [after his death]. In order to forestall such an assumption, at the moment of his passing Rebbe said: "I need my sons." As if to say: "Even though I am now ascending to divine service of a transcendent order, I nevertheless remember you, and I shall remember you wherever I shall be. Moreover, in whatever lofty levels of ascent I may find myself, your divine service matters to me—'I need my sons.'"[38]

The disciples of a rebbe believed that nothing could break the bond of *devekut*, not even death. In fact, the day of a tzaddik's death is know as his *Yom Hilula* (יום חילולא), " a day of celebration." The term originally referred to a wedding day but was adapted by Chassidim to describe the return of the tzaddik's soul to HaShem, i.e. a "mystical marriage."[39] Rebbe Schneerson writes:

> In one of his letters, his honorable holiness, my teacher and father-in-law, the Admor Rayatz expounds on the greatness of the practice of observing the yom hillula of a tzaddik through study and a farbrengen. In that letter he recounts the events of the yom hillula of the 9th of Kislev … At the farbrengen that took place then, his Honorable Holiness the Admor, may his soul rest in Eden, said the following: "The observance of a yom hillula through studying the teachings of the tzaddik who passed away on that day and through prolonging the farbrengen constitutes a pidyon nefesh that one gives to that tzaddik."[40]

The anniversary of the death of a tzaddik is not a time of mourning but of connection with his disciples. The chassidim celebrate the return of the rebbe to HaShem.

> A Tzaddik is like a son of G-d. There is still a barrier separating him from his Father. G-d has a great longing for the Tzaddik, just as the Tzaddik yearns to return and come close to G-d.[41]

The presence of one's rebbe is said to be even stronger in his death than before it.

---

38 Rabbi Menachem M. Schneerson, *Proceeding Together* (3 vols.; Brooklyn, NY: Sichos in English, 2000), 1:35–36. Cf. Matthew 28:20.

39 "Hillula," *Encyclopedia Judaica* 9:119.

40 *Torat Menachem* 5711, 1:106.

41 Rabbi Nathan, *Rabbi Nachman's Wisdom* (trans. Aryeh Kaplan; Monsey, New York: Breslov Research Institute, 1973), 125.

Therefore we have learnt that the tzaddik, even when he departs from this world, does not really disappear from any world, since he is to be found in all of them more than in his lifetime. (*Zohar* III, 71b [Soncino])

Commenting on this the *Tanya* states, "That is he is to be found more even in this world of action ("this day to do them [Deuteronomy 7:11]"), because the action keeps growing."[42] That is to say that after the tzaddik dies, his actions and influence are increased and become even greater than when he was alive.[43] Hence, it can be said that a tzaddik can always be said to be "living."[44]

Additionally, it is taught that once a tzaddik dies, his *ruach* (spirit, רוח) is freed from the earthly soul (*nefesh*, נפש) and can now be freely received much more abundantly by his students.

> [Because the *ruach* has been freed of the limitations of the *nefesh*,] each one of [the *tzaddik's*] students and all those who are close to him can receive a portion of his *ruach* which is in *Gan Eden*. For it is no longer material, nor is it contained within a vessel … In contrast, during the lifetime of the *tzaddik* when his *ruach* is enclothed in his soul, and his soul attached to his body, his students and the Jewish people as a whole can receive [his influence] through his holy words and thoughts. When, however, the *ruach* is separated from the *nefesh*, [the *ruach*] can shine forth to every one of his students according to the individual level … It can be understood that any one of [the *tzaddik's*] students can receive their portion and their teachings from the *ruach* of their master in any place.[45]

DEAD CHASIDIM

Ordinarily, after the passing of a rebbe, a new rebbe rises up to take his place at the head of the Chasidic community. In a few Chasidic sects, however, the disciples' connection to their rebbe, even after his death, is so strong that no replacement is possible. The Chasids of the dead rebbe remain devoted to their deceased leader's teachings and refuse to accept a new rebbe in his place. For example, although Chabad elected a succession of six consecutive rabbis after the death of their founder Schneur Zalman of Liadi, they have not found a successor for the seventh and late Rabbi Menachem Mendel Schneerson. Though he died in 1994, no replacement is being sought. Schneerson's charisma and connection to his followers was at such an exalted level that it would be too difficult for anyone to take his place.

---

42 *Igeret HaKodesh* 26 (Kehot).

43 See also b.*Chullin* 7b where the example of Elisha's bones (2 Kings 13:21) is used to prove the greater power of the righteous after their death.

44 *Or HaChayim* on Genesis 23:2.

45 *Whispers Between Worlds*, 29–32. See also *Kav HaYashar* 71. Cf. the Master's words about the *ruach*, "Nevertheless, I tell you the truth: it is to your advantage that I go away, for if I do not go away, the Helper will not come to you. But if I go, I will send him to you" (John 16:7) and "When the Spirit of truth comes, he will guide you into all the truth … He will glorify me, for he will take what is mine and declare it to you" (John 16:13).

The most famous example of a Chasidic sect clinging to a deceased rebbe is the Breslover Chasidim; the sect was founded by Rabbi Nachman of Breslov. Rabbi Nachman died in 1810, but to this day, the Bresolver Chasidim have never elected anyone to take headship over their sect. Rebbe Nachman told his followers, "My fire will burn until Mashiach comes."[46] Other Chasidic schools refer to the Breslovers as the *Toytn Chasidim* ("Dead Chasidim," טויטן חסידים) i.e., they serve a rebbe who is no longer alive in the physical sense.[47] Many Breslovers make a declaration of connection (*hitkashrut*, התקשרות) before beginning a prayer time or performing certain mitzvot:

> I hereby bind myself in my every thought, word and action all through the day to
> … the True Tzaddik, the "flowing brook, the source of wisdom …" Rabbi Nachman
> the son of Feige, may his merit protect us.[48]

In this way Breslov Chasidim see themselves still attached in spiritual fellowship with Rabbi Nachman, even generations after his passing.

INTERCESSION

Another important part of the *tzaddik/devekut* equation is intercession. The tzaddik makes intercession for his followers, petitioning God on their behalf. In some cases, the tzaddik is imagined continuing to do so even after his death. The precedent of intercession is biblical and is derived, once again, from the life of Moses. Moses was unique, the man in whom God found favor (*chen*, חן)—that is, "grace."

> The LORD said to Moses, "I will also do this thing of which you have spoken; for you
> have found favor [*chen*] in My sight and I have known you by name." (Exodus 33:17)

Because of his favor in God's eyes and the intimacy he had with God, Moses' prayers of intercession on behalf of the people are heard by God, often even reversing God's own judgment on the people. For example we find in Numbers 11:22 that when a fire broke out, "the people therefore cried out to Moses, and Moses prayed to the LORD and the fire died out."

The *Talmud* states, "Whosoever has a sick person in his house should go to a sage who will invoke [heavenly] mercy for him."[49] James also alludes to the concept when he says that "the effective prayer of a righteous man [tzaddik] can accomplish much" (James 5:16).

Joel Marcus writes about Rebbe Shcneerson:

---

46   Rabbi Nathan, *Until Mashiach Comes*, 158.

47   See Appendix Two, J. Ungwarer, *The Dead Chasidim*.

48   Yitzchok Breiter, *Seven Pillars of Faith and A Day in the Life of a Breslover Chassid* (Monsey, NY: Breslov Research Institute, 1989), 43. See also Rabbi Nachman, *Rabbi Nachman's Tikun* (trans. Avraham Greenbaum; Monsey, NY: Breslov Research Institute, 1984), 11 and Rabbi Nathan, *The Fiftieth Gate* (trans. Avraham Greenbaum; 2 vols.; Monsey, NY: Breslov Research Institute, 1992), 1:25. Such declarations are not unique to Breslovers only but are found in other Chasidic circles, e.g., Rabbi Menachem Nochum of Chernobyl, *Me'or Einayim, Beshalach* [end].

49   b.*Bava Batra* 116a. This is then codified as halachah in the *Shulchan Aruch, Yoreh Deah* 335:10.

Those who encountered [the Rebbe] often remarked on the way in which his piercing but compassionate gaze seemed to uncover their hidden needs and desires. The Gospels, similarly, stress what A. Ambrozic has called Jesus' 'possessive gaze,' a glance by means of which he looks into and takes hold of the life of the follower. [50]

The tzaddik is said to have the power to nullify evil decrees and even transform the wicked. The Lubavitcher Rebbe writes:

> We must add that especially at the time of *chevlei mashiach* ["birth pains of Messiah"] and harsh decrees, God forbid (b.*Sanhedrin* 97b), it must be the case that the "Holy One, blessed be He, enacts and decrees, and the tzaddik annuls it." He accomplishes this by his causing a sinner to become a penitent.[51]

Even when the tzaddik himself is not present to pray on behalf of someone, praying in the tzaddik's name is believed to recall his righteousness, merit, and favor before God. The prayer offered in the name of a tzaddik will be answered on his merit. An example is seen in the Breslov prayer quoted above where it says, "May his merit protect us." In other words, "As we bind ourselves to him, hear our prayers based on his merit and favor." Rebbe Nachman taught:

> And every person must bind his prayers to the tzaddikim of the generation. For the tzaddik knows how to match the gates to the prayers and raise each and every prayer to its appropriate gate. (*Likutey Moharan* 2, 9:4 [Mycoff])[52]

Moreover he added that "the true tzaddkim atone for sins"[53] and that he himself was "a river which cleanses from all stains."[54] Even after his death Rebbe Nachman stated that he himself "will still intercede for anyone who comes to my grave," where he will pull "him by his *Peyos* out of Gehinnom!"[55] It is for this reason that every year his most devout followers still make the difficult

---

[50] Joel Marcus, "The Once and Future Messiah in Early Christianity and Chabad," New Testament Studies 46 (2000): 381-401. E.g., Mark 1:16, 19; 3:34; 10:21. Ambrozic argues that these are not pointless references to him looking at someone, but "rather, a description of Jesus' taking possession by means of a thorough 'inspection.'" See Aloysius M. Ambrozic, "New Teaching with Power (Mk 1.27)," in *Word and Spirit: Essays in Honor of David Michael Stanley* (ed. Joseph Plevnik; Willowdale, Ontario: Regis College Press, 1975), 113–149.

[51] *Likkutei Sichos* 4, 1257.

[52] Also *Likutey Moharan* 1, 2:6. See also Rabbi Nathan, *Rabbi Nachman's Wisdom*, 413 and *Likutey Etzot, Tzaddik* 15–16.

[53] *Likutey Etzot, Tzaddik* 14 [Greenbaum].

[54] *Chayei Mohoran* 332 [Greenbaum], also *Chayei Mohoran* 87.

[55] *Rabbi Nachman's Wisdom* (trans. Aryeh Kaplan; Monsey, New York: Breslov Research Institute, 1973), 275 n.472.

pilgrimage to his grave in Uman on Rosh HaShannah, the day of judgement.[56] When they travel to him on this auspicious day it is thought that "all severe judgements are mitigated."[57]

YESHUA THE TZADDIK

The parallels between Chasidic thought and the apostolic scriptures are astounding. Yeshua too was declared a tzaddik on many occasions. His disciple John tells us, "we have an Advocate with the Father, Yeshua the Messiah the righteous [tzaddik]."[58]

Yeshua is the ultimate tzaddik, the only truly sinless person to walk the face of the earth. The concepts of *devekut*, tzaddikism, and *yechidut* can teach us a great deal about our relationship to Yeshua.

In the Master we have *yechidut* ("oneness") where we are brought into a type of marriage relationship with Him. The Apostle Paul draws on this theme frequently in his epistles:

> So husbands ought also to love their own wives as their own bodies. He who loves his own wife loves himself; for no one ever hated his own flesh, but nourishes and cherishes it, just as Messiah also does the church, because we are members of His body. "For this reason a man shall leave his father and his mother, and be joined to his wife; and they shall become one flesh." This mystery is great; but I am speaking with reference to Messiah and the church. (Ephesians 5:28–32)

In Ephesians 5, Paul transitions back and forth seamlessly between a literal marriage and Messiah's relationship to His disciples. Much like the mystical musings of the Chasidic concept of *yechidut*, Paul calls this a great mystery. The marriage relationship between Yeshua and His disciples is taken so seriously that Paul calls a breach of it adultery:

> Shall I then take away the members of Messiah and make them members of a prostitute? May it never be! Or do you not know that the one who joins himself to a prostitute is one body with her? For He says, "The two shall become one flesh." But the one who joins himself to the Lord is one spirit with Him. (1 Corinthians 6:15–17)

Marriage is a form of *devekut*. The man is commanded to "join [*davak*] to his wife."[59] Paul brings in this imagery to illustrate his point. The language here is also very reminiscent of *yechidut*. Our spirit is joined with Messiah's, and we have become one. To break from this relationship is paramount to marital unfaithfulness.

---

[56] See *Uman! Uman! Rosh HaShanah! A Guide to Rebbe Nachman's Rosh HaShanah in Uman* (Monsey, NY: Breslov Research Institute, 2001). Breslovers find an early reference to this practice in b.*Rosh HaShannah* 29b where people would travel to the *beit din* (i.e., a group of *tzaddikim*) to hear the shofar blown on Rosh HaShannah. Also note the custom of visiting the graves of *tzaddikm* on Erev Rosh HaShannah in *Whispers Between Worlds*, 18.

[57] *Likutei Moharan* 1, 61:7 (Mycoff).

[58] 1 John 2:1. See also Matthew 27:19, Luke 23:47, Acts 3:14, 7:52, and 22:14.

[59] Genesis 2:24.

The Master Himself prays "that they may be one, just as We are one."[60] His desire is to draw us to the Father in perfect unity. Just as He is united with HaShem, so we will be united with Yeshua. The perfect unity is summed up by Rebbe Schneerson:

> Just as "Israel and the Torah and the Holy One, blessed be He, are all one"—i.e., not only is Israel connected to the Torah and the Torah is connected to G-d, but they are all absolutely one—so, too, in the bond between [disciples] and their Rebbe, these are not like two entities which unite, but they become absolutely "all one." And the Rebbe is not an intermediary who intercepts,[61] but an intermediary who connects.[62] Accordingly, for the [disciple], he and the Rebbe and the Holy One, blessed be He, are all one.[63]

Paul tells us that Messiah, like with the exalted tzaddik, is the head "from whom the whole body, nourished and knit together through its joints and ligaments, grows with a growth that is from God" (Colossians 2:19). It is through our head, Yeshua, that we receive life from the Father.

The imagery continues with the picture of a tree, its roots, and its branches. Rebbe Schneerson also points out:

> Chasidus [Chasidic teaching] and Chasidim are a "tree of life." In a tree, there is a root, which is connected to the *ko'ach ha'tzome'ach* (power/vitality in plants, הצומח כוח), the body, and the branches. Through the root and the body of the tree, the branches receive abundant life and, therefore, bring forth various fruit.

> In the Chasidic tree of life, the rebbes represent the root. The body of the tree is Chasidus, and the Chasidim are the branches.

> Every Chasid is a branch from the "tree of life." Through the root and body of the tree, do the Chasidim (which are the branches) receive eternal life in order to bring forth fruit. "What is the fruit? Mitzvot"[64]—performing mitzvot with an eternal life.[65]

Rebbe Schneerson's metaphor is strikingly similar to the Master's words in John 15:5: "I am the vine, you are the branches; he who abides in Me and I in him, he bears much fruit, for apart from Me you can do nothing." We connect the vitality of HaShem through Messiah; He is the trunk and the roots connecting us to the life-giving soil. In Him we produce good fruit, i.e. good deeds.

According to the Gospels and the Epistles, connection and unity in Messiah should permeate the entire scope of our behavior day to day. It is not just about mystical philosophies, but rather

---

60 John 17:22.

61 Literally: "an intermediary who separates" (*memutza mafsik*, ממצע מפסיק).

62 Literally: "an intermediary who connects" (*memutza mechabber*, ממצע מחבר).

63 Schneerson, *Proceeding Together*, 39.

64 b.*Sotah* 46a.

65 Menachem M. Schneerson, *Sefer HaMa'amarim 5708* (Brooklyn, NY: Kehot, 1986), 262. Translation by Michael Murray.

about personal transformation. Connection and intimacy with the Master should inspire us to live a life dedicated to Torah as He draws us closer to the Father. A true one-on-one encounter with Yeshua is life-changing.

Like the interceding *tzaddik*, the Master makes intercession on our behalf, "since He always lives to make intercession for [us]."[66] Yechiel Lichtenstein points out that when the Master tells us to pray in his name (John 14:14) that it means to pray "in his merit."[67]

The Chasidic background can also be applied to the Master's parting words: "I am with you always, even to the end of the age."[68] The bond that we have with Him is eternal and transcends even the grave. Though He is not here with us now physically, He is alive and ever present in our lives. Like the rebbe of the Breslov Chasidim, our Master is no longer with us in the bodily sense, yet we experience a spiritual connection with Him that transcends physical parameters. He remains as the connection between us and the Father. We even hear a genuine Chasidic ring in the Evangelical quip, "Yeshua is in my heart."

CONCLUSION

We are a frail and sinful people. We need a mediator between ourselves and the Father. We are in need of a savior. The ancient sages, as well as the modern Chasidic movement, realized the need for an intermediary. They understood that without one, man cannot hope to cling to HaShem. The same ideas form the central teachings of the Apostolic Writings.[69]

The Gospels' ideas of the divine nature of Messiah, His oneness with the Father, His intermediary role between man and HaShem, and the concept of having a personal relationship with Him, should not be considered foreign to Judaism. Instead concepts like these are central to Chasidic Judaism's philosophy and theology.

---

[66] Hebrews 7:25. Cf. Romans 8:34.

[67] R. Yehiel Zvi Lichtenstein, *Commentary on the Books of the New Testament: John* (Leipzig: Professor G. Dahlman, 1897) on John 14:14.

[68] Matthew 28:20.

[69] It is interesting to note that Yaffa Eilach speculates that the Chasidic concept of the *tzaddik* was heavily influenced by a dissenting sect of the Greek Orthodox Church. See Eliach, "The Russian Dissenting Sects and Their Influence on Israel Baal Shem Tov, Founder of Hassidism," 76.

APPENDIX 2

SKETCHES OF THE CHASIDIC WORLD

In his mission journal, *Christ and the Jews,* Levertoff frequently attempted to communicate the essence and flavor of Chasidic piety to his Christian readers. He did so by offering excerpts from *Love and the Messianic Age* and by printing various articles about Chasidus. We have collected three examples from the journal and reproduced them in this appendix.

"The Hidden Christ Among the Jews"[1] is Levertoff's translation of an article on Chasidism by a Russian-Jewish believer, Elizabeth Belenson. As the title implies, Belenson sees Chasidism as a veiled form of the Master's teaching at work within Judaism. "The Dead Chasidim"[2] is Levertoff's translation of an original Yiddish article written by another Jewish believer, J. Ungwarer, who had been impressed by his contact with Breslov Chasidim. Ungwarer highlights the similarity between Breslov devotion to Reb Nachman and a believer's devotion to Yeshua of Nazareth and the inner-spiritual transformation. "The Wisdom of the Chasids"[3] is Levertoff's own fictional depiction of real-life Chasidic pilgrimages to visit a Tzaddik-Rebbe.

Additionally, we have also included three of Levertoff's articles from the German language missionary journal *Saat auf Hoffnung* ("Seed of Hope") that Vine of David has translated into English. The English translations have never been previously published. In these articles, Levertoff offered further windows into the Chasidic community and its personalities.

"The Life of the Baal Shem"[4] is a brief biographical sketch of the founder of Chasidic Judaism, Rabbi Israel ben Eliezer—the Baal Shem Tov. In "Kabbalistic-Chasidic Miracle Stories,"[5] Levertoff writes about a tale of the wonder-working Rabbi Isaac Luria and his disciples. Finally, "From the Kabbalistic-Chasidic World of Thought"[6] Levertoff creates a question and answer dialogue between a Chasid and a non-Chasid about the world of Chasidic Judaism.

---

[1] Elizabeth Belenson, trans. Paul P. Levertoff, "The Hidden Christ Among the Jews," *Church and the Jews* 95 (April 1933): 8–10.

[2] J. Ungwarer, trans. Paul P. Levertoff, "The Dead Chasidim," *Church and the Jews* 90 (January 1932): 19–21.

[3] Paul P. Levertoff, "The Wisdom of the Chasids," *Church and the Jews* 89 (October 1931): 23–30.

[4] Translation from "Aus dem Leben des Baal-Schem," *Saat auf Hoffnung* 55 (1918): 7–19.

[5] Translation from "Kabbalistisch-chassidische Wundergeschichten," *Saat auf Hoffnung* 55 (1918): 113–118.

[6] Translation from "Aus der Kabbalistisch-Chassidischen Gedankenwelt," *Saat auf Hoffnung* 51 (1914): 19–27; 78–89.

THE HIDDEN CHRIST AMONG THE JEWS

ELIZABETH BELENSON

We are glad to publish the following short sketch on Chasidism by a Russian Jewish lady belonging to the Roman Communion. The original is in Russian. (Paul P. Levertoff)

The sick soul of Israel in exile is kept alive by the still constant expectation of the miraculous coming down of the angel of the Lord to "move the water." At times, in order that this soul may not finally fall into the sleep of death, the Lord kindles it with a burning Messianic vision, which He conveys to His people by means of His chosen messengers.

The last such outburst of spiritual life among the Jews was Chasidism, which originated in Podolia and Volivnia at the end of the 18th century, when the Jews, having been recurrently disappointed in their expectation of an earthly Messianic Kingdom, were ready to fall into the indifference of despair. Then the Lord, in His pity for His blind children—who, although they turn their back to Him are in fact eagerly, though perhaps unconsciously, longing for Him—raised from among them the great Israel ben Eliezer (commonly known as Besht, the initial letters of Baal Shem Tov, i.e., "Master of the Good Name"), and he, the founder of Chasidim, awakened among the Jews living in remote towns and villages in the southeast of Poland, Rumania, and the Ukraine, an ardent inward piety and a glowing longing for redemption.

It is not intended to give in this little sketch a characterization of this remarkable personality and of the other prominent representatives of the Chasidic movement, nor even a summary of Chasidic teaching. It is intended merely as a vindication of the theory that this movement is indeed a *praeparatio evangelica* ["preparation for the gospel"].

It is told of a Chasidic saint [i.e., tzaddik] that such was his expectation of Redemption, that if he heard a tumult in the street he was at once moved to ask what this meant, and whether a messenger had not arrived; and always when he went to sleep he told his servant that he must wake him the moment the messenger drew nigh. For the coming of the Deliverer as a swiftly approaching event was as constant an expectation to him as the return of a beloved only son from a strange country is to the father who stands on the watchtower with longing in his eyes, and peers through every window, and, if the door is opened, hastens out to see if his son is not yet come.

Chasidism teaches concerning Scripture that not only the black letters but also the white spaces between them are meant to teach us something, with the only difference that the latter we cannot read. But a time will come when the Lord will unlock the hidden mysteries of the Torah and reveal its glory to our eyes. And these "white spaces" between the lines, which have yet to be revealed, are just the hidden rays of Christ in Chasidism, which, when perceived, can enlighten the whole structure of thought with new meanings and with fresh significance.

The central theme of Chasidic teaching is the need of spiritual regeneration, the call for the transformation of the World, for the sanctifying of the whole of life.

The way to God is prayer and active, creative love. Love is the first and the last word on the lips of a Chasidic saint. There were many such saints [i.e., tzaddikim] and all of them, having had different gifts, have served differently: one by prayer, another by wisdom, a third with the simple devotion of his heart. But for all of them prayer was love; love, wisdom; and wisdom proceeded from a heart illumined by love. Chasidism teaches that humility cannot and ought not to be "commanded," for then it can easily lead to hypocrisy and pride. True humility is the natural result of a true knowledge of God. Before the presence of the Holy One, the false garments of pride and vainglory in which the soul is wrapped are torn away. Two truths one must always have in mind: "For my sake was the world created," and, "I am just dust and ashes."

Prayer must be freed from the ballast of personal needs and desires. When a man stands in prayer and hungers to take firm hold of the eternal, and strange thoughts come and go unbidden in his mind, these are the holy sparks which have sunk down, and which wish to be uplifted and set free by him, and these sparks belong to him and are akin to the roots of his soul; by virtue of Him they shall be liberated. He liberates them when he sends every sad thought back to its pure source, and when he sinks all the individual impulses of his mind in the one universal and God-like impulse and lets all that is separate be merged into one unity.

A spiritual boldness in regard to the bringing down of the kingdom of heaven, ardent prayer, love for one's neighbor, and loving-kindness for the whole of creation—these intentions form the basis of Chasidic teaching.

The words of the Chasidic teachers sound sublime and solemn, and at the same time are extraordinarily simple.

THE DEAD CHASIDIM

J. UNGWARER

The following sketch from Jewish life in Poland is a translation from a Yiddish manuscript written by a talented young Jewish Christian friend. It is taken from life. (Levertoff's editorial note)

"Surely you have heard of the Uman Chasidim? What, not even of the Breslov ones? But I take it for granted that you have heard of the dead Chasidim. Those are we!" This is the way Shimeon Henech, a little, lean Jew, usually introduces himself to short-coated, i.e., modern, young men, inviting them to enter the little Chasidic synagogue to which he belongs.

"In other synagogues they wouldn't allow 'bowler hats' (a sign of modernity) even to cross the threshold … But we are different. On the contrary, we look out for such as you."

Noticing that you are rather startled by his missionary fervor, he gathers courage and becomes more oratorical, looking upwards, as if he were in the act of "sanctifying the new moon," at the same time casting an occasional glance at you, to find out whether it is worth his while to continue his talk, or whether it is merely casting pearls before swine. But on this occasion, seeing—or rather feeling—that he has before him a serious-minded person, he warms up and tells you why he is on the lookout for "such as you."

"It is because the Rabbi, blessed be his memory, taught that even the greatest sinner can be awakened to repentance, as his soul is a part of God. Alas! Alas! Through sin man falls deeply into the mire and his soul is smothered in it. Deep, deep in the soul, however, a spark still glows which cannot be quenched. Only when all the filth which covers it, all the lusts, all those things which hide the face of God from us, are removed, then can the wind fan it, so that it may become a bright fire … Every Jew has moments in his life when the spark strives to flicker up, when he thirsts for the living God. To some these moments come in the season of repentance, between the New Year's Day and the Day of Atonement; to others, when they are in great tribulation; to the most wicked ones, when they are in the clutch of death. Rabbi Nachman, blessed be his memory, shows, however, in his writings that there can be a daily awakening of the soul.

"Moreover, a sinner who repents is so great …" (He draws out the "great," and looks at you with an expression of envy, but confesses that he also was once a sinner like yourself).

He used to live like most Jews: absorbed in his business, in his daily ambitions and worldly cares. But he was restless. He was not satisfied with himself. Something was lacking. He became more pious, spent more time in the synagogue, gave more time to the study of sacred writings, even consulted a Chasidic Rabbi, but no peace came that way. "I longed to pour out my heart, to reveal the anguish of my soul to a sympathetic friend. I wanted to confess my sins …

"All at once I heard of the dead Chasidim, and I resolved to visit them. They were at prayer. What ecstasy! What contemplation! They were so absorbed in their devotions that they did not even notice my entrance. I felt at once that here I would find what I wanted. And, thanks be to God, I was not disappointed. After prayer one of them talked to me, and all my sins stood before me, and I wept bitterly. I was not the only one; they all wept, as though it were the Day of Atonement, and yet it was but an ordinary weekday. One of them explained to the congregation passages from the *Likkutei Maharan* (a collection of sayings of the Chasidic teacher, Rabbi Nachman of Breslov).[7] How shall I explain? The words were sweeter than honey. For instance, the teaching concerning true repentance and the joy that follows it, and the new stream of life from above fills the soul …

"You understand my joy … I also saw how they confessed their sins to one another and how united they were. And the sacred dancing! Surely, it is not a small thing to be able to say with the Psalmist: 'All my bones say, O Lord, Who is like unto Thee?' Previously I used to mumble my prayers as quickly as possible, just as a matter of duty. Now I feel reluctant to cease praying … The whole world looks different from what it had ever looked before. It is a beautiful world. Now my fondest wish is to draw souls into the shelter of the wings of the Shechinah.

"Why are we called 'The dead Chasidim'? Because we do not visit the *living* Chasidic rabbis. We make pilgrimages to the 'Tent' (grave) of Rabbi Nachman, may his memory be blessed!"

"So you are called 'Dead Chasidim' because you are attached to a dead Rabbi?"

"Nay, but he is alive, alive!"

---

7   [Translated into English as Rabbi Nachman of Breslov, *Likutey Moharan* (trans. Moshe Mykoff et al.; 12 vols.; New York: Breslov Research Institute, ongoing).]

THE WISDOM OF THE CHASIDS[8]

PAUL PHILIP LEVERTOFF

The founder of Chasidism has left nothing in writing, with the exception of some letters. This is the case also with most of the leaders of the first generation of the Chasidim. They could all say, with the great Kabbalist Isaac Luria: "As soon as I want to express in words something of what is going on in my soul, the ideas begin to fill me so much, and the waves of thought come on with such profusion, that they break through the boundaries of words. Then I seek and seek after some means to conquer the thoughts, and to find a narrow outlet through which I could impart them to you; I seek for words in which to concentrate the mysteries which move me so deeply." To the Chasid, a stammering movement of the tongue, a hinted suggestion simply, is of more value than a clearly defined system.

Most of the Chasidic writings (about two hundred) are collections of saying or reports of miracles of the great Tzaddikim ["Righteous Ones"]. Those writings that describe the sayings and miracles of "the Besht" (Baal Shem Tov) are the most popular (*Shivhei HaBesht* [Kopyst: 1814]).[9] Also Rabbi Nachman of Breslov attracted a certain literature around his life and doings (*Sichot HaRan*).[10] A collection of some sayings of the Tzaddikim is contained in the books called *Leshon HaChasidim* and *Derech Chasidim* (Lemberg: 1876).[11] The crude colors, a mixture of rabbinical casuistry with Kabbalistic realism in describing supernatural relationships, as we find them especially in the "Chabad" writings, are things which could scarcely be translated into any other language. Buber has not touched on these (for instance, *Tanya,* or the mystical commentaries to the Old Testament of Rabbi Shneur Zalman)[12] but has gathered up many of the legends about the Tzaddikim from the other simpler sources, and tells them in his excellent German in the former book, while the latter contains their pithy sayings drawn from the same sources; and, as I read, my mind sets the stage, as it were, to frame them.

---

[8] See Martin Buber, *Der grosse Maggid und seine Nachfolge (The Great Maggid and his Succession)* (Frankfurt: Rütten & Loening, 1922) and *Das verborgene Licht (The Hidden Light)* (Frankfurt: Rütten & Loening, 1924).

[9] Cf. Martin Buber, *Die Legende des Baalschem* (Frankfurt: Rütten & Loening, 1908). [In English Martin Buber, *The Legend of the Baal-Shem* (trans. Maurice Friedman; New Jersey: Princeton University Press, 1995). *Shivhei HaBesht* was translated into English: Jerome R. Mintz and Dan Ben-Amos, *In Praise of the Baal Shem Tov (Shivhei Ha-Besht): The Earliest Collection of Legends about the Founder of Hasidism* (New Jersey: Jason Aronson, 1994).]

[10] Cf. Martin Buber, *Die Geschichten des Rabbi Nachman* (Frankfurt: Rütten & Loening, 1906). [In English Martin Buber, *Tales of Rabbi Nachman* (New York: Humanity Books, 1988). *Sichot HaRan* was translated into English: Rabbi Nathan, *Rabbi Nachman's Wisdom* (trans. Aryeh Kaplan; Monsey, New York: Breslov research Institute, 1973).]

[11] [Both were written by Rabbi Nachman Goldstein (the Tcheriner Rav, d. 1894) who was a disciple of Rebbe Nachman. These works are compilations of the teachings of the Baal Shem Tov and his major disciples.]

[12] Cf. Paul Levertoff, *Die religiöse;* cf. Also Paul Levertoff, "Chasidic Parables," *The Quest: A Quarterly Review* (January 1925).

PILGRIMAGE TO THE REBBE

It is springtime, and the long flat roads are soft and slushy with melted snow, which the spring rains have not yet cleared away. Tomorrow is the Eve of Passover, and along these roads for the week and more pilgrims have been travelling from far-out-lying villages and little towns to the famous Tzaddik of B.

They are now almost in sight of their destination, and the throng of footsore and weary ones has been added to by some in carriages and on horseback.

Here, in a well-upholstered landau drawn by a pair of high-stepping, swift-footed, Russian horses with glossy black coats and long tails, lolls one of the wealthy. To his credit, may it be said, he has taken up into it also two women and their babes, in spite of their evident muddiness. The spirit that prevails among the Chasidim is, especially at these times, one of real fellowship.

On two heavy mounts are two elderly Jews, their long caftans tucked up round their waists out of their way, their fur caps well rammed down upon their heads.

In a large farm wagon drawn by two oxen sit at least three families with their belongings, and their voices are shrill with excitement at the prospect of visiting the Tzaddik, tales of whom have enlivened the whole of the long tedious journey for them all.

Plodding in the mire are men and women and even some older children, for to make this pilgrimage on foot is of special merit. Their clothing is in a sad state, bespattered and frowsy with travel, but their faces are full of expectant rapture.

Repeat these types many times and the procession is before your eyes. Each side of the sodden road are deep ditches, full of dirty snow and water, and beyond, stretch the acres of brown earth with here and there a patch of brilliant green, denoting the tender shoots of winter-sown barley. Overhead is a sky of April blue. In the river the ice floes are bumping and cracking as they travel to the distant sea. The villages through which they go are unspeakably dingy and sodden, but that mysterious feeling of awakening and promise that spring brings, is in the air; and even the most unwashed peasant feels it, much more so this multitude of seekers and potential mystics.

Psalms are sung to lilting tunes, and joyous hymns of praise. Merry jokes and quips greet them in the villages and are returned in good measure. Kindness and friendly curiosity follow them even among the non-Jewish population.

At last, on the outer edge of the last village, a little wood is reached, and through the trees the friendly chimneys of the Tzaddik's mansion can be seen. Louder and gayer are the tunes the sight draws forth, until they fain must stop for want of voice to sing with.

THE REBBE'S TABLE

As they draw near the wide-thrown hospitable doors an awe-struck silence falls, and those who have anything to say speak now in whispers, as though this was indeed a sanctified spot.

The wife of the Tzaddik is there in silk attire, and gems gleam on her hands, her neck, and in her ears. This arouses no envy, for what subject envies the queen? All the splendor of the mansion only fills each breast with pride, for each one feels it belongs also to him; he has helped, he, the poorest there, to contribute to its splendor, and intends to contribute still more as long as he has life and health to do so.

The women and children go off to the women's apartments with the Tzaddikah. The men are conducted by the numerous servants to the baths and to their rooms; and then all is silence while preparation is being made for the evening meal.

The evening sky darkens, the evening star shines out, and the faithful gather in the great hall, set with tables literally groaning under the abundance of the fare. The gourmet views it all with delight, not less than that of the poor peasant who has never seen such wonderful food even in his wildest dreams.

The Tzaddik is not yet present. He is alone in a room set apart for prayer and contemplation.

By and by, when he comes, the entry of him they have come so far to see is dramatic.

The door opens at the top of the room, and a frail figure in white stands framed an instant in the doorway. He scans the multitude with his keen black eyes. Someone catches sight of him, and in a flash the news goes round the room in some imperceptible manner. There is silence, then a long rustle, a sound of chairs being pushed back, and everyone is on his feet. The slight figure glides softly to the head of the central table and seats himself on the throne-like chair that has been awaiting him.

Again he flashes his piercing glance over all, then drops his eyes, and in silence they all resume their seats.

Rapidly he makes the blessing, breaks his unleavened bread, takes his glass of wine and, blessing it, takes a sip. His nearer neighbors almost fight to serve him, but his meal is very frugal.

Suddenly, without any preliminaries, he begins to expound the scripture of the day, or some point connected with the feast they are celebrating.

In the breathless silence he goes on talking rapidly in snatches, with long silences between. Sometimes his listeners are bewildered at this flow of language, in which he strives to express the deep and mystic thoughts that rise within him. Yet, a word, a snatch of a sentence, even the stammer of the tongue, has its significance here. Only the initiated can really follow his thoughts, and even they not always. But then, what matter? Can they understand all the works and words of the Creator? Is not the Tzaddik practically divine? He has lived so much in the presence of God, that His spirit lives in him to such an extent that it raises him even above the angels.

When he has ended, he rises to leave the table and retire to his room again. They all rise. He blesses them with outstretched hands.

As he turns away, the remnants of his meal, every crumb of it, are carefully gathered up by the adoring ones. Does not every crumb touched by him now contain a small spark of the Divine, to assimilate which in the body is gain in sanctity? The scramble for these scraps is an eager one.

This table is as an altar to them all, ever since the master has come to it; the meal, a sacrament. From his line, the Messiah may perhaps come. To sip from the wine his lips have touched brings the life of the soul (the Tzaddik) to them, the body.

The fortunate ones rejoice, and faith works miracles in these devoted ones; their sorrows are lightened, their sicknesses—physical, mental, or spiritual—are healed, and the life of their souls is deepened by this mystical agency.

TALES OF THE CHASIDIM

Tales are told of the powers of speech, wisdom, and healing of the master. He comes from a family of Tzaddikim, and tales of his ancestors are mingled with tales about himself. As the years go by, the tales get intermixed and enlarged.

Then, with prayer, praise, joyous hymns, and ecstatic dancing, the evening draws to a close.

Some of the pilgrims are guests of the house—a much sought-after honor—while the greater number sleep in the adjoining village.

The Tzaddik sleeps little, from habit. He roams about among the sleepers, blessing, watching and praying as he goes.

On the third day the Tzaddik holds his court, and there the pilgrims come to lay their gifts at his feet and to tell him their troubles.

Solomon has a daughter to marry off and she has no dowry; something must surely be done for her. And it is done. Solomon goes away satisfied. Mother Rachel leads little Miriam by the hand; she suffers from twitchings of her whole body, poor child. She begs … a special blessing for the little one. She retires with a radiant face.

Mendel has some business trouble; he unfolds it to the master who ponders on it, asking a few piercing questions. With a parable he makes the whole thing clear, and ends his advice with some pithy words, which become a proverb from that moment.

So the scene goes on. The faithful feel they cannot be born, married, die, or be buried without the holy Tzaddik. He must share their every joy and sorrow. He says: "I will carry each one of you written upon my very heart. You are always with me."

The journey home is one of joyous satisfaction. The history of it will make ample conversation for a whole year.

IN THE BEIT MIDRASH

Another scene comes before me. It is night, and the hall is alight in the Tzaddik's house. Here, the most diligent students are remaining to pass the night in study, prayer and contemplation.

In one corner sits a young man, his head thrown back, his face rapt, his eyes fixed. So he will sit for hours, meditating on some deep kabbalistic sentence, and seeing, probably, wonderful visions.

Bending over a table in another part of the room is an old, old man, all shriveled and yellow with age. His rheumy eyes are dim as he searches the pages of the *Zohar* open before him in his near-sighted manner. His body sways to and fro and his lips move soundlessly, but in his head runs the music with which he had intoned all this long, long ago, when he was young. Yet he is not sad. Fresh treasures come to the surface at every new search, and the new mystical life is almost within his grasp now, when his strength will be renewed as the eagle's.

Here, also swaying to and fro, but with much energy and vigor, is a group of men in the prime of life. Their voices rise and fall as they chant.

Beyond them is a pair of children, boys who have just reached their teens. They scan the page before them with sleepy eyes. They strive to conquer outraged nature by listening to the chanting of the enthusiasts, but nature has her way ere long; and the heavy eyelids drop, and their heads fall on their arms upon the open books. Their breath comes softly and evenly.

The lights grow dim. The fire dies down. It grows cold; the enthusiasts have dropped to an undertone. Only the old seeker after truth, with the sleeplessness of extreme old age, outlasts them all. The door opens softly, and the Tzaddik comes in to visit his disciples.

The air is heavy with sleep and breathing. But do the dim lights really flame up? Is there really a breath of perfumed air like the fresh spring breeze? His disciples would swear to it. They rouse themselves, sleep flies away, leaving them refreshed and strong to continue. He calls them to him, the old and the young, and seated in their midst, he exhorts and expounds, and thrills them with his teaching. They almost worship him. He is the mediator between them and God. He brings the Holy One near. It seems as though the heavens open and angels come down and mingle with them. The grey dawn comes all too soon, when warm and happy they retire to their beds for a few hours' sleep.

THE REBBE'S YAHRTZEIT

Scenes of village weddings, circumcisions, miracles worked at sickbeds, festivals, and funerals, at all of which the Tzaddik plays the central role—on these space forbids my entering. So the next I select is this:

The Tzaddik is dead and has been buried now these many years. His son reigns in his place, and is gaining in fame as the years go by.

The old Tzaddik's grave is apart from the rest. Over it today a tent is erected. To it a procession of pilgrims is wending its way. What is it that troubles the faithful? Is it plague or persecution? Some trouble it must be. They come singing, as usual, and in their hands are lighted tapers. As they reach the tent, as many as can do, enter. The grave is as an altar in the midst, and on it the tapers are placed and petitions laid. Amid a torrent of prayer the departed one is besought to listen and lend aid to his faithful followers; he is begged to intercede for them favorably. The service over, those who had failed to get in take the place of those who come out, and lay their petitions and place a taper on the altar.

Perhaps it is the anniversary of the Tzaddik's death? Then they come to the synagogue where he was wont to attend worship.

What is this? The place is full of light and color—gay draperies and many, many candles. Death is no hideous angel of mourning here. Death opens the mystic door to Life Eternal. Greet the knowledge with every evidence of joy.

The faithful shout and sing the most happy hymns and psalms. Then they gather close and listen to tales of the wondrous words and works of the old Tzaddik from those who knew him; and, as time goes on, these tales are told by old men who were once the children of the pilgrims of long ago.

As they talk and compare the present Tzaddik with his ancestors, it seems to them that the whole long line of these holy ones is present, too, and awe falls upon them.

The hour grows late and, as the mysteriousness of the midnight quiet falls upon them, they shudder together in a rapture of mystic joy and fear.

THE LIFE OF THE BAAL SHEM

PAUL PHILIP LEVERTOFF

At the end of the 17th century, the situation of the Jews in Poland was bleak. The bloody years of 1648–1655, which the Jews referred to as *getzuros tag* (Yiddish: "the day of troubles"), had left a deep impression on Jewish spirituality. The Cossacks had soaked the whole country with Jewish blood. The yeshivas had been destroyed. For a long time, Kabbalah had blossomed there. The Sabbatarian movement[13] had spread across all of Poland, and even though the false messiah was already dead, he still had faithful followers there. It was out of this messianic movement in Poland that the sects of the Chasidim were born. These Chasidim attempted to bring deliverance and freedom from asceticism.[14] Among the leaders of this movement were two famous Kabbalists, Yehudah Chasid and Chayim Malach. Though the movement amounted to nothing, one vestige remained: It left a lasting impression among the common people that miracles could still happen.

It was around this time, in a tiny little village in Walachia, that the father of modern Chasidism was born: Rabbi Israel Baal Shem Tov (also known as the Besht).

No one knows exactly where or in what year the Besht was born. Limited information can be gleaned from the writings which his disciples have left behind and which were spread abroad by his followers shortly after his death. All that can be said with certainty is that he was the child of poor, common parents. His father, Eliezer, was a simple, pious Jew; his mother was a midwife, and she supplied the needs of the whole family. Israel was their only son.

His birth is shrouded in the following legend: Once upon a time, the savage Tartars fell upon and attacked the village where the parents of the Baal Shem lived. The Tartars were accustomed to plunder homes, take the inhabitants of the village captive, and sell them as slaves; this is what they did here as well. Among these prisoners was the father of the Baal Shem Tov. (His mother was rescued and barely escaped.) This took him to a distant country in which no Jews lived. There, the man whose slave he had become made him overseer of his household.

Eliezer decided to escape, but he then received a sign from heaven that he should stay where he was. His master had developed a fondness for him and gave him as a gift the position of vice-regent. One day, it came about that his master and the Sultan, whom his master represented, needed the advice of a wise man—and Eliezer was just that wise man! As a result, the Sultan overwhelmed him with honors and loaded him down with riches. Additionally, he received the most beautiful young maiden of the land as a wife. However, he kept his distance from her. She was confused; she could not understand the reason for this. She repeatedly asked him for an explanation, but every time she asked, he was always able to appease and pacify her. However, one day it happened that he could no longer dissuade her, and he confessed to her, with tears in his eyes, that he was a Jew. She gave him some costly presents, said goodbye to him, and sent him away.

---

13   [Led by the false Messiah, Shabbatai Tzvi.]

14   [Judaism at the time was characterized by asceticism and the intellectual discipline of Torah study, perceived by some as dry and lifeless.]

Along the way, robbers fell upon him and took away everything that he had. But "in order to comfort him, the prophet Elijah revealed himself and announced to him that God would send him a son who would open the eyes of the Jewish people. And so," the legend concludes, "the founder of modern Chasidism, Rabbi Israel Baal Shem Tov, was born."

His father died while Israel was still very young. Before his death, Eliezer took his son in his arms and said to him, "As you can see, my child, the time has come for me to make my departure from this world. I am certain that you will be a great man of God. Remember this well, my son: that God will always be with you, so you don't need to be afraid of anything."

These last words of Israel's dying father made a deep impression on his soul which, it seems, the Baal Shem Tov never forgot. His mother probably also died soon after that, and apparently some strangers must have taken him in.

Just like every other Jewish boy, he went to *cheder*.[15] The Jewish philosopher Solomon Maimon sketched quite a dreary picture of the Jewish elementary schools of that era. "The *cheder*," he said, "is a dirty, narrow little room full of smoke. Some of the children sit on benches; the rest of them sit on the floor. The teacher is clad in a dirty old vest-like shirt, and he sits at his table with a heavy stick in his hand. This stick serves a double purpose: he tamps down his tobacco with it, which is in a little snuff box next to him on the floor; and, when necessary, he swings it and strikes the shoulders and heads of the students."

Besides the teacher, there is also an "assistant" in the *cheder*. The children are more afraid of him than they are of fire itself. He beats them even more than the teacher. To top it all off, whatever the mothers have sent with their children for lunch, this "assistant" steals and eats.

What was supposed to be learned in *cheder*? Prayers, and the Torah with Rashi's commentary; the older children would also learn a little Talmud. But all of this occurred unsystematically.

Such was the *cheder* in which Israel found himself, but he had no desire to learn. He always wandered off into the woods, where there was no teacher and no assistant teacher, and where he didn't have to look at the gloomy faces of the other schoolchildren. He often disappeared for the whole day, and if someone finally found him in the woods, he was in a dream-like state as if in a trance. The trees and the hills worked their special magic upon him; and the "mistress of music" was something that he loved very much as child.

His disciples often related that the Baal Shem could determine the character of any man just by paying attention to his singing and the music that he made.

"In the little synagogue," the Chasidim would explain, "where the Baal Shem was in the habit of praying, there was a Jew who had a rather slow, untalented child who couldn't even read. The father, who lived out in the countryside, was ashamed to bring the lad with him to the synagogue in the city. Even during the festivals he left him at home. It went on this way until the boy was thirteen years old. Once, when it was Yom Kippur, the father was afraid to leave the boy at home alone. He wasn't sure, but he felt that perhaps the boy might learn something in spite of his ignorance. He might find something to enjoy on this great fast day."

---

[15]   [An elementary school for Jewish boys.]

"The boy had a little flute. While he was tending the sheep in the field, he played wonderful, beautiful melodies with it. It was this same flute that the lad brought with him into the synagogue—but his father knew nothing about it."

"The whole day, the boy sat in the synagogue and watched with his mouth wide open as the Jews were praying. He felt sorry that he couldn't participate at all. At one point, he took out his flute to show what he was able to do, but his father noticed it and took the instrument away, holding on to it firmly. Finally, the boy couldn't stand it any longer, and he tore the flute out of his father's hand and blew … You can imagine the onlookers' astonishment. The Baal Shem turned to the congregation and said, 'This boy has sent all of our prayers to heaven. In the eyes of God, his flute is worth more than all of your prayers.'"

Understandably, the guardians of the Baal Shem were not happy with their ward, and at last they wanted nothing more to do with him, so that he had to fend for himself even at his tender young age.

A short time later we find him back at the *cheder*, but no longer as a student. He was an assistant.

As an assistant, he was the exception to the rule in his chosen profession. He soon won the hearts of the young children. He got into the habit of not only teaching them in the school but even of going home with them, and going with them into the synagogue and helping them with their prayers. This brought him great joy.

After a while, he became an attendant at the synagogue. They were pleased with him, although his personal habits seemed a little strange: He would stay up all night learning and sleep during the day.

Why did he stay awake at night at the synagogue? What was he doing? What was he learning? His biographies give us no specific answer to these questions. But it is safe to assume that the imaginative young man was already, even in his youth, so spiritually and mystically minded that he simply couldn't spend too much time with the Talmudic casuistry and argumentation so common in his day. Rather, he had probably been immersed in the Kabbalistic literature since his youth.

His biographers frequently mention that the Kabbalistic bible, namely the Zohar, was his favorite work. This mystical work is full of legends and profound thoughts, and is written in an enchanting style. It certainly must have made a deep impression upon the young man's tender soul.

"In this book," he used to say to himself, "God has hidden light for the righteous ones, light which he created during the six days of creation."

He also loved our Kabbalistic writings as well as the haggadic (narrative) part of the Talmud.

The legends further tell of secret manuscripts which miraculously came into young Israel's hands when he was an attendant in the synagogue.

"In a certain country," so it is said, "there lived at that time a holy man, a certain Kabbalist by the name of Rabbi Adam. This man once found in a cave a bundle of sacred manuscripts through which he was able to perform miracles. He was a very poor man. Once a great king wanted to visit him with his entire army, and the holy man conjured up a large palace in the blink of an eye; he was likewise able to produce a royal meal fit for a king."

Before his death, it was revealed to Rabbi Adam from heaven that the manuscripts belonged to someone by the name of Rabbi Israel, the son of Eliezer, who was to be found in the city of Okup.

Rabbi Adam had an only son, and before his death, he ordered him to give the writings to their true owner. The son went to Okup, found the head of the Jewish community there, and explained to him what his father had commanded him to do: He was supposed to marry a woman from that place. So he married the daughter of a very rich man.

After the wedding, he began to look for Rabbi Israel. But all he found was a fourteen-year-old boy by that name who was an attendant at the synagogue. Watching the boy, he allowed a few of the secret manuscripts to fall carelessly from his pouch. He saw that the boy became very agitated, and with trembling hands he picked the manuscripts up. Rabbi Adam's son realized then that this was the one he had been searching for.

As a result, the two of them became fast friends. The son of the Kabbalist handed the rest of the manuscripts to Israel, and asked him if he would allow him to learn along with him. Israel agreed, but only on the condition that the world would know nothing about it. To all outward appearances, he would simply be his servant.

The young man asked his rich father-in-law for permission to build a little study-hall room on the outskirts of the city where he could study undisturbed. There the two devoted themselves especially to the study of the mysterious manuscripts, which were filled with secrets. They also tried to perform miracles with them, as Rabbi Adam used to do, but they were unable. On the first attempt, they started a fire; the second attempt ended in a very serious accident: Rabbi Adam's son was killed.

When Israel was serving in the synagogue, and was still very, very young, he was given a wife. However, she died at the same time as his friend. So Israel was by himself again, and lonely. He became an assistant in various schools; his profession, though, did not bring in much income.

His love for solitude and his love for nature drove him to abandon his position as a teaching assistant; instead he became a teacher in the home of a Jewish farmer.

The Jewish farmers at that time were a strange lot. Solomon Maimon reminisced in his autobiography that "poverty and ignorance reigned in the home of every farmer." The farmers were unlearned; they couldn't understand a word of Hebrew nor could they speak Yiddish. Their language was a butchered form of Russian. Their huts were blackened with smoke. Their one-room houses comprised at once the sleeping quarters, the living area, the dining room, and the classroom for instruction.

In time, Israel gained a reputation—not only among the Jews, but even among the Polish landowners—as a highly respected man of honor, and he was frequently sought out to solve disputes as an impartial judge. Among those who were accounted as learned, well known, and reputable in the city of Brody, there was a certain man by the name of Ephraim of Kotev. He had a dispute with another very eminent man and wanted to travel to Brody to present his case there before the Rabbi.

But since his opponent portrayed Israel as an objective judge and a clear-sighted man, they both agreed that it would be better to take their dispute to Israel for settlement. Rather than going to Brody, they traveled to Tlost. Israel made such an impression on Rabbi Ephraim that Ephraim offered him his own daughter in marriage. Israel immediately accepted this offer, as it was apparent to him that Ephraim's daughter was destined to become his wife. The engagement contract was drawn up. Yet Ephraim wanted to keep Israel's true character a secret, even though he was a Talmud scholar himself and therefore had the desire to marry his daughter to a scholar, so he wanted to omit all of Israel's credentials and honorary titles from the *ketubbah,* leaving only the name of the learned groom. On the return trip, however, Rabbi Ephraim died, and his son Gershon, a scholar of great reputation in his own right, was quite surprised to see that in his father's papers was an engagement contract, from which it was apparent that his sister was to marry a man who seemed to be an *am-ha'aretz* [עם הארץ]; that is, an unlearned man. He did not want his sister involved in this marriage. But she refused to accept any objection to a marriage to which her father had agreed.

Before the wedding, the groom had a serious talk with his bride. He told her the truth about his identity; she swore that she would tell no one until a later, agreed-upon time. After the wedding, the brother-in-law's attempts to instruct Israel proved to be futile, so he decided to free himself from them for the present time. Gershon gave his sister an ultimatum: separate from her husband, or leave the city with Israel. She chose the latter. The two of them left Brody, and began a life of poverty and hardship. For his new home, Israel chose a place to live in one of the foothills of the Carpathian Mountains. There were no Jews living there; Israel and his wife lived separated from their fellow believers—a life of complete isolation.

Israel worked in the canyons of the mountains and mined chalk, and his wife sold it in the nearby city. Their life seemed to be one of deprivation. Nevertheless, the harder their life became outwardly, the more Israel rose to spiritual greatness. In his times of solitude, he gave himself over to the practice of prayer, worship, and religious observance. It became his habit to climb to the top of the mountain and to wander around at the peak in an ecstatic state. He fasted, prayed, and performed incessant washings, and he observed all the ceremonial laws with exacting care.

Gershon must have been aware of the bitter poverty his sister was enduring. After seven years, his compassion for them prevailed. He brought his sister and her husband back to Brody. At first, he made Israel his chauffeur, but he was totally unsuitable for this job. So he rented for them a little inn in a village a few miles away, and he housed his sister and her husband there. "It was in this inn," as the Chasidim tell the story, "that the Master revealed his majestic splendor. He was about 36 years old when he was commanded from above to emerge from his humble circumstances and reveal his true greatness."

One day, a guest came down to the inn who was a lesser rabbi, a student of Rabbi Gershon. Israel waited on him alone. At the Sabbath table, this scholar recognized the hidden greatness of this seemingly uneducated innkeeper. Israel urgently pleaded with him not to reveal this to his brother-in-law. He was only to visit the pious Jews of the nearby city and say to them, "A great star has arisen in our midst, and you have known nothing about it." After that, Israel no longer lived in obscurity.

The founder of modern Chasidism revealed himself to the great masses as a miracle worker first, as a *ba'al Shem* ("master of the Name," בעל שם). This calling brought him into close contact with thousands of Jews, and even Christians, who believed in his holiness and goodness.

He was not the first or even the only *ba'al Shem* among the Jewish people. At that time there were stories all over Poland, Galicia, and Bohemia about the miracles which various wonder-working rabbis were performing. The physical and spiritual condition of the Jewish masses was pitiable. In the eyes of the Polish nobility, the Jews were worthless. Even Christian carpenters had to suffer hardship; how much more so the Jews. The *responsa* of the rabbis of that time are full of questions and answers regarding women who didn't know what to do or what had become of their husbands; in most cases, the landowners had simply slaughtered them.

It is no wonder that such treatment by "Christians" had a chilling effect on the Jews, who ended up hating everything Christian—so much so that even learning the Polish language or reading its literature was viewed as a sin. A rabbi, for example, might be heard to address his fellow Jews: "If a father made a vow that his son should not learn anything about the Polish language, it is a sin to do so even if the father was talking about something as simple as reciting the alphabet."

The miracle workers found a rich field for their activity not only in Poland and Galicia but also in other regions of Europe. Their clients were not limited to Jews; Christians (especially rich women) came to these holy men in order to seek relief for their physical and spiritual ailments. These miracle-workers are analogous to the modern-day disciples of "Christian Science" in America and England.

In contrast to most "miracle-workers," Israel really believed in his power to heal the sick, to free the possessed, and to foretell the future. He was so thoroughly permeated by his belief in the omnipresence of God that it would have been unthinkable for him to imagine that men who are connected to God would find themselves unable to experience and reveal the power of God. He traveled from place to place and became well known everywhere. Hundreds of men from all social strata traveled to see him in order to hear his teachings. After a while, he decided to abandon the life of an itinerant miracle-worker, and instead chose to take on the role of a teacher of the deepest kind of piety.

He especially emphasized the immanence of God, and—as is the case with Christian mystics—his concept of God and creation was colored with pantheism. Since God is present in all things, there must be some good in all things. It was on the basis of this principle that the Besht developed his ethical principles and especially his love for the sinner. One of his favorite slogans was, "No one has sunk so deep that God cannot make him a saint." He mingled often with sinners and tried to convince them that God was just as close to them as to the pious, and that he would seek them out to save them.

He was a great opponent of asceticism, which had been raised almost to the level of a non-negotiable dogma through the influence of Lurianic Kabbalah.

Intimate, fervent prayer meant much more to him than all other forms of outward piety and Torah study. Above all else, every man should be "a living Torah." "Actually, every man is a Torah in himself," said a student of the Baal Shem Tov, "because he is bearing the image not only of the Torah's Abraham and Moses, but also of the Torah's Balaam and Haman. He must strive to be someone who drives out Balaam and develops Abraham inside of himself." Each of a man's actions should be a pure manifestation of God. We should do what the Law requires, not to find grace in the eyes of God but rather in order to learn how we are to properly love God and to become one with him. It does not depend upon us or upon how many rules we observe but upon how we do God's will and with what kind of spirit.

In general, the Chasidim differ most sharply from all other Jews in the way that they pray; this is true even today. The Chasidim believe that the professional cantor is, for the most part, "the one with the most beautiful voice, but the one with an empty head," who regards his profession as nothing more than a business—and he is despised by the Chasidim. Among the Chasidim, the cantor must be a *tzaddik*—an extremely pious person. The prescribed hours for the holding of public worship are of little consequence to them; for Chasidim, prayer begins—just as among the Quakers—as soon as they get into the proper frame of mind for prayer.

Frequent washings, the study of Kabbalistic literature, stories of miracles done by the *tzaddikim* ["righteous ones," צדיקים]—these things are the means which help the Chasidim to achieve the right state of mind, the proper condition of the soul. The prayers themselves are accompanied by bizarre manifestations of religious excitement. In the zeal of prayer, some of them begin to dance like whirling dervishes; others become so absorbed in prayer that they are lost in catatonic ecstasy; some pray loudly, others in solemn silence.

The master, or guiding force, for the Chasidim—in fact, the very embodiment of their teachings and their lives—is their system of ongoing revelation. There is, outside of Chasidism, no other system in Judaism in which the attachment of the pious man to a tzaddik is viewed as being so absolutely essential.

KABBALISTIC-CHASIDIC MIRACLE STORIES

PAUL PHILIP LEVERTOFF

RABBI ISAAC LURIA AND HIS DISCIPLES

A holy man, Rabbi Solomon Luria, lived in the Holy Land and spent his life in prayer and study. One day as he stood alone, deep in prayer in the synagogue, the Prophet Elijah appeared to him and said, "May your soul not be troubled that you have no children, because the Lord has heard your prayer and will send you a son. You shall call his name Isaac. He will be a holy man who will penetrate the secrets of Torah and will be a benefactor of his people Israel."

The righteous man asked, "When will this happen?"

Elijah answered, "I cannot tell you; I can only tell you that when he does come, then you must wait for me until the eighth day after his birth, because I myself will perform the circumcision."

Full of joy and hope, Rabbi Solomon prayed to God that he would fulfill his promise.

When the child came into the world, the whole household of the pious ones was filled with light.

On the eighth day, they carried the child to the synagogue so that he could be circumcised there. Many had gathered there in order to attend the sacred rite and to go to the sacred meal. An hour went by; two hours went by, and more; and the people waited. They looked at the father with wonderment, and finally they asked him why he was still waiting. He answered, somewhat distressed, that he was still waiting for a guest.

When it was late, and the evening shadows were lengthening, and the prophet still had not appeared, the pious man went into a corner and began to cry, and prayed, "Holy God, your sinful servant has fulfilled your promised requirements, for the sake of your name."

His prayer was heard, and lo and behold, the prophet appeared. He performed the sacred ceremony and the father gave the son the name Isaac. However, the community noticed neither the prophet nor the carrying out of the deed. Astonished, they left the synagogue.

Three years passed, and the little Isaac began to go to school. It hardly needs to be said that he was a child prodigy. When he was eight years old he could already read the Talmud and the various commentaries. Just about then, his father died. After the seven days of mourning had passed, the mother spoke to her son: "I am too poor to buy you the holy books that you need. We will both travel to Egypt where your rich uncle lives."

Once in Egypt, the uncle took the boy to the famous Rabbi Bezalel Ashkenazi in order that he should be taught the Torah. After only two years, great Egyptian scholars were coming to little Isaac in order to learn from him. Rabbi Bezalel ordered that the young man should be called "rabbi." The uncle married him to his daughter, and he devoted himself to his studies in the Beit Midrash undisturbed. One day young Isaac was sitting in the Beit Midrash and saw a kabbalistic work in the hands of a completely unfamiliar Jew.

When he was asked who he was, the stranger answered that he was descended from those who had been forced to become Christians. Now he had fled, but he was not able to understand anything from this book. Rabbi Isaac gave him a siddur and asked him for the kabbalistic work. He immersed himself in it and discovered great secrets, and this work unfolded for him many puzzles in the holy Zohar. Every night, the soul of the young rabbi ascended to Paradise where a new secret was revealed to him. Once it was proclaimed to him that if he wanted to delve into even deeper secrets, he would have to separate himself completely from this world.

Six years went by in this manner. During this time, the prophet Elijah revealed himself to Isaac frequently. He led a life full of holiness and purity. One night, the prophet said to him: "Know that your years are numbered; leave Egypt and travel to Safed in Galilee. Rabbi Chayim Vital, who is now living in Damascus, you must visit in your official role as a prophet, because he is a holy man and has a spark of the soul of Rabbi Akiva in him. Share with him everything—whatever he asks you about."

Rabbi Isaac and his family moved to Safed. When he arrived there, all his wisdom vanished, and he forgot all the secrets that had been revealed to him in Egypt. He fell into despair and wrestled with God. An old man appeared to him and said to him, "You must start a new life, because all the wisdom that you have attained and achieved in Egypt cannot endure in the Holy Land."

He began again. He immersed himself in the divine secrets all over again, until he was like an angel, holy and pure. He understood the language of the angels, animals, and birds. And he could tell just by looking at the face of a man at what level his soul was. There was never a fly at his table, and in his room there blew the wind of Paradise itself. When he saw a man, he knew what would be determined on the Day of Atonement concerning him. However, he did this all in such a way so that the reputation of the holy Rabbi Moses Cordovero, who also lived in Safed, would not be affected.

One day, Rabbi Moses fell ill. He allowed his disciples to visit him, and he blessed them and said, "You need to know that my successor has been chosen. The one who has been determined to succeed me will notice a pillar of cloud at my funeral. This pillar of cloud will accompany me to my grave. He is a great Kabbalist, and he will open your eyes so that you will be able to see things which you were not able to see through me. You should follow him!"

Rabbi Moses died, and the whole city followed his body. Among these was Rabbi Isaac. Suddenly he cried out: "There is a pillar of cloud here!" The community understood what he meant. They showed him great honor, but he did not reveal himself to them at this time.

Ten pious Jews, among them our Rabbi Isaac, formed a community whose special assignment it was to bring the sinner to God. One day several of them noticed a well-dressed woman going with a man to a hidden place and talking with him quietly. They came and told Rabbi Isaac. However, he said, "Let this woman alone, she is not a sinner; her husband is in a distant land, and he sent her a message which instructed her to speak to several people about things which others should not hear. Go to this woman and ask for her forgiveness, because you have [wrongly] suspected her of sinning."

From that time on they were afraid to look the holy man in the face. However, two of his disciples had questions about him. They came to him in order to test him, and said, "Rabbi, are you a prophet?"

He answered them and said, "I am not a prophet, nor the son of a prophet!" Then they noticed someone walking past, and he touched the robe of the Rabbi, and Rabbi Isaac spoke to this person and said, "God forgive you; because of you I will have to immerse myself today because of contamination."

His disciples followed this man and said to him: "If you want your soul to be saved, then tell us what sin you have committed, and then we will gladly provide a means by which you will receive forgiveness of sins."

The man realized the sins which he had committed the day before, and was frightened. He was very scared. So this disciple also believed in Rabbi Isaac, and his reputation as a holy man spread everywhere.

That very night, the soul of Rabbi Isaac talked with the soul of Chayim Vital in Damascus. The soul of the first one (Rabbi Isaac) said to the other one: "Come here to Safed and great secrets will be revealed to you. Become my disciple!"

The next morning, Rabbi Chayim told his disciples, and they were surprised that he, the one who had written a commentary on the holy Zohar, should go to Safed in order to allow himself to be taught by an unknown Rabbi Isaac.

Three months passed and Rabbi Chayim noticed more and more that his wisdom was disappearing. Therefore, he decided to go to Safed. There, he tore his clothing and sprinkled ashes on his head and prayed to God that the rabbi would accept him as a disciple. He went to Isaac and asked him if he would like to take him on as a disciple. Isaac answered: "You have repented, and your prayer has been heard. Come and learn!"

He came and learned and understood everything; however, the angel of forgetfulness came over him and he could no longer retain the content of what he learned for longer than one day. Then the holy man [Isaac Luria] took him down to Miriam's well, and he drank from its water, and was healed.

FROM THE KABBALISTIC-CHASIDIC WORLD OF THOUGHT

PAUL PHILIP LEVERTOFF

"THE GREAT DEBATE"[16]

Benjamin of Slonim, a disciple of the Rabbi Elijah of Vilna,[17] one of the most resolute opponents of the Chasidim, once prepared a letter to a young friend of his, Rabbi Joseph of Nemirow, a disciple and an adherent of the famous Chasidic teacher, Rabbi Levi Isaac of Berdichev.[18] Rabbi Benjamin discusses in his letter nineteen questions about Chasidism, which he addressed to a naïve Chasid from his city, and he shares the answers to these questions as well. The Chasid, so he writes, did not at first want to discuss "spiritual things" with him at all, because to do so, it would be necessary for Benjamin to have "a special ear." But when Rabbi Benjamin assured him that he was simply searching for the truth with his heart, then he was willing to answer his questions. Several of the things which the Chasid said greatly pleased the rabbi, but for several of the others he wanted to have clarification from his young friend.

---

[16]   *Vikucha Rabbah* [ויכוחא רבה], "The Great Debate," is the title of a short Hebrew dialogue. It originates from the Golden Age of Chasidism. If the American philosopher of pragmatism, Prof. James, had been acquainted with the contents of this little work, which holds the reader in suspense until the last moment, he certainly would have given it a prominent place in his book, *Varieties of Religious Experience*. But now, as far as I know, the writing is only mentioned by Graetz (*The History of the Jews: Volume 9*, note 2), even though it shows more than one proof of a speculative or legendary product of the Kabbalistic-Chasidic tendency of the religious swing of mystical Judaism. For the work contains neither speculation, nor anything legendary, but only genuine religious experience. The duel took place in 1785–1786.

The writing abounds, as do most Chasidic works, with printing errors; there are many abbreviations, but no source information. For an example which I have in my possession, there is a bound volume under the name *Hashavat Aveida*, in which an unknown stranger wanted to prove to his Jewish people that he could be a great blessing. So he found several nasty passages about Jesus in the Talmud, in Kimchi's commentary to the Psalms, in Abraham ben Chissas' astronomical treatise (a writing from him which was translated in 1116 by Plato Tibertinus into Latin), which had been banned by the censors, and he reprinted them! May libel have such a fate!

[17]   1720–1797. He was honored with the title "Gaon" by his contemporaries and is called "The Vilna Gaon" to this day. Among his numerous writings (textual criticism and commentary on both Talmuds, the *Tosefta*, *Mechilta*, *Sifra*, *Sifre*; commentary on the Zohar; explanations to almost all the books of the Old Testament; a Hebrew grammar; a topographical description of the land of Palestine), there is to be found even a work about trigonometry and algebra. But to the Chasidim, he appeared to be like Saul to them.

[18]   Author of the *Kedushat Levi*. Rabbi Levi Isaac's love of the Jews has endeared him to the Jewish people to this day. Based on the verse in Numbers, "No harm is in sight for Jacob, no woe in view for Israel, the Lord their God is with them," he taught that those who look favorably on the people of Israel have God on their side. Rabbi Levi Isaac appreciated the Jewish masses in a way few others did, and they, in turn, have lovingly preserved his memory. Many of the incantations and special prayers attributed to him are in Yiddish, the language of the people. In times of trouble, Jews have recited them; in the same way, they have clung to the amulets he left behind. In modern times, poets like Zalman Shneur, Uri Zvi Greenberg, and Itzik Manger have called upon Rabbi Levi Isaac of Berdichev to save the Jewish people from the wrath of God.

Question 1: What attracted you in particular to a Chasidic rebbe? Why do other people from his city not travel to their own rebbe?

The Chasid's answer went like this: It is well-known that healthy people do not need a medical cure;[19] how much less those who are actually sick, but do not know that they are sick, and who imagine themselves to be healthy.[20] But those who are sick and feel the pain search out a doctor, even if it is at night. So it is with me. I saw my miserable need; I recognized the predicament of my soul and my sins, which were always before me.[21] I examined myself, weighed my options, and found that I was a long way from being good. So I thought to myself: "I will not rest until I have found a cure for my sickness." And since I had heard that there was a competent soul-doctor, I travelled to see him in the hope that he could perhaps provide a remedy or cure for me.

As far as my fellow countrymen are concerned, they do not go out to the *tzaddik* for two reasons: either they are completely healthy and not in need of a doctor, or they are so sick that they so not recognize their sins at all.

Question 2: So tell me, did you find a cure with the rabbi?

Answer: I saw that it would be a very protracted, long-term illness, which could not be healed in a short time, because all my own characteristics were a mixture of good and bad. It would take a lot of time to separate the good from the evil. But I had at least one advantage from this: that the sickness would not become even more serious, because I had recognized the root cause of my illness. And when the root cause of the illness has been eliminated, then the sickness itself can also be cured.

Question 3: You speak in parables. Tell me now, clearly and plainly: What did you experience there?

Answer: When I went to the Rabbi and stepped into his little *shul*, in order to pray there, I heard his prayer; it was like the sound of many waters, which broke the hearts of those who heard it. My hair stood on end, and I heard an impassioned voice, the likes of which I had never before heard, not even once. My heart broke, because I recognized my miserable poverty. My prayers until this time had been a babbling chatter. After the prayer, I went into the room of the rabbi. He seemed to be to me like an angel of God, and I was totally filled with awe. I stayed there until the Sabbath. What I saw there was a pure and holy life. I saw how he sat at his table, and I said to myself, "Yes indeed, it is true, what I have heard about him. But they didn't tell me even the half of it—of what I am seeing here." I was deeply moved and warmly inspired, for I had now seen the light. The impression remained fixed in the depths of my heart, even after I returned home. Every time I prayed, I remembered this experience and the words of the rabbi, which I had heard "from the fire," and my heart was warmed, and then I prayed the same way. But when this became a mere habit for me, and I again began to fall asleep spiritually, then I travelled back to the rabbi once more.

---

[19]   Cf. Mark 2:17.

[20]   Cf. John 9:41.

[21]   Cf. Psalm 51:5.

Question 4: Why haven't you told me about the root cause of your [spiritual] illness, which you recognized? You are telling me here that you "fell asleep again," but sleep is the sixtieth part of death! [22]

Answer: The origin of this deep sleep, which was so pleasant to me, and from which I could not rouse myself, I now realize. I asked the rabbi if he might have some advice for me as to how I might be freed from my own miserable characteristics. He answered that I had not described all of my sins, which were the source of all my evil, to him. Whereupon I said to him, "O master, I have hidden nothing from you." Then he said that I could not feel the worst characteristic [of my personality] at all. When I asked him what that might be, he said, "Pride. God and you, you cannot live together." Because God, on account of my pride, cannot dwell within me—this is the reason for this illness; therefore it follows that all bad personality traits are only branches of this root. Because man cannot recognize his own sins, he says, "Peace, peace, when there is no peace." And about such people it is said, "Woe to 'those who are lost in the land of Assyria!'[23] For although they seem to themselves to be good and fortunate, they are going to be lost, for they do not long from deliverance" (Asshur = Assyria = Ashir [עשיר], to have good fortune). So I said to myself, "No, that cannot be! How can I be so proud?"

His answer was that mankind by nature is very proud, and that he must desire to rise above the creature [the animal instinct inside him]. So we see this is already the case with children, whose nature it is to rise up and to beat everyone else with a stick, even if there is no good reason. As a child grows, so pride grows along with him.

For this reason a man also does not recognize his own sins, because they have become like a second nature to him. Likewise, a man also cannot feel the air, because it has surrounded him since his birth, and it has been a life-giving element for him. Likewise, the fish do not feel the water, because they were created in it and it is their life-giving element. For this reason they cannot tolerate the air, but it stands in opposition to their nature. [A fish cannot live outside of water in air alone; it is against the nature of a fish to do so.] However, just as a man cannot live in water, so also can a man recognize his own conceited self-importance only through the opposite. If someone, for example, mocks and despises him, then he is distressed and cannot tolerate the insult. By this, one can recognize that he has a personal characteristic which is exactly the opposite of humility and self-abasement. He is like one who grew up on a high mountain and never came down from it. Such a person is of the opinion that he is standing upon a level plain, but he will not believe it as long as he remains on his high observation point; until he one day begins to go down onto the flat lands below, and now realizes what a valley is. Only then does he understand that he previously had been standing upon a mountain.

So this is what happens to a man, when he first recognizes [the prideful state] of his own heart—when he has descended [to a lower level]. Now it is true that I had understood all of this before [in my head], but not with my heart. When I came back to my hometown and everyone who saw me mocked me, then I was angry and experienced in my own person the truth of all this—what the rabbi had told me.

---

22   b.*Berachot* 57b.

23   Isaiah 27:13.

Question 5: Don't we have a physician in our own town? Yes indeed, we have many holy writings, which the doctors have given us for the illness of the soul. Also, in them there is much talk about humility and pride.

Answer: We know that for an external medical problem, one doesn't need a specialist, because there are many doctors who can cure these things easily. But when it is an internal illness, whose cause is not so easy to determine, and about the root cause of which the doctors themselves are still in controversy, with each doctor offering a different diagnosis, then you need a highly competent doctor, one upon whom you can depend to make an accurate diagnosis. But when the source or root cause of an illness is unknown, medicine or treatment cannot help at all—yes, it could even do harm.

So it is with the sicknesses of the soul. For them, you need a specialist who can accurately examine the patient with precision in every detail. Men are different from one another according to the specific mixture of the four elements in them.[24] The one who is strong in the element of fire is inclined by nature to pride. The one in whom the element of water predominates tends toward joy. The bad qualities come from the "evils" in the four elements of mankind and their opposites; there are also good qualities which flow from and result from the "good" in the four elements, as well. The natural souls in Jews are indeed composed of good and evil.[25] It is also a given in the mixture of good and bad characteristics that healing and sorting is necessary. The one who is proud by nature will not recognize his pride at all, because his nature has hidden it from him. The one who is dominated in his nature by the element of earth tends toward melancholy, greed, and miserliness. He also will tend not to recognize his sins, just as it was in my case. I did not realize my own illness until I went to the rabbi and he gave me his "soul-diagnosis" and correctly specified my sickness.

The *tzaddikim* who discard the evil and choose the good, and transform the evil into the good, possess "knowledge of mankind," so that they can recognize and diagnose the root cause of the sins in anyone. But if someone wants to see a description of the evil inclinations of man in a book, that will not help much, because the sin still remains. Why? Because by nature a man does not recognize his sin. Even if there are bad characteristics which are to be blamed, the man says to himself, "Why, I certainly haven't done that!"

Question 6: Yes, there is a medicine that can heal all, which is the Torah; as our sages have said, "If a man has head, neck, or any other kind of pain, he should occupy himself with the Torah. And if a man studies Torah all day long, he does not need to read any other edifying writings."[26] This is what I was once told by the Vilna Gaon, my master. One time, when his disciples asked him to recite something witty for them, he answered: Someone spanked a child so that he should get going to school; but if he is already on his way to school, then you certainly don't need to spank him. Even so, if someone studies Torah, that person does not need mussar [מוסר].[27]

---

[24] Cf. *Etz Chayyim* 50:2.

[25] Cf. *Sefer Ha'Gilgulim*, 1, and *Tanya*, 10.

[26] b.*Eruvin* 54a.

[27] *Mussar* means both chastisement, or castigation, and edifying instruction.

Answer: The witnesses upon which you depend are very reliable, but I wonder how the Gaon could say that "building up" or "edification" doesn't first require a broken heart. Isn't man evil by nature? Certainly, our sages have also said, "The goal, the purpose of knowledge is repentance and good works."[28] This doesn't always happen; someone reads the Torah and studies the Talmud, and then goes and abuses his parents. Someone can act wickedly after learning something. Then the Torah which one has learned does not ascend upwards into the heavens. So it also says in the Zohar: "Torah, without fear and love (for God), does not rise upward but remains below." And if the Torah is not studied for its own sake, it can neither protect against sin nor rescue from sin. For this reason, even the Torah could not protect Doeg and Ahithophel,[29] because within them their souls were polluted, and the light of God could not dwell there.[30] The light of God can only be drawn down through true repentance, just as it stands written: "Repentance is a great thing, because it brings a cure into the world."[31] So it is also the case with an outward or external illness, in which a part of the body, when it has developed an illness via the blood, can no longer maintain life, and must first be healed by some medicine, in order to remove the illness. Then, after a return to a menu of light food, life returns to the diseased member, and it again goes well with the soul.

If it is polluted, then the light of God cannot dwell there, unless, of course, one repents. But through Torah study alone, the stain is not removed, because the light of God does not dwell in a polluted place, unless, of course, one repents. For this reason the Torah is also called bread, as it has been written: "Come, and eat my bread,"[32] and, "Your Torah is in my inward parts."[33] How this bread strengthens the heart of man! Because if a man does not eat, then he becomes weak; food keeps body and soul together, but food cannot bring the soul back to the body [once it has left it]. It is the same with Torah study. It strengthens the soul; however, if one does not occupy himself with the Word of God, then he will find that he has no strength to enlighten his soul, even if he has love for God and fear of him. So this is how it is, for example, with the man who eats sweet fruit but no bread: He stays weak. So it is with the Torah: it strengthens the soul, but it cannot bring the soul back again if it has become dead through sin. Indeed, when man is sinning, then even the Torah becomes for him like a deadly poison.[34]

And that is the meaning of the word of the Talmud: If someone has a headache, etc., that is, if a man is weak and if his soul has no strength, but he has not yet completely fallen, then the Torah is able to strengthen him. However, who can be so brave as to say, "I am pure, I have sanctified my works, and I don't need anything. How in the world am I to feel remorse, be contrite, and repent about my [good] works?"

---

28 b.*Berachot* 17a

29 Cf. b.*Sanhedrin* 106b.

30 Cf. 1 John 1:6

31 b.*Yoma* 86a.

32 Proverbs 9:5.

33 Psalm 119:11; Jeremiah 31:33.

34 b.*Yoma* 72b.

PART 2

Rabbi Benjamin had a hard time agreeing with the Chasid about the importance of Torah learning. In the Talmud it does indeed say, "Rabbi Judah said in the name of the Rabbis: 'One should still learn the Torah, even if this is happening when the Torah is not being learned for its own sake. Because if you occupy yourself with the Torah, even for selfish reasons, in the beginning, so it may happen that in time that you do study Torah for its own sake.'"[35]

Yet the *Tossafists*[36] proposed the question: "Indeed, it is said in another place, that if the Torah is not studied for its own sake, it would be better for him if he had not entered the world."[37] And they explain it this way: that the latter ones might arrive at the same destination as those who occupy themselves with the study of Torah in order to be able to triumph over their friends in a disputation. The former ones, however, refer to the one who occupies himself with the Torah in order to be called "rabbi."

Now granted, most people who are diligent in Torah study in their youth do so from a desire to become more learned; later on, they give themselves to Torah study out of love for it. However, if someone had to wait until he could study Torah out of entirely pure motives, then he generally would not get around to it; this is just like the story of a great rabbi who once heard that it was the devil who was preventing research into the Torah for selfish reasons, and also from doing a good deed for selfish reasons.

The Chasid refers again to the words of the Zohar, that Torah observance, without having fear and love, does not penetrate the realm above, because it is the spirit that gives it wings and which raises Torah and good works to a higher level. So, just as nothing can fly without wings, so also the Torah and good works cannot rise aloft without fear and love for God, but will remain [below], bound by Satan.

Of course, if the Torah is studied for its own sake, it will be given wings to rise up and ascend on high, even if it had previously been learned only from self-interest. However, you must still repent of everything that was formerly done out of selfish motives and free yourself from the grasp of Satan, so that it can then rise upwards. When the rabbi says that most people apply themselves to Torah study in their youth so that they might become educated people, it is indeed true, but such people are like children who still have insufficient knowledge about the true nature of Torah. And for those who study for this reason—so that they might know exactly what the Law says, yet they also wish at the same time to be regarded as someone great—that is not in itself a bad thing. This is just like the child, who first begins to learn when he goes off to school for the sake of the nuts and candy [he is given]. Then, when he gets bigger and his reason and his character have developed a bit more, he learns on account of the nice clothes which will be given him.[38] Later on, he learns in order to become a rabbi. By this time he has likely discovered so much more, so that he under-

---

[35] b.*Pesachim* 50b.

[36] The Northern French Glassatoren (commentators) of the Talmud in the twelfth to the fourteenth century of the Middle Ages. This was the era of Rabbi Shlomo Yitzhak (Rashi).

[37] Cf. *Sifre* at Leviticus 26, 3; b.*Berachot* 17a.

[38] Cf. Maimonides at m.*Sanhedrin* 11.

stands the true meaning of the Torah, and he immerses himself in God's Word, but not to receive a reward for it. And the opposite of this is what Rabbi Benjamin calls the temptation of the devil, and the Rabbi holds firmly to this view: namely, that Satan persuades a man to believe that Torah study would be something great for any reason, even if this Torah study is happening for selfish motives; so that everything becomes sheer habit, and one never recognizes his sins, and he even says that he is not lacking anything. For *kavanah* (intention)[39] is the main thing, both in halachic piety and in Torah study. Without *kavanah*—intention—there is only compromise with sin. It is better to have little with proper *kavanah* than much without it.

Then Rabbi Benjamin said, "These words are good. Unfortunately, there are many learned people who sing their own praises, that only they hold everything good; their own sins, however, they do not admit. Certainly, they are fortunate— those who go to the rabbi and receive [sound] advice from him as to how they can be cleansed from all stain—these righteous ones are to be praised."

Rabbi Benjamin now further expresses his amazement that so many Chasidim seem to have gotten no benefit from their visit to the Chasidic Rabbi, since one could observe in them no real change at all for the better. Even more so, he had the impression that after their return from the Rabbi, they had an exaggerated self-confidence and were even more filled with spiritual pride.

The answer of the Chasid is simple: Many are called, but few are chosen. And as it says in the Talmud in reference to Ecclesiastes 7:28: "A thousand men visit the study hall, but only a hundred of them become Torah scholars, only ten of them Mishnah scholars, and only one of them a Talmud scholar." [40] How much more so is this the case in spiritual things, where you need to decide to do something which forces you to strive against your [sinful] nature, namely: [achieve] holiness. Having said all that, there are still inner conversions which are hidden from man, which are known only to God. In addition to all that, the attachment of the Chasid to his rabbi is, in and of itself, something great.

It says in the Talmud that "he who attaches himself to a Sage, it is as if he had attached himself to the Shechinah." [41] And who is wise, if not he who possesses the higher wisdom, namely, he who ascends into God and is inwardly bound with him?[42]

This is like when men go to war. When some of them become sick, they carry them on their shoulders, but the dead they let lie. So it is when men are soul-sick: they will want to be brought to those who are truly pious, and they will adhere to them.

However, what self-confidence the Chasid has—now, compare the sinner with someone who approaches an old king; in order to be able to come into the presence of an old king, a person must have a great amount of self-confidence![43]

To the question how it came about that while he happened to be praying, he would cry out so loudly, and fall into ecstasy, the Chasid himself said he had realized how inappropriate it would

---

[39] Cf. b.*Berachot* 31a.

[40] *Leviticus Rabbah* 2:1; *Ecclesiastes Rabbah* 7:41.

[41] Cf. b.*Berachot* 10b; b.*Pesachim* 22b.

[42] Cf. *Zohar*, III, 138b, 139a.

[43] b.*Nedarim* 32b, Cf. Luke 14:31-33, Ephesians 6:10–21.

be if he would be able to suddenly fall into prayer and be transformed, and could reach the highest level of righteousness, the *hitlahavut*.[44] The Chasid humbly answered that his crying out did not result in such an ecstatic experience of immersion of himself into God, but that he cried out because of the realization of his own sins. For it is precisely in prayer that it becomes clear how far away he still is from God, and how ineffective all the preparations were, which he undertook before praying, in order to allow himself to be controlled by God. He is like a man who must be operated upon because of blood poisoning, and will gladly undergo all the pains of the operation, in order to be saved from death. However, how great his pain must be, and how loud his cries, when he is shown that even after the operation, all of the poison has not totally disappeared!

"One should serve God with joy,[45] and the pious ones have forbidden[46] sorrow altogether, and especially in prayer. Can you explain this?"

The answer of the Chasid was that one must differentiate between simple sorrow and contrition (over one's sins). The first example [the one who feels only sorrow] has pride as its source,[47] and hardness of heart and spiritual death is the result. The pain felt over sins, however, leads to joy and to life.[48] The more a man suffers in this way—true contrition, so that he realizes his sins before the holy God, the deeper will the light of godly joy penetrate into his heart.[49]

For this reason, a man should certainly do this before he approaches God in prayer: He should divert his will away from this world, and purge his heart of all filth. Then the attributes of a man will be accompanied by his will. And just as medicine can only help the sick when his body has first been purged inwardly, so only then can God's penetration into our souls through prayer occur, and then create life and joy in us, when we turn our own will away from the [things of this] world, and focus on our Father in heaven.

Rabbi Benjamin says that this must probably be true, what the Chasid has said about the will, and his own experience confirms this: that if a man's will is focused on something else other than God, he cannot pray. However, he was not so sure how a man could come to this point, to focus the will entirely upon God and to drive out all other thoughts from the soul.

---

44 *Hitlahavut* [התלהבות], ecstasy; and *hitdavkut* [התדבקות], the attachment to God (Cf. Deuteronomy10:20; 11:22; Psalm 63:9) are, just as Philo has already said, "the focal point" of Chasidic mysticism. *Hitdavkut* reminds us also of the Indian concept of *Bhakti*, in the *Bhagavad Gita*, and especially in the *Ramayana*. Cf. in addition, also Johann Gottlieb Fitche, *System der Sittenlehre* (Jena, Leipzig: C. E. Gabler, 1798) *Werke* IV, 254.

45 Psalm 100:2.

46 b.*Berachot* 31a, b.*Shabbat* 30a et al. Cf. Philippians 4:4.

47 Cf. *Tanya* 26 and 27.

48 Cf. 2 Corinthians 7:10: "Godly sorrow works towards sanctification. The sorrow of the world, however, works death." The joy belongs, in contrast to older Jewish mysticism, to the basic principles of Chasidic piety. "Faith in the light of the face of the Living King—that is the main thing! And he is absolutely Good. Therefore we will want to rejoice in him always! He who is sorrowful denies the love of God!" See *Tanya* 232.

49 Cf. Matthew 5:4; Luke 6:21.

The Chasid mentioned that prayer took up a lot of his time, and Rabbi Benjamin could explain this in no other way than that he was controlled by Lurianic[50] mysticism, and he was occupied in prayer especially with the concentration of his thoughts upon a specific name of God, with gematria, with combinations and permutations of the [Hebrew] letters. Now Rabbi Benjamin said that he would also like to penetrate the depths of Kabbalah, and he asked the Chasid if he would introduce him into the esoteric practices of his master.

The Chasid answered that he was a simple, sinful man, who would not dare to attempt to achieve the deepest concentration, which was possible only for the true *tzaddikim*, who, because they were totally free from materialism, could even "pull out" of the holy letters material things, and penetrate into the essence of an object.

However, as far as he, the Chasid, was concerned, the main thing in prayer was to speak from the heart in simple faith and with joy. However, as to introducing him into the esoteric observances of prayer, the Chasid would not be able to fulfill the wish of rabbi Benjamin, since he was just like his master, and just like the other Chasidic disciples, who simply stimulated heart-piety, and who could explain to him nothing about the secrets of Kabbalah.

But why does he pray for so long? Because prayer requires much effort and work.

Is it easy to totally disengage and be free from sensuality and carnality? When someone draws near to God in prayer, the Satan is right there opposing him, trying to confuse his thoughts.[51]

Yes, prayer is a battle. Prayer is work.[52] Prayer means ascending totally into God.

In prayer, man should immerse himself in the secret of the omnipresence of God and realize that he is "all in all." Prayer means concentrating upon God, and that is not so easy!

Rabbi Benjamin wondered about the inconsistency of the Chasid; to wit: Sometimes he prayed so fervently, but sometimes so coldly. He also observed how often the Chasid, instead of living in the higher regions after prayer, remained adhered to everyday life, and seemed to get excited if someone was not doing what he wanted to do. How would this be any different from those whose prayers he considered to be nothing more than an outward "babbling of the lips"? How much better indeed are the ordinary pious ones, who do not only not belong to a Chasidic sect, but who simply pray regularly according to the *Siddur*, and conduct their lives on a daily basis in a meek and humble way! That is probably what the Vilna Gaon meant, when he spoke about the sect of

---

50 Isaac Luria (1534–1572), from Jerusalem, established the new Kabbalah. Living in a lonely house on the Nile River, he saw nightly visions the prophet Elijah, the man who revealed the deepest secrets to him. He moved to Safed in Upper Galilee, the city of "saints and men of action," where "even all the air was saturated with mystical thoughts." Only a two-year stay was enough for him to make it the focal point of the famous Kabbalist circle. He systematized the Zohar, but the real goal of his teaching was to prepare for the Messianic redemption. Prayer is for him the most important means for accomplishing this. Every sound in prayer, beneath its literal meaning, has deep mystical significance.

51 Cf. Salomon Maimon, *An Autobiography* (1792), 1, 222: "It was amusing to see how they (the Chasidim) would often pray, making all sorts of strange sounds and breaking into comical movements (which were able to be seen—like the threats and abusive words against their enemy, Satan, who tried to disturb their concentration). And, how they worked themselves into a frenzy in the process, so that they regularly fainted, falling down at the end of their prayer, completely spent and out of energy." Cf. also the *Tanya* 28.

52 Cf. *Sifre* at Deuteronomy 11:13; y.*Berachot* 4:1.

the Chasidim—that they have their origin in the "outer-shell" (*kelippat nogah*, [קליפת נגה]),[53] and for this reason they are confusing good and evil with each another.

The Chasid answered this criticism in the following way:

Either way, such people ought to pray regularly every day, so that for these people who will be completely dominated by the divine power, even their animal soul (*nefesh*)[54] rejoices with God in prayer. However, ordinary men do not possess such a spiritual condition, because for them, it is like someone who is color-blind; they lack the organ for it. Such a saint will certainly always focus his heart upon his Father in heaven.

However, some people are of a lower sort, who remain totally unmoved in prayer by the power of God and who pray only habitually, from an outward, external sense of duty. However, he who belongs to neither the first nor the second class cannot always pray in the same way, since his spiritual condition is influenced by his physical, and his physical by his spiritual, condition.

As far as the non-Chasidic saints are concerned, they are for this very reason all the more regular in prayer, and so humble in their dealings with men, because they either belong to those who have become perfect, complete saints, or they belong to those whose piety is only outward and external, and pray according to a prescribed *Shulchan Aruch*, and act in a humble way according to the same *Shulchan Aruch*, without warmth, without intimacy.

What is the difference between the chasid and the *mitnaged*? The latter know neither what sin [really] is nor how to fight against it. They are satisfied with themselves and with their level of piety. But the former knows the power of sin and longs for salvation.

The Vilna Gaon's characterization of the Chasidim, however, stands in stark contrast to the doctrine of the soul in the Kabbalah, according to which every Israelite, whether he be good or bad, possesses two souls. The one comes directly from God, and just as the child's toes have their origin in the parents, so their spiritual souls of even the greatest sinners have their origin in God.

The other soul of the Israelite emanates from the "shell," which is penetrated by rays of lights and which is embodied in the four natural elements, from which the evil nature as well as the good attributes or characteristics come. The difference between good and bad Israelites consists only in this: that the souls of the former ones descend into this world in order to transform the natural, animalistic part in their being and make it pure, and in order to force the evil qualities [of their being] into the service of the good.

---

[53] The material world, a world existing as separate and independent is, according to the Kabbalah only a phantom, an empty shell, the "backside" or "other side" of the divine. The distinguishing sign of the "backside" is the striving for separation, for something different, as opposed to the "divine side," which is striving to bring unity from multiplicity. But for now, the "other side" or "backside" needs to be considered from two different viewpoints: 1) as a complete, anti-divine flip-side, which represents the evil thoughts, the evil desires, and the evil deeds, which are called "the three unclean shells" and which form total darkness; and 2) on the other hand the *sitra achra* or "other side" is more of an intermediary between the divine and the anti-divine "outer shell," which is able to be penetrated by beams of light, and where the Divine Light shines into the empty world. From the first shell comes all sins, all evil, all idolatry. The second shell represents, as it were, the ordinary course or way of this world, where good and evil are mixed together.

[54] In the Kabbalistic doctrine of the soul, into which we occasionally go in detail, *neshamah* is hereby understood as πνευμα, spirit. *Neshamah* forms the third, higher level of the five levels of the soul, which are preceded by the two lower levels: *nefesh* (animal soul) and *ruach*. Cf. also Saadia, *Kitab al-Amanat wal-I'tikadat* 6:4; *Zohar* 2:141b, Rabbi Moshe Cordovero in *Pardes Rimonim* at several places.

With the souls of the idolaters, however, this is not the case; they are emanating from the three impure shells which create total darkness.[55] Only how could the Vilna Gaon say that the souls of the Chasidim have their origin in the "outer shell"? He probably just heard something about their forms of worship, and to deter simple, ordinary people from joining the Chasidim, he said what he said.

Certainly, Rabbi Benjamin wanted to know why the Chasid spent so much time in prayer, since it was indeed much more important to spend time in the study of the Holy Scriptures. The Talmud does speak about men like this, who neglect that which has eternal worth, and who occupy themselves instead with things which have only temporal, worldly value.[56]

The Chasid replied that true prayer must bear the character of the one who is offering it; and just as the offered animal must go up in fire on the altar, so must the animal soul (*nefesh*) of the man go up through the fire of his love towards God, in order to become one with him. As soon as the prayer rises, through the immersion in the Holy Scriptures, the divine light comes down. Now the ancients, because they had highly developed souls, and because they were so holy, only had to sacrifice a little, for they gave most of their time to the Torah. We, however, must be first cleansed through prayer.

Why do the Chasidim maintain that prayer must play such a major role, when it is not pre-scribed in the times of the Talmud? Among the *vatikin*, the old Chasidim, it was even reported that they observed the first breaking of the rays of the sun on the horizon so that they could recite the Shema at the break of day.[57] But why do the Chasidim not worry about a *minyan* (whether there are at least 10 worshipers present), but will pray alone, each man praying by himself?

"That just shows how outward your piety is!" said the Chasid. While you are praying, it is all about *kavanah*, devotion, and "a prayer without *kavanah* is like a body without a soul." Now it is certainly nice when you can pray early, as the ancient Chasidim did, but you must be sure to pray with deep sincere *kavanah*, turned away from this world.[58]

"You, on the other hand, are only seeking to imitate the ancients outwardly, even though you are not mentally or physically prepared to pray as you should." You also should not forget that even in the old days, there were only a small number of chosen ones who could pray so. Their body was pure, because their spirit had the dominant authority over it; their body was a holy temple of God.[59] But we, who have so little holiness, and are also outwardly unclean, and are also so bound to this world, must first prepare ourselves for a long time, in order to speak with God.

It is like a king who loved music very much. He selected some great musicians, and ordered them to come early every morning, at a set time, and play for him. He arranged for them to receive rich rewards, especially those who came to play before the crack of dawn.

---

[55] Cf. Vital, *Sha'ar haKedusha* 1; *Etz Chayim* 50:2; *Tanya* 10, 11. Cf. also the classification of humanity into categories, which according to their nature are different among the Gnostics. The Valentinians especially distinguish between the Pneumatics, the Psychics, and the Hylikers. See G. Heinrici, Die *Valentinianische* Gnosis und die *heilige Schrift* (1871); Adolf Harnack, *Lehrbuch Der Dogmatik Und Dogmengeschichte* (1888), 1.2, 222.

[56] Cf. b.*Shabbat* 33b, b.*Betza* 15b.

[57] b.*Berachot* 9b, 25b, 26a.

[58] Cf. b.*Berachot* 32b.

[59] 1 Corinthians 3:16.

Now, there were two classes of musicians among them. The first class consisted of musicians whose music could penetrate the soul, and whose instruments were first-rate, and they loved the king more than their reward. Because they didn't have to prepare ahead of time, they brought special joy to the king, by always coming before the appointed time.

The second class consisted of others like them, but who were not as good. Also, their instruments were not perfect. But because they also loved the king, they were well-prepared ahead of time, and they came at the appointed time. The king was also very pleased with their playing.

Then their children came to be their successors as musicians for the king. However, most of them understood very little about the nature of music, and their instruments were of poor quality as well. To make matters worse, they didn't even love the king, but thought more about the pay they would receive for their playing.

And so the sons of those great musicians tried to imitate their fathers. But they came before the king unprepared, with their poor quality instruments, only to receive the big reward. The sons of the others, who weren't as good at being musicians, also acted like their fathers, and arrived on time, right at the appointed time. But the king was not pleased with their music.

Several of them noticed this, and decided to learn some basic music, and to prepare themselves ahead of time. So this is what they did, and came every day a little before the appointed time. Now their playing was certainly not perfect; but the king noticed how much effort they were putting into it, and how sorry they were that they couldn't play better, and even though their instruments were not perfect, he now enjoyed it more when they played for him.

APPENDIX 3
PRIMARY SOURCES USED BY LEVERTOFF

Address to the Greeks: Written by Tatian, who was a believer of the second century CE in Assyria and known for his works on theology. After becoming a believer, Tatian became a disciple of Justin Martyr and later opened a school in Rome. His oracles are a defense of the Christian faith as well as a denunciation of Greek culture.

Antiquities of the Jews: Written by the Jewish historian Josephus in the late first century CE, it tells the story of the Jewish people from the creation account until Josephus' own era.

Aphraates Homilies: Aphraates, the first of the Syriac Church Fathers, lived in the early fourth century. His Homilies (also known as the *Demonstrations*) are a collection of writings on Christianity and the Christian faith.

A Treatise on the Soul: Written by Tertullian (also known as Quintus Septimius Florens Tertullianus) who was an early church father in Africa from the late second century to early third century. His *A Treatise on the Soul* is a doctrinal work on the nature of the soul.

Chovot HaLevavot: "Duties of the Heart," a work written by Rabbi Bachya ibn Pakuda, who lived in Spain in the eleventh century; he is more commonly known as Rabbeinu Bachya. The work was originally written in Arabic under the title *Al Hidayah ila Faraid al-Kulub* and later translated into Hebrew under the title *Chovot Halevavot* by Judah ibn Tibbon. Based on his observation that the majority of rabbis devoted attention to outward observance of the Torah and ignored the matters of the heart, he sought to compile the ethical teachings of rabbinic literature into a complete system.

Clementine Homilies: One of several pseudepigraphal works ascribed to Clement of Rome. The *Homilies* contain various discourses that Clement is said to have sent to James the brother of our Master as well as an account of the dispute between Peter and Simon Magus. Although it is a forgery in that it does not go back to Peter or James, its apparent Jewish origin is a matter of academic discussion.

Didache: Lit. "Teaching." A collection of teachings purportedly passed on from the twelve apostles that dates to the late first or early second century CE. The contents concern moral and communal instructions to primarily Gentile believers in Yeshua. The full title of the *Didache* is "The Teaching of the Lord through the Twelve Apostles to the Gentiles." Although scholars agree that it does not date back to the original twelve apostles, it is certainly of Jewish-Christian origin.

Etz Chayim: Written by Rabbi Chaim Vital (1543–1620). The teachings he received from Rabbi Isaac Luria explaining the system of Lurianic Kabbalah.

1 Enoch: Also known as the Ethiopic Enoch. This work describes a vision revealed to Enoch in which he is taken up to the heavens and shown the secrets of heaven and earth. After returning from the heavens, Enoch explains his visions to his family before being taken back up into heaven, as described in Genesis 5:24. The book of Enoch is quoted in the Epistle of Jude 1:14.

2 Enoch: Second Enoch, also known as the Slavonic Enoch, is part of the Pseudepigrapha and is traditionally dated to the first century BCE. Likely authored by an Alexandrian Jew, the majority of this work describes the various levels of the heavens; it concludes with Enoch's admonition to his offspring and his eventual ascent into heaven.

Epistle to the Ephesians: Written by St. Ignatius, who was the second bishop of Antioch of Syria (some sources say the third bishop) and was martyred under the reign of Trajan (98–117 CE). His Epistle to the Ephesians urges them to strengthen themselves in their unity and allegiance to their bishop.

4 Ezra: Also known as 4 Esdras in the Latin Vulgate. This work is also known by the title 2 Esdras (when the biblical books of Ezra and Nehemiah are not counted as 1 and 2 Esdras respectively). Due to internal language, the work appears to be from the late first century CE.

Hegion HaNefesh: "Contemplation of the Soul." A work written by Rabbi Avraham bar Chiyah, who lived in Spain from the late eleventh to the early twelfth century.

Igeret HaKodesh: "Sacred Epistle." The fourth section of the *Tanya* written by Rabbi Schneur Zalman of Liadi. It primarily discusses how to walk out the way of God according to Chasidic thought.

Igeret HaTeshuvah: "Epistle of Repentence." The third section of the *Tanya* written by Rabbi Schneur Zalman of Liadi. It discusses the concept of repentance in Chasidic thought.

Kav HaYashar: "The Just Measure." The *Sefer Kav HaYashar* is a work of *mussar* ("ethic teachings") written by Rabbi Tzvi Hirsch Kaindenover (died 1712).

Keter Shem Tov: A collection of teachings by the founder of Chasidus, Rabbi Israel "Baal Shem Tov." The teachings were compiled by Aharon ben Tzvi HaKohen. The work was originally published in Zholkva in 1794–95.

Ketonet Pasim: A compilation of writings by Rabbi Yaakov Yosef HaCohen of Polonnoye, who was one of the chief disciples of the Baal Shem Tov and author of the famed *Toledot Yaakov Yosef* (1870). *Ketonet Pasim* was published posthumously in Koretz. Other works of Rabbi Yaakov Yosef include *Ben Porat Yosef* (1781) and *Tzafnat Paneach* (1782). The above works are some of the major sources for the teachings of the Baal Shem Tov and often speak against the elitist Jews who ignored the masses.

Kuntras HaHitpa'alut: The "Essay on the Awakening," it is a work authored by Rabbi Dov Ber Schneuri, the Mittler Rebbe (1773–1827), the second Rebbe of Chabad-Lubavitch. This work, also known by the title "Essay on Ecstasy," is a discussion of the five levels of spiritual emotion and the corresponding five levels of the soul, as well as how these emotions are found within both the animal soul and the godly soul.

Letter of Aristeas: A pseudepigraphical work dating to 200 BCE. This is a letter written to a certain Philocrates describing the origin of Greek translation of the Torah by the seventy-two elders at the request of the librarian of Alexandria. Josephus mentions the account in *Antiquities* 12:2.

Likkutei Ramal: Authored by Rabbi Moshe Leib of Sassov (1745–1807), a disciple of Reb Shmelke of Nikolsburg. He also authored *Toras Ramal HaShalem* and a collection of insights on the *Talmud* called *Chiddushei Ramal*.

Likkutei Torah: Authored by Schneur Zalman of Liadi (1745–1813), who was the founder of the Chabad-Lubavitch sect of Chasidic Judaism, it was originally published in Zhitomir in 1848. This work is a collection of homilies on the books of Leviticus, Numbers, Deuteronomy, Lamentations,

Esther, and Song of Songs, as well as discourses relating to Rosh Hashanah, Yom Kippur, and the feast of Sukkot.

Mechilta: Also known as the *Mechilta De'Rabbi Yishmael*, this work is a halachic midrash (although large portions are aggadic in nature) on the book of Exodus from the school of Rabbi Yishmael ben Elisha. The *Mechilta* was redacted by the third century CE and written in Mishnaic Hebrew, with some words in Greek and Latin.

Midrash Rabbah: A compilation of homiletic and halachic teachings on scriptural expositions by the various sages of the Tannaitic era. The *Midrash Rabbah* is arranged according to the weekly Torah readings based on the one-year cycle. The books of Torah are covered in the midrash as well as the five *Megillot*: Lamentations, Ruth, Ecclesiastes, Esther, and Song of Songs.

Mishnah: The Oral Torah as compiled by Rabbi Meir and eventually committed to writing by Rabbi Yehudah HaNasi, dating from approximately 200 CE.

Nachmanides' Commentary on the Torah: Nachmanides (1194–1270) was a Torah scholar and mystic. His commentary encouraged a critical examination of the text of the Torah and provided simple explanations for the weekly sections of the Pentateuch on Sabbaths and festivals.

Odes of Solomon: A Jewish pseudepigraphical work composed of forty-two odes written toward the end of the first century CE. The extant manuscripts are predominately in Syriac, with a relatively few in Coptic and Greek. The odes bear resemblance to themes in the Dead Sea Scrolls and the Gospel of John, and are believed to be the work of the early Jewish believers.

Or HaShem: A work written by Rabbi Chasdai ben Avraham Crescas (1340–1411) that speaks against the use of Aristotelian philosophical systems in understanding the Jewish faith, feeling that doing such led one to misunderstand Judaism.

Perek HaShalom: "Chapter of Peace." This work is a midrashic collection of sayings on the subject of peace from various rabbis of the Talmudic era. It is found in the Minor Tractates of the *Talmud* in *Derech Eretz Zuta*.

Philo: A Hellenized Jewish philosopher who lived from 20 BCE to 50 CE. In his writings, he attempted to harmonize Judaic Torah and Greek philosophy. His writings give us a historical glimpse into the world of the Second Temple period. Many similarities exist between Philo's writings and the theology of the Gospel of John, and there are some similarities to Paul and the Epistle to the Hebrews. Among Philo's works cited by Levertoff are *Allegorical Interpretations, Concerning Noah's Work as a Planter, On Abraham*, the *Fragment on Exodus*, and *The Special Laws*.

Pirke DeRabbi Eliezer: A collection of *midrashim* attributed (perhaps pseudepigraphically) to Rabbi Eliezer ben Hyrcanus (first and second century CE) on the book of Genesis as well as parts of Exodus and a small portion of Numbers. Internal content indicates that the work was amended by a later scribe, due to its mention of Talmudic sages who lived after the time of Rabbi Eliezer.

Pirkei Avot: A collection of ethical teachings from the sages. Found in the *Mishnah* tractate *Seder Nezikin*.

Prayer of Azariah: The prayer that comprises the first part of *The Song of the Three Children* is found in the Septuagint and contains an account of the praises offered to God by Hananiah, Mishael, and Azariah while in the furnace. The prayer takes place after Daniel 3:23 in the Hebrew texts. Verse 1 is an introduction; verses 2–26 contain a prayer by Azariah (Abednego); verses 27–66 contain a song of praise by the three children (*Hymn of Praise*); and verse 68 is a conclusion to the text.

Reishit Chokmah: A work written by the sixteenth-century Tzfat mystic Rabbi Eliyahu de Vidas, who was a student of the Rabbi Moshe Cordovero. *Reishit Chokmah* explains the preliminaries to begin the study of the mystical wisdom.

Schneur Zalman's Siddur: A siddur titled *Siddur Torah Or* that was compiled by the Alter Rebbe of Chabad, Schneur Zalman of Liadi. Schneur Zalman sought to compose a prayer book based primarily on the Jewish mystical school of Rabbi Isaac Luria of Tzfat. Schneur Zalman later compiled a siddur without the mystical meditations that was titled *Tehillat HaShem*.

Seder Eliyahu Rabbah: The first section of a larger work known as *Tanna de'Vei Eliyahu*. Although the final redaction of this work occurred in the tenth century CE, the actual dating of much of the work is earlier, as found by a reference to it in the *Talmud* in b.*Ketubot* 106a, which mentions the teachings therein being committed to Rabbi Anan, a third-century Amora of Babylon. The work is a collection of teachings on the commandments and study of the Torah as well as other topics of Judaism.

Sha'ar HaKedushah: A work authored by Rabbi Chayyim ben Yosef Vital that describes the proper conduct of those seeking to enter into mystical studies.

Sha'ar HaTefillah: "The Gate of Prayer" is a work written by Dov Ber of Chabad, which is found within the collection titled *Sha'arei HeTeshuvah*.

Sha'arei Avodah: "The Gates of Service." A continuation and expansion of the teachings of the Alter Rebbe by Rabbi Aharon HaLevi that outlines the idea that divine service and self-nullification come by displaying spiritual emotion openly.

Sha'arei HaTeshuvah: "The Gates of Repentance." A work authored by Dov Ber, the second rebbe of Chabad. It is a collection of discourses on the subjects of repentance, free will, and prayer, as well as Jewish education.

Sha'arei HaYichud Ve'Emunah: A work authored by Rabbi Aharon HaLevi Horowitz, one of Rabbi Schneur Zalman's chief disciples, which is an elaboration on the section of *Tanya* titled *Sha'ar HaYichud VeHa'emunah* ("Gate of Unity and Belief"). HaLevi's work discusses the creation and its relationship with God. The book also speaks on the subject of the infinitude and omniscience of God.

Shnei HaMeorot: Another title authored by Dov Ber, *Shnei HaMeorot* is an early Chasidic work explaining the origin of Chasidic mysticism within the Torah, thus attempting to establish the biblical roots of Chasidus with special reference to Schneur Zalman's *Likkutei Amarim*, the *Tanya*.

Shomer Emunim: Written by the Italian rabbi and mystic, Rabbi Yosef ben Immanuel Ergas (1685–1730), a student of the Ramaz (Rabbi Moshe Zacut). *Shomer Emunim*, published in Amsterdam in 1736, is dialogue between a philosopher and a Jewish mystic. It is seen as a basic introduction to the primary thoughts in Jewish mysticism.

Siddur Sha'arei HaTefillah: The Siddur known as "The Gates of Prayer."

Sifre: A midrash on the books of Numbers and Deuteronomy from the Tannaitic era. The *Sifre* to Numbers reflects the teachings from the school of Rabbi Ishmael ben Elisha, while the majority of the *Sifre* to Deuteronomy reflects that of Rabbi Akiva.

Talmud: A voluminous record of rabbinic discussions about the *Mishnah*. The text of the *Talmud* contains both the *Mishnah* and later argumentation about the *Mishnah*. The later argumentation is called the *Gemara*. It contains legal disputes, ethical instruction, midrash, stories about the sages, Jewish customs, and historical anecdotes. Two different compendiums of *Talmud* exist. The *Jerusalem Talmud* (the *Yerushalmi*) contains the discussions of the sages in the land of Israel, and the *Babylonian Talmud* (*the Bavli*) contains the discussions of the sages in Babylon. The *Talmud*s were completed in the fifth and sixth centuries but also contain material dating back to Ezra's time.

Tanya: This work is also known by other titles, which include *Sefer Shel Beinonim* ("Book of the Intermediates") and *Likkutei Amarim* ("Collected Discourses"). It is often called *Tanya* ("It was taught") after the first word of the book, which is a quote from the *Talmud* (b.*Niddah* 30b). The *Tanya* was authored by Rabbi Schneur Zalman of Liadi (1745–1813), who was the founder of the Chabad-Lubavitch sect of Chasidic Judaism; it was first published in Slavita in 1796 under the title *Likkutei Amarim*. It is a systematic exposition of the teachings and philosophy of Chasidus and serves as a guidebook for life for many adherents to Chabad today.

Testament of the Twelve Patriarchs: A Jewish pseudepigraphical work written between the second century BCE and the end of the first century CE. The contents are essentially the last will and testament of the twelve patriarchs of Israel, the sons of Jacob. Each patriarch gives a biographical summary of his past that includes a confession of sins committed and concludes with a prophetical oracle of sorts. The texts are extant in Greek, Armenian, and Slavonic; an early date of composition may be attributed to the Testament of the Twelve due to Aramaic fragments of the testaments that were found in the Dead Sea Scrolls and Cairo Genizah.

The Shepherd of Hermas: Also known as *The Pastor of Hermas*, the work dates from the late first to early second century CE. Numbered among the apostolic fathers, Hermas was a Christian who compiled his *The Shepherd* based on a series of visions he received. *The Shepherd* speaks of the virtues of repentance and Christian virtues.

Tomer Devorah: The "Palm Tree of Devorah," a work of Jewish mysticism written by the sixteenth-century Tzfat mystic Rabbi Moshe Cordovero (1522–1570). The work teaches one to imitate the attributes of God.

Torah Or: A collection of homiletical discourses on the first two books of the Torah, Genesis and Exodus, that was authored by Schneur Zalman of Liadi (1745–1813), who was the founder of the Chabad-Lubavitch sect of Chasidic Judaism, and originally published in Kopust in 1837.

Tosefta: Lit., "Addition." Rabbinic writings of supplementary material to the *Mishnah*. Although it was not compiled until after 200 CE, it contains material that dates back to an earlier period, sometimes even further back than the *Mishnah* does.

Tractatus Theologico-Politicus: A work written in Latin by Benedictus de Spinoza (1632–1677) that criticizes religious intolerance and speaks in defense of the secular government.

Wisdom of Ben Sira: This deuterocanonical work, which dates to around the second century BCE, is also known as *Ecclesiasticus, Ben Sirah, Sirach,* or *The Wisdom of Jesus the Son of Sirach*. The subject matter of the book concerns itself with Torah observance and how it is the center of attaining wisdom.

Wisdom of Solomon: A deuterocanonical known in Latin as *Sapientia* that was likely written sometime between the second and first centuries BCE in Alexandria. The *Wisdom of Solomon* addresses authorities on earth and admonishes them to hearken to the wisdom of God; the latter half of the work contains Solomon's musings on his attainment of wisdom from God as well as various prayers.

Zohar: A deeply mystical commentary on the Torah, traditionally believed to be authored by Rabbi Shimon bar Yochai (second century CE) while he was hiding from the Romans in a cave. It is organized to follow the weekly Torah portions. Critical scholarship argues for a later date of composition in the medieval period, though it is likely a compilation of earlier traditions that are attributed to Shimon. Quotes from the *Zohar* by figures predating the medieval era also suggest the antiquity of several of its portions.

BIBLIOGRAPHY

Altmann, A. "'Eleazar of Worms' *Hokhmath Ha-'Egoz.*" *Journal of Jewish Studies* 11 (1960): 101–113.

Ambrozic, Aloysius M. "New Teaching with Power (Mk 1.27)." Pages 113–149 in *Word and Spirit: Essays in Honor of David Michael Stanley.* Edited by Joseph Plevnik; Willowdale, Ontario: Regis College Press, 1975.

Belenson, Elizabeth. Translated by Paul P. Levertoff. "The Hidden Christ Among the Jews." *Church and the Jews* 95 (April 1933): 8–10.

Berger, David. *The Rebbe, the Messiah, and the Scandal of Orthodox Indifference.* Oxford: Littman Library of Jewish Civilization, 2001.

Berlin, Rabbi Naftali Zvi Yehudah. *The Path of Torah.* Translated by E. Greenman. Jerusalem, Israel: Urim, 2009.

Bloomberg, Craig L., and Mariam J. Kamell. *Exegetical Commentary on the New Testament: James.* Grand Rapids: Zondervan, 2008.

Braude, William G. *The Midrash on the Psalms.* 2 vols. New Haven, CT: Yale University Press, 1959.

Breiter, Yitzchok. *Seven Pillars of Faith and A Day in the Life of a Breslover Chassid.* Monsey, New York: Breslov Research Institute, 1989.

Buber, Martin. *Tales of Rabbi Nachman.* New York: Humanity Books, 1988.

Buber, Martin. *The Legend of the Baal-Shem.* Translated by Maurice Friedman. New Jersey: Princeton University Press, 1995.

Catchpole, David. "You Have Heard His Blasphemy." *Tyndale Bulletin* 16 (October 1965): 10–18.

Charitonov, Sholom. "Our Generation: What Makes Us Different." *Beis Moshiach* 320. No Pages. Cited 27 January 2009. Online: http://www.beismoshiach.org/Moshiach/Moshiach320/moshiach320.htm.

Charles, R.H. *The Apocrypha and Pseudepigrapha of the Old Testament.* 2 vols. London: Oxford University Press, 1913.

Climacus, John. *The Ladder of Divine Ascent.* Translated by Colm Luibheid and Norman Russell. Mahwah, NJ: Paulist Press, 1982.

Cooper, Stephen Andrew. *Marius Victorinus' Commentary on Galatians.* New York: Oxford University Press, 2005.

Cordovero, Moshe. *Pardes Rimonim.* Translated by Elyakim Getz. Rhode Island: Providence University, 2007.

Cordovero, Moshe. *Tomer Devorah*. Translated by Dov Fink and Shimon Finkelman. Brooklyn: Tomer Publications, 2007.

Coxe, A. Cleveland. *Ante-Nicene Fathers*. Edited by Alexander Roberts and James Donaldson. 10 vols. Peabody, MA: Hendrickson, 2004.

Culpepper, R. Alan. *John, the Son of Zebedee*. Columbia, SC: University of South Carolina Press, 1994.

Dan, Joseph. "*Hokhmath Ha-'Egoz*, Its Origin and Development." *Journal of Jewish Studies* 17:1–2 (1966): 73–82.

DovBer, Shalom. *Kuntest Umaayan: Overcoming Folly, A Chasidic Treatise by Rabbi Shalom DovBer of Lubavitch*. Translated by Zalman Posner. Brooklyn: Kehot Publication Society, 2006.

Dubnov, Shimon. *Toldot HaChassidut*. Tel Aviv, Israel: Dvir Co., 1959.

Eliach, Yaffa. "The Russian Dissenting Sects and Their Influence on Israel Baal Shem Tov, Founder of Hassidism," *Proceedings of the American Academy for Jewish Research* 36 (1968): 55–83.

Epstein, Baruch HaLevi. *My Uncle the Netziv*. Brooklyn, NY: Mesorah, 1988.

Finkel, Avraham Ya'akov. *Sefer Chasidim: The Book of the Pious*. New Jersey: Jason Aronson, 1997.

Gendle, Nicholas, and John Mewendorff. *Gregory of Palamas: The Triads*. Mahweh, NJ: Paulist Press, 1983.

Gieschen, Charles A. "The Seven Pillars of the World: Ideal Figure Lists in the Christology of the Pseudo-Clementines." *Journal for the Study of the Pseudepigrapha* 12 (1994): 47–82.

Gold, Rabbi Avie. *Hoshanos: A New Translation with a Commentary Anthologized from Talmudic, Midrashic and Rabbbinic Sources*. Brooklyn, NY: ArtScroll Mesorah, 1980.

Green, Aurthur. "The Ẓaddiq as *Axis Mundi* in Later Judaism." *Journal of the American Academy of Religion* 45:3 (1977): 327–347.

Harris, Rendel. "Rivers of Living Waters." *The Expositor* 8th series 20 (1920): 197–202.

Hecker, Joel. "The Blessing in the Belly: Mystical Satiation in Medieval Kabbalah." Pages 257–279 in *Food and Judaism: A Special Issue of Studies in Jewish Civilization Volume 15*. Edited by Leonard J. Greenspoon, Ronald A. Simkins, Gerald Shapiro; Omaha: Creighton University Press, 2005.

Herczeg, Rabbi Yisrael Isser Zvi. *The Torah: With Rashi's Commentary Translated, Annotated, and Elucidated*. Brooklyn, NY: Mesorah Publications, 2005.

Hertz, Joseph H. *Sayings of the Fathers*. New York: Behrman House, 1945.

Horowitz, Rabbi Isaiah. *Shney Luchot Habrit*. Translated by Rabbi Eliyahu Munk. 3 vols. Jerusalem: Lambda Publishers, 1999.

Idel, Moshe. "Enoch is Metratron." *Immanuel* 24/25 (1990): 238.

Idel, Moshe. *Kabbalah: New Perspectives*. New Haven, CT: Yale University Press, 1988.

Idel, Moshe. *Messianic Mystics*. New Haven, CT: Yale University, 1998.

Jacobs, Louis. "Eating as an Act of Worship in Hasidic Thought." Pages 157–166 in *Studies in Jewish Religious and Intellectual History*. Edited by Siegfried Stein and Raphael Loewe; Alabama: The University of Alabama Press, 1979.

Jacobs, Louis. "The Doctrine of the 'Divine Spark' in Man in Jewish Sources." Pages 87–114 in *Studies in Rationalism, Judaism and Universalism*. Edited by Raphael Loewe. London: Routledge and Kegan Paul, 1966.

Kaindenover, Rabbi Tzvi Hirsch. *Kav HaYashar*. 2 Vols. Edited by Rabbi Avrohom Davis. Monsey, NJ: Metsudah Publications, 2007.

Kittel, Gerhard, and Gerhard Friedrich, eds. *Theological Dictionary of the New Testament*. Translated by Geoffrey W. Bromiley. 10 vols. Grand Rapids: Eerdmans, 2006.

Klein, Rabbi G. *Der älteste christliche Katechismus und die jüdische Propaganda-Literatur*. Berlin: G. Reimer, 1909.

Kohler, Kaufmann, and Ludwig Blau. "Preexitence." Pages 182–184 in vol. 8 of *Jewish Encyclopedia*. Edited by Isidore Singer. 12 vols. New York: Funk and Wagnalls, 1901.

Lachs, Samuel Tobias. *A Rabbinic Commentary on the New Testament: The Gospels of Matthew, Mark, and Luke*. Hoboken, New Jersey: KTAV Publishing House, 1987.

Lancaster, Daniel. *Torah Club Volume Five: Rejoicing of the Torah*. Marshfield, MO: First Fruits of Zion, 2006.

Levertoff, Beatrice. "Thirty Years Work." *Church and the Jews* 180 (July 1954): 3–4.

Levertoff, Beatrice. "Ten Years at Holy Trinity, Shoreditch." *Church and the Jews* 94 (January 1933): 18.

Levertoff, Olga. *The Wailing Wall*. London: A. R. Mowbray & Co. Ltd., 1937.

Levertoff, Paul P. "Worship." *Church and the Jews* 94 (January 1933): 6–13.

Levertoff, Paul P. *Die religiöse Denkweise der Chassidim*. Leipzig: J. C. Hinrichs, 1918.

Levertoff, Paul P. "Some Aspects of Jewish Mysticism." *Church and the Jews* 100 (July 1934): 20–23.

Levertoff, Paul P. "The Wisdom of the Chasids." *Church and the Jews* 89 (October 1931): 23–30.

Levertoff, Paul P. "Chasidic Parables." *The Quest: A Quarterly Review* (January 1925).

Levertoff, Paul P. "Some Aspects of Jewish Mysticism." *Journal of the Transactions of the Victoria Institute* 65 (1933): 71–87.

Levertoff, Paul P. "The Religious Tragedy of Judaism." *Church and the Jews* 100 (July 1934): 11.

Levertoff, Paul P. "The Shechinah Motif in the New Testament Literature." Lecture, Society of the Study of Religions, 1951. Republished in *Messiah Journal* 100 (Spring 2009), 43–49.

Levertoff, Paul P. *St. Matthew*. London: Thomas Murby & Co., 1940.

Levertov, Moshe. *The Man Who Mocked the KGB*. Brooklyn, NY: self published, 2002.

Lichtenstein, R. Yehiel Zvi. *Commentary on the Books of the New Testament: John*. Leipzig: Professor G. Dahlman, 1897.

Liebes, Yehudah. "Christian Influences in the Zohar." *Immanuel* 17 (Winter 1983/84): 43–67.

Likutei Amarim: Tanya. Translated by Nissan Mindel et al. Brooklyn: Kehot Publication Society, 1998.

Lossky, Vladimir. *In the Image and Likeness of God*. Crestwood, NY: St. Vladimir's Seminary Press, 2001.

Majeski, Rabbi Shloma. *The Chassidic Approach to Joy*. Brooklyn, NY: Sichos in English, 1995.

Majeski, Rabbi Shloma. *A Tzaddik and His Students*. Brooklyn, NY: Sichos in English, 2008.

Majeski, Rabbi Shloma. *Yechudis: The Essence of Chosid-Rebbe Relationship*. Audiotape lectures. Brooklyn, NY: Sichos in English. 4 cassettes.

Marcus, Joel. "The Once and Future Messiah in Early Christianity and Chabad," *New Testament Studies* 46 (2000): 381–401.

Marcus, Yosef B. *Sefer Tehillim: Ohel Yosef Yitzchak*. Brooklyn: Kehot Publication Society, 2004.

Matt, Daniel C. *The Zohar Pritzker Edition: Volume Three*. Stanford, CA: Stanford University Press, 2006.

Mendel of Kasover, Rabbi Menachem. *Sefer Ahavat Shalom*. Jerusalem: Ma'yan haHasidut, 1995.

Menzi, Wilder, and Zwe Padeh. *The Tree of Life*. New York: Arizal Press Publications, 2008.

Midrash Rabbah. Translated by Dr. H. Freedman et al. 10 vols. London: The Soncino Press, 1992.

Mintz, Jerome R., and Dan Ben-Amos. *In Praise of the Baal Shem Tov (Shivhei Ha-Besht): The Earliest Collection of Legends about the Founder of Hasidism*. New Jersey: Jason Aronson, 1994.

Moo, Douglas J. *The Letter of James*. Grand Rapids: Eerdmans, 2000.

Nadler, Allan. "Holy Kugel: The Sanctification of Ashkenazic Ethnic Foods in Hasidism." Pages 193–214 in *Food and Judaism*. Edited by Leonard J. Greenspoon, Ronald A. Simkins, and Gerald Shapiro. vol. 15 of *A Special Issue of Studies in Jewish Civilization*. Omaha: Creighton University Press, 2005.

Odesser, Rabbi Israel Dov. *Israel Saba: Conversations of the Holy Rabbi Israel Dov Odesser*. Jerusalem, Israel: Keren Rabbi Israel Dov Odesser, 2007.

Palmer, G. E., Kallistos T. Ware, and Philip Sherrard. *The Philokalia*. 4 vols. England: Faber & Faber, 1986.

Patai, Raphael. *The Messiah Texts*. Detroit: Wayne State University Press, 1988.

Pirke de Rabbi Eliezer. Translated by M. Friedlander. Skokie, IL: Varda Books, 2004.

Philo. Translated by F.H. Colson et al. 12 vols. Loeb Classical Library. Cambridge, MA: Harvard University Press, 1991.

Pines, Shlomo. "Form(s) of God: some Notes on Metatron and Christ." *Harvard Theological Review* 76:3 (1983) 269–288.

Porter, Frank Chamberlin. "The Pre-Existence of the Soul in the Book of Wisdom and in the Rabbinical Writings." *The American Journal of Theology* 12:53 (January 1908): 53–115.

Rabbi Dov Ber of Mezeritch. *Tract on Ecstasy*. Translated by Louis Jacobs. Portland, OR: Vallentine Mitchell, 2006.

Rabbi Nachman. *Likutey Moharan*. Translated by Moshe Mykoff et al. 12 vols. New York: Breslov Research Institute, ongoing.

Rabbi Nachman. *Rabbi Nachman's Tikun*. Translated by Avraham Greenbaum. Monsey, New York: Breslov Research Institute, 1984.

Rabbi Nachman. *Restore My Soul*. Translated by Avraham Greenbaum and Aryeh Kaplan. New York: Breslov Research Institute, 1980.

Rabbi Nachman. *The Essential Rabbi Nachman*. Translated by Avraham Greenbaum. Jerusalem, Israel: Azamra Institute, 2006.

Rabbi Nathan, *Likutey Etzot: Advice of Rebbe Nachman*. Translated by Avraham Greenbaum. Monsey, NY: Breslov Research Institute, 1983.

Rabbi Nathan. *Rabbi Nachman's Wisdom*. Translated by Aryeh Kaplan. Monsey, New York: Breslov Research Institute, 1973.

Rabbi Nathan. *The Fiftieth Gate*. Translated by Avraham Greenbaum. 2 vols. Monsey, New York: Breslov Research Institute, 1992–3.

Rabbi Nathan. *Tzaddik: A Portrait of Rebbe Nachman*. Translated by Avraham Greebaum. New York, NY: Breslov Research Institute, 1987.

Rabbi Nathan. *Until the Mashiach Comes: Rabbi Nachman's Biography*. Translated by Aryeh Kaplan. Far Rockaway, NY: Breslov Research Institute, 1986.

Safrai, Chana. "The Kingdom of Heaven and the Study of Torah." Pages 169–189 in *Jesus' Last Week*. Edited by R. Steven Notley, Marc Turnage, and Brian Becker. Boston, MA: Brill, 2006

Sanday, W., and Arthur C. Headlam. *International Critical Commentary to the New Testament: A Critical and Exegetical Commentary on the Epistle to the Romans*. New York: Scribner, 1896.

Sarna, Nahum. The *JPS Torah Commentary: Genesis*. Philadelphia, PA: Jewish Publication Society, 1989.

Schaff, Philip, and Henry Wace. *Nicene and Post-Nicene Fathers*. 14 vols. Peabody, MA: Hendrickson, 2004.

Schneerson, Menachem M. *Likutei Sichos*. 37 vols. Brooklyn, NY: Kehot Publishing Society, 2000.

Schneerson, Menachem M. *Proceeding Together*. 3 vols. Brooklyn, NY: Sichos in English, 2000.

Schneerson, Menachem M. *Sefer HaMa'amarim 5708*. Brooklyn, NY: Kehot, 1986.

Schneerson, Menachem M. *Sichos in English Volume 17*. Brooklyn, NY: Sichos in English.

Schneersohn, Yosef Yitzchak. *Chassidic Discourses*. Translated by Sholom B. Wineberg. 2 vols. Brooklyn: Kehot Publication Society, 1999.

Schnurr, Günther. "Eucharist," Page 170–171 in vol. 2 of *The Encyclopedia of Christianity*. Edited by Erwin Fahlbusch et al. 5 vols. Grand Rapids, MI: William B. Eerdmans Publishing Company, 2001.

Schochet, Jacob Immanuel. *The Mystical Dimension*. 3 vols. New York: Kehot Publication Society, 1995.

Schochet, Jacob Immanuel. *Tsava'at Harivash: Testament of Rabbi Israel Baal Shem Tov*. New York: Kehot Publishing House, 1998.

Scholem, Gershon. *Kabbalah*. New York, NY: Meridian, 1978.

Scholem, Gershom. *Major Trends in Jewish Mysticism*. New York: Schocken Books, 1961.

Scholem, Gershom. *On the Mystical Shape of the Godhead*. New York: Schocken, 1997.

Scholem, Gershom. "Zohar." Page 202 in vol. 16 of *Encyclopedia Judaica*. Edited by Fred Skolnik. 22 vols. Jerusalem: Keter Publishing House, 1996.

Schoneveld, Jacobus. "The Torah in the Flesh: A New Reading of the Prologue of the Gospel of John as a Contribution to a Christology without Anti-Judaism." *Immanuel* 24/25 (1990): 77–94.

Silberman, Lou H. "Joy." Pages 470–471 in vol. 11 of *Encyclopedia Judaica* (Second Edition). Edited by Fred Skolnik. 22 vols. Jerusalem: Keter Publishing House, 2007.

Stauffer, Ethelbert. *Jesus and His Story*. London: SCM Press, 1960.

Stone, Rabbi Abraham. *Highlights of Moshiach*. Brooklyn, NY: Sichos in English, 1992.

Tanna Debe Eliyyahu. Translated by William G. Braude and Israel J. Kapstein. Philadelphia: Jewish Publication Society, 1997.

The Bahir. Translated by Aryeh Kaplan. Lanham: Rowman & Littlefield Publishers, 2004.

The Septuagint with Apocrypha: Greek and English. Translated by Lancelot C.L. Brenton. Peabody: Hendrickson Publishers, 2005.

The Tosefta. Translated by Jacob Neusner. 2 vols. Peabody: Hendrickson Publishers, 2002.

The Zohar, Translated by Maurice Simon, Harry Sperling, and Paul P. Levertoff. 5 vols. London: The Soncino Press, 1973.

Touger, Eliyahu. *To Know and To Care: An Anthology of Chassidic Stories about the Lubavitcher Rebbe*. 3 vols. Brooklyn, NY: Sichos in English, 1993.

Triipolitis, Antiona. *The Doctrine of the Soul in the Thought of Plotinus and Origen*. Roslyn Heights, NY: Libra Publishers, 1978.

Twersky, Rabbi Menachem Nachum. *Me'or Einyam*. Translated by Rabbi Eugene J. Cohen. USA: Xlibris Corporation, 2003.

Uman! Uman! Rosh HaShanah! A Guide to Rebbe Nachman's Rosh HaShanah in Uman. Monsey, NY: Breslov Research Institute, 2001.

Ungwarer, J. Translated by Paul P. Levertoff. "The Dead Chasidim." *Church and the Jews* 90 (January 1932): 19–21.

Wagshul, Yitzchok Dovid. *Words of the Living G-d: Torah Or, Volume One: The Book of Genesis*. New York: Purity Press, 2007.

Weiss, Joseph. "The Kavvanoth of Prayer in early Hasidism." Pages 95–125 in *Studies in Eastern Jewish Mysticism*. Edited by David Goldstein; New York: Oxford University Press, 1985.

Weiss, Joseph. "The Ṣaddick—Altering the Divine Will." Pages 183–193 in *Studies in Eastern Jewish Mysticism*. Edited by David Goldstein; New York: Oxford University Press, 1985.

Whispers Between Worlds. Translated by Rabbi Eliyahu Touger. Brooklyn, NY: Sichos in English, 2009.

Williams, Frank. *The Panarion of Epiphanius of Salamis: Book I*. New York, Brill, 1997.

Wolfson, Elliot R. *Along the Path*. New York: State University of New York Press, 1995.

Wolfson, Elliot R. "Inscribed in the Book of the Living: *Gospel of Truth* and Jewish Christology." *Journal for the Study of Judaism* 38 (2007):234–271.

Wolfson, Elliot R. *Language, Eros, Being*. New York: Fordham University Press, 2005.

Wolfson, Elliot. *Through a Speculum that Shines: Vision and Imagination in Medieval Jewish Mysticism*. Princeton: Princeton University Press, 1994.

Yosef, Mordechai. *Living Waters—The Mei HaShiloach: A Commentary on the Torah by Rabbi Mordechai Yosef of Isbitza*. Translated by Betsalel Paul Edwards. Northvale: Jason Aronson, 2001.

Zalman, Schneur. *Journey of the Soul: A* Chasidic *Discourse by Rabbi Schneur Zalman of Liadi.* Translated by Ari Sollish. Brooklyn: Kehot Publication Society, 2004.

Zalman, Schneur. *Selections From Torah Or and Likkutei Torah: Festivals Vol. 1.* Translated by Rabbi Eliyahu Touger. Brooklyn, NY: Kehot, 2009.

Zalman, Schneur. *Transforming the Inner Self.* Translated by Chaim Zev Citron. Brooklyn: Kehot Publication Society, 2004.